What They Say about Us

"One organization with a long record of success
in helping people find jobs is The Five O'Clock Club."
FORTUNE

"Many managers left to fend for themselves are turning to the camaraderie offered by [The Five O'Clock Club]. Members share tips and advice, and hear experts."
The Wall Street Journal

"If you have been out of work for some time . . . consider The Five O'Clock Club."
The New York Times

"Wendleton has reinvented the historic gentlemen's fraternal oasis and built it into a chain of strategy clubs for job seekers."
The Philadelphia Inquirer

"Organizations such as The Five O'Clock Club are building . . . an extended professional family."
Jessica Lipnack, author, *Professional Teams*

"[The Five O'Clock Club] will ask not what you do, but 'What do you want to do?' . . . [And] don't expect to get any great happy hour drink specials at this joint. The seminars are all business."
The Washington Times

"The Five O'Clock Club's proven philosophy is that job hunting is a learned skill like any other. The Five O'Clock Club becomes the engine that drives [your] search."
Black Enterprise

"Job hunting is a science at The Five O'Clock Club. [Members] find the discipline, direction and much-needed support that keeps a job search on track."
Modern Maturity

"Wendleton tells you how to beat the odds—even in an economy where pink slips are more common than perks. Her savvy and practical guide[s] are chockablock with sample résumés, cover letters, worksheets, negotiating tips, networking suggestions and inspirational quotes from such far-flung achievers as Abraham Lincoln, Malcolm Forbes, and Lily Tomlin."
Working Woman

What Job Hunters Say

"During the time I was looking for a job I kept Kate's books by my bed. I read a little every night, a little every morning. Her common-sense advice, methodal approach, and hints for keeping the spirits up were extremely useful."

> Harold Levine, coordinator, Yale Alumni Career Resource Network

"I've just been going over the books with my daughter, who is 23 and finally starting to think she ought to have a career. She won't listen to anything I say, but you she believes."

> Newspaper columnist

"Thank you, Kate, for all your help. I ended up with four offers and at least 15 compliments in two months. Thanks!"

> President and CEO, large banking organization

"I have doubled my salary during the past five years by using The Five O'Clock Club techniques. Now I earn what I deserve. I think everyone needs The Five O'Clock Club."

> M. S., attorney, entertainment industry

"I dragged myself to my first meeting, totally demoralized. Ten weeks later, I chose from among job offers and started a new life. Bless You!

> Senior editor, not-for-profit

"I'm an artistic person, and I don't think about business. Kate provided the disciplined business approach so I could practice my art. After adopting her system, I landed a role on Broadway in *Hamlet*."

> Bruce Faulk, actor

"I've referred at least a dozen people to The Five O'Clock Club since I was there. The Club was a major factor in getting my dream job, which I am now in."

> B. R., research head

"My Five O'Clock Club coach was a God-Send!!! She is truly one of the most dynamic and qualified people I've ever met. Without her understanding and guidance, I wouldn't have made the steps I've made toward my goals."

> Operating room nurse

"The Five O'Clock Club has been a fantastic experience for my job search. I couldn't have done it without you. Keep up the good work."

> Former restaurant owner, who found his dream job with an
> organization that advises small businesses

What Human Resources Executives Say about
The Five O'Clock Club Outplacement

"This thing works. *I saw a structured, yet nurturing, environment where individuals searching for jobs positioned themselves for success. I saw 'accountability' in a nonintimidating environment. I was struck by the support and willingness to encourage those who had just started the process by the group members who had been there for a while."*

Employee relations officer, financial services organization

"Wow! I was immediately struck by the electric atmosphere *and people's commitment to following the program. Job hunters reported on where they were in their searches and what they had accomplished the previous week. The overall environment fosters sharing and mutual learning."*

Head of human resources, major law firm

*"The Five O'Clock Club program is **far more effective** than conventional outplacement. Excellent materials, effective coaching and nanosecond responsiveness combine to get people focused on the central tasks of the job search. Selecting The Five O'Clock Outplacement Program was one of my best decisions this year."*

Sr. vice president, human resources, manufacturing company

"You have made me look like a real genius *in recommending The Five O'Clock Club [to our divisions around the country]!"*

Sr. vice president, human resources, major publishing firm

Go to our website
www.fiveoclockclub.com
Join our mailing list and receive FREE periodic
emailings on job search or career development.

The Five O'Clock Club®

Find your personal path in job search and career success

TARGETING
A GREAT
CAREER

KATE WENDLETON

CENGAGE
Learning®

Professional • Technical • Reference

Australia • Canada • Mexico • Singapore • Spain • United Kingdom • United States

CENGAGE Learning

Professional • Technical • Reference

Targeting a Great Career
Kate Wendleton

Vice President, Career Education SBU: Dawn Gerrain
Director of Editorial: Sherry Gomoll
Publisher and General Manager,
Cengage Learning PTR: Stacy L. Hiquet
Associate Director of Marketing: Sarah Panella
Manager of Editorial Services: Heather Talbot
Senior Marketing Manager: Mark Hughes
Acquisitions Editors: Martine Edwards and Mitzi Koontz
Developmental Editor: Kristen Shenfield
Editorial Assistant: Jennifer Anderson
Director of Production: Wendy A. Troeger
Production Manager: J.P. Henkel
Production Editor: Rebecca Goldthwaite
Technology Project Manager: Sandy Charette
Director of Marketing: Wendy E. Mapstone
Channel Manager: Gerard McAvey
Marketing Coordinator: Erica Conley
Cover Design: TDB Publishing Services
Text Design: Bookwrights

CENGAGE and CENGAGE LEARNING are registered trademarks of Cengage Learning, Inc., within the United States and certain other jurisdictions.
All ot her trademarks are the property of their respective owners.
All images © Cengage Learning unless otherwise noted.
Cartoons courtesy © Jerry King of Cartoons, Inc.

For product information and technology assistance, contact us at Cengage Learning Customer & Sales Support, 1-800-354-9706
For permission to use material from this text or product, submit all requests online at cengage.com/permissions
Further permissions questions can be emailed to permissionrequest@cengage.com
Cengage Learning PTR
20 Channel Center Street
Boston, MA 02210
USA
Cengage Learning is a leading provider of customized learning solutions with office locations around the globe, including Singapore, the United Kingdom, Australia, Mexico, Brazil, and Japan. Locate your local office at: international.cengage.com/region
Cengage Learning products are represented in Canada by Nelson Education, Ltd.
For your lifelong learning solutions, visit cengageptr.comVisit our corporate website at cengage.com

For information, please contact: The Five O'Clock Club®
300 East 40th Street
New York, New York 10016 www.fiveoclockclub.com
Library of Congress Cataloging-in-Publication Data
     Targeting a great career / Kate Wendleton.
     p. cm.
     "The Five O'Clock Club."
     Includes index.
     ISBN 978-1-285-75342-3
                                                      2013934077

NOTICE TO THE READER

If you haven't the strength
to impose your own terms upon life,
then you must accept the terms it offers you.

T. S. Eliot,
The Confidential Clerk

To my parents,
who showed me that compassion is the most important virtue

Preface

Dear Member or Prospective Member of The Five O'Clock Club:

Have you ever asked yourself the question, "What should I be doing with my life?" This book will help you find the answer. It is the first in a four-part series for job hunters, career changers, freelancers, and consultants who want some guidance about what to do in this changing economy. None of us can depend on our employers to help us through this—we have to figure it out for ourselves. And if we do, we will all be better off.

Learning how to manage our own careers is the only job security we can expect from now on. And this book will show you how to do it. *Targeting a Great Career* is the most extensive and thorough book on the subject. It is important to do the exercises in this book. The results are the only things that will keep you calm and secure in this stormy market.

Taken together, the books in this series prepare you to deal with the continuous change we are all experiencing, figure out where you fit in, and help you get what you want.

The books present the strategies we use at The Five O'Clock Club, our national job-search strategy program. *The Five O'Clock Club* series is the result of over 25 years of research into how successful people plan and manage their careers, and land the most satisfying jobs—whether on payroll or on assignment—at the best pay. These books provide the most sophisticated and most detailed explanation of the process:

- *Targeting a Great Career* (this book) tells you where to look for a job. It is a relatively painless way to think about the career-planning process. It also contains an extensive overview of the entire Five O'Clock Club approach to the job search.

- *Packaging Yourself: The Targeted Résumé* is quite simply the best résumé book on the market. It uses the résumés of real people and tells you their stories. It refers to more than 100 industries and professions.

- *Shortcut Your Job Search: Get Meetings That Get You the Job* tells you how to get job leads—part-time or full-time, freelance or consulting. It also contains worksheets that you may copy for your own use. In addition, it contains the most comprehensive job-search bibliography around.

- *Mastering the Job Interview and Winning the Money Game* teaches you the consultative approach to job interviews, how to turn those interviews into offers, and how to get the best compensation package—whether for full-time, part-time, freelance, or consulting work.

Running The Five O'Clock Club is the most gratifying thing I do. Those who coach job hunters privately or in our small-group strategy sessions agree that nothing gives them more satisfaction than helping someone figure out a career path, and then coaching that person to land a great job at a great salary. And that's what I do in my spare time when I work with young men who have aged out of foster care. Nothing is more gratifying.

Even those who have been unemployed a long time find help with us. Do not become discouraged if you have been searching a long time. You may be doing something wrong. Some of our best stories are about people who had been unemployed two years or longer, and found the job that was perfect for them at just the right salary. All of the case studies in this and our other books are of actual people.

All of this information is based on the highly successful methods used at The Five O'Clock Club, where the average, regularly attending member finds a job within 10 weeks. For a packet of information on joining the Club and subscribing to *The Five O'Clock News*, call 1-800-538-6645, or see the Application Form in the last section of this book or on our website.

We are guided by the original Five O'Clock Club, where the leaders of Old Philadelphia met regularly to exchange ideas and have a good time. Today's members are the same—they exchange ideas at the Club or through our LinkedIn group, operate at a high level, brainstorm to help each other, and truly enjoy each other's company. In addition, they work closely with a Five O'Clock Club career coach to find the best strategies for their search.

I hope these books will assist you as they have so many others. Thank you for supporting The Five O'Clock Club through your purchase of this book. Because of people like you, we can keep the program going so we'll be there when you need us. Our goal is, and always has been, to provide the best affordable career advice. And—with you as our partners—we will continue to do this.

Cheers, God bless, and good luck!

Kate Wendleton
New York City, 2013
www.fiveoclockclub.com

Acknowledgments

With appreciation to my husband, Richard, my knight in shining armor, life partner and supporter of all of my wild dreams. He is still a dream in my Forty-Year Vision. To our children, both the former foster kids and the birth children, who have added so much to our lives. They are one of my top Seven Stories.

I appreciate all of The Five O'Clock Club members, old and new, some of whose stories are contained herein: Members provide feedback on our techniques, which allows our approach to evolve continually with the changing job market. Members also give us information for our database, so we can track trends and know what is going on. And members support and encourage each other, a key element of The Five O'Clock Club philosophy.

I thank our career coaches, a highly trained and dedicated group, especially those who give speeches in the community, providing a valuable public service by making The Five O'Clock Club known to more people. I thank our small-group coaches, who have brought this high-quality program to others with enthusiasm and dedication.

I thank the excellent back office staff of The Five O'Clock Club, who keep our office running smoothly, and who keep tabs on the job hunters and coaches alike, making sure that people do not fall through the cracks.

Special mention to Dr. David Madison, the Director of our National Guild of Five O'Clock Club Career Coaches, Dr. Richard Bayer, our Chief Operating Officer, Rickey Allen, head of I.T., Ahmed ElMasry, head of accounting, Jerry Iannaccone, SVP, Operations and Michael Payan,VP, Client Relations and Major Accounts. And, finally, Vanessa Gathers, our long-time head of Administration.

I thank the human resources professionals who care enough about the employees they have to let go that they choose The Five O'Clock Club as their outplacement provider despite the many alternatives they have. And those HR people who care about their current employees who need executive coaching to do well in their present or future positions, and allow us to help them in this effort.

Finally, my deepest appreciation to my parents, who taught me the power and importance of compassion. Although they had nine children, they always had room for more. Although they were not rich, they were always generous to their church and to those in need. In her late-eighties, my mother was still visiting the "elderly woman" who lived two doors away from her. My father took care of my ill mother when Mom was in her early nineties and he considered it an honor, as we all must when we care for those in need. As my husband has often said to me: "The strong need the weak and the weak need the strong."

My father gave me my drive, energy and spunk. He urged me to go into computer programming in the '60s when few women were in that field and inspired me to be an entrepreneur because of his own and his family's history in that area. Mom and Dad encouraged my husband and me when we decided to volunteer in a hospital, then a prison, and then to work closely with young, African-American men who had aged out of foster care. My parents taught me to be grateful for what you have, count your blessings and never be jealous or resentful of those who seem to have more.

As the Dalai Lama says, "If you want others to be happy, practice compassion. If you want to be happy, practice compassion." We are on this earth to take care of each other.

Hence, the Five O'Clock Club philosophy, which is carried out by our members:

"The Garden of life is abundant, prosperous and magical. In this garden, there is enough for everyone. Share the fruit and the knowledge. Our brothers and we are in this lush, exciting place together. Let's show others the way. Kindness, Generosity, Hard work, God's care."

K.W.
New York City, 2013

Contents

PART THREE   ## How to Select Your Job Targets: Brainstorming Possible Jobs

PART FOUR   ## How to Manage Your Future

The Five O'Clock Club®

PART ONE

The Changing Job Market

HOW IT WORKS TODAY

You and the New Job Market

I'm going to fight hard.
I'm going to give them hell.

HARRY S. TRUMAN
REMARK ON THE PRESIDENTIAL CAMPAIGN, AUGUST 1948

Five O'Clock Clubbers know that they should first do the assessment exercises in this book to determine what they want to do now and what they want to do 15 – or even 40 – years from now. Because of our powerful assessment process, 58% of those who attend the Club end up changing careers – they decide to change the field or industry they are now in.

The process works for people at all levels. For example a truck driver who was downsized went through our assessment process. He could drive a truck for anyone, but, when working with his coach he revealed that he'd always wanted to drive a truck for an ice cream company, such as Ben and Jerry's. He contacted the local Ben & Jerry's distributor, said that working for them would be his ideal job, and he got an offer.

Sometimes, you may have to take a job that is not right for you or do consulting work. Don't say to yourself, "So this is where my life has ended up." This is not the end. It's a blip. We all have to cope with this kind of situation, but it's temporary. Get through it. Do what you can to keep body and soul together, but also keep plugging ahead in the direction you want to go. Even while you work in something that's not perfect, you can still make strides by building your contacts and skills for the long term.

We give this advice to executives and also to those kids who have aged out of foster care. If you can't find the exact right job right now, be sure to keep your foot in the game by building your skills and your connections until you are in the career you want.

Your Employer Has Got to Be Sharper— and So Do You

In a growing but stable economy, the market favors the job hunter. There are more jobs than there are job applicants. Sloppy job-hunting techniques work *well enough*. Organizations can hire more people than they need and hope someone will do the job right.

In today's ever-changing economy, job hunters face greater competition for the jobs that are available. Everyone has to be sharper. Just as your employer cannot be sloppy when competing in world markets, you cannot be sloppy when competing in job markets. Your prospective employers have to be more serious about every position they fill. You, too, must take your job hunt more seriously.

Labor is the superior of capital, and deserves much the higher consideration.

ABRAHAM LINCOLN

Don't Be Scared by the Headlines

Job hunters are starting to realize that a large number of people may be laid off in one part of an organization, while different kinds of people are hired in other parts of the same organization. In the news, you will hear about the layoffs, but you will not hear about the hiring—the organization would be deluged with résumés.

Get used to the headlines. Organizations must react quickly to changing world circumstances, and they no longer have time to figure out where the laid-off people could fit into other parts of the same organization. Some organizations now allow laid-off employees to job hunt both inside and outside the organization. It can be an efficient way for the organization to change direction, and save perhaps 10 percent of the laid-off employees who can fit into the new direction.

The laid-off employee is usually able to find a position outside more quickly because, by definition, there are more positions outside. No matter how big the old organization is, it is small compared to the outside world. A smart employee would devote 10 percent of his efforts to an inside search, and 90 percent outside.

A Changing Economy

Today, we know that doing a good job is not enough. Our career prospects can now change for reasons that have nothing to do with our personal job performance, but with the performance of our employers. It's a new economy—a world economy—and the changes are not going to slow down. Not only will things not return to the way they were, the amount of change will increase.

Government statistics show the impact of change on job hunters:

The average American has been in his or her job only four years.

The average American getting out of college today can expect to have five careers during his or her lifetime—that's not five jobs, but five separate careers!

We will probably have 12 to 15 jobs in the course of those five careers.

Ten years from now, half the working population will be in jobs that have not yet been

"Joe took the day off to go to the ball game. I'm his dog, I'll be sitting in for him until he returns."

Cartoon Courtesy © Jerry King

invented. Let's make that more personal: Ten years from now, half the people reading this book will be in jobs that do not exist today. That's okay. We'll tell you where some of the new jobs are, but you'll have to do research as well.

Ten years from now, half the working population will be in nontraditional forms of employment. This means that half of us will not be working full-time, on payroll, for one employer—a wrenching change in our mind-sets. Some of us may work two days a week on payroll for one employer, and three days a week for another. Or three days a week on payroll, with consulting or freelance work on the other days. Or we may be paid by one company that farms us out to another. The variations are endless—and changing.

More and more, organizations are hiring workers as consultants. People find themselves going from consulting work to on payroll and back to consulting again. The situation is unsettling—to say the least. However, we cannot fight it. In this time of dramatic change, few organizations really know where they are heading, but some are learning what kind of workers they need: flexible, self-aware ones who continually improve their skills. Gone are the days when it was good enough for employees to simply do their assigned jobs well. America wants and needs a new kind of workforce.

Employees too are learning that they must take care of themselves and remain marketable so they are not dependent on one employer. They are proactively figuring out what they bring to the party, while finding out—and fitting into—the new directions their organizations and industries are taking.

A few smart organizations have wisely embraced a process of helping employees take charge of their own careers. More and more, The Five O'Clock Club is being asked to deliver career development programs for essentially every employee in the organizations. Or we are asked to provide leadership development or executive coaching programs to help one or a dozen employees better lead their staffs. Most of us, however, will have to develop career plans on our own, and this book can help you do just that.

Security is mostly a superstition. It does not exist in nature, nor do the children of men as a whole experience it. Avoiding danger is no safer in the long run than outright exposure. Life is either a daring adventure or nothing.

HELEN KELLER, *THE OPEN DOOR* (DOUBLEDAY, 1957)

Continual Career Development—An Enlightened Approach

All of this fits in with what we have taught at The Five O'Clock Club since 1978: It is best for both the employee and the employer if job hunting is seen as a continual process—and not just something that happens when a person wants to change jobs. **Continual job search means continually being aware of market conditions both inside and outside of our present organiza-**tions, and continually learning what we have to offer—to both markets.**

With this approach, workers are safer because they are more likely to keep their present jobs longer: They learn to change and grow as the organization and industry do. And if they have to go elsewhere, they will be more marketable. Organizations are better off because employees who know what is going on outside their insular halls are smarter, more sophisticated, and more proactive, and make the organization more competitive. Every industry is going through dramatic change—and hence needs a more aware and flexible workforce.

The New Technology Companies Employ Relatively Few People

One issue is that the "largest" companies today – measured by revenue – employ far fewer people than the giant companies of the recent past. As of this writing, Apple, the largest company by revenue, employs fewer than 50,000 people. Facebook, the country's latest darling, employs only 3,000! This makes Facebook far and away the smallest employer of the five top names in tech (Google, Amazon, Apple, and Microsoft are the other four). Google, the next smallest, has 10 times as many employees, with just over 32,000. Technology companies have high valuations, but employ relatively few people. Those new technology companies, whether LinkedIn (2,900), Microsoft (89,000), or Ebay (15,500), do not have the employee headcount of the old fashioned Fortune 100 companies such as GE, (134,000), GM (68,000 in the U.S. after all of the staff cuts), or Citigroup (259,000).

Here are the largest employers in the U.S., measured by number of employees:

1. Wal-Mart Stores Inc., 2.1 million employees
2. International Business Machines Corp. 436,000
3. United Parcel Service 400,000
4. McDonald's Corp. 400,000
5. Target Corp 355,000

6. The Kroger Co.	338,000
7. Hewlett-Packard	324,000
8. Sears Holdings Corporation	312,000
9. PepsiCo, Inc.	294,000
10. Bank of America Corporation	288,000

The economy is changing too fast for you to use the same old career planning techniques or the same old attitudes about job hunting. The unemployment rate has been high for many years now, and many of the new jobs created are lower paying. We all have to think harder about what we want to do with our careers.

People are always blaming their circumstances for what they are. I don't believe in circumstances. The people who get on in this world are the people who get up and look for the circumstances they want, and if they can't find them, make them.

GEORGE BERNARD SHAW, MRS. WARREN'S PROFESSION

Technology Is the Most Pervasive, followed by the Global Economy

Probably no change will affect our careers more than technological change. It's not like a stock market crash, or tearing down the Berlin Wall. It doesn't make the headlines, because it's happening everywhere—every day. When you want money from a bank, you can go to a machine. The human—the middleman doing the drudgery—is no longer required in that job. People are required in new jobs—to design and make the machines, service them, sell them, and so on—jobs that did not exist a few years ago.

As a result of technology, new industries are possible, such as direct marketing and the express-mail industry. Desktop publishing has affected the publishing, typesetting, and printing industries. Books, magazines, newspapers and newsletters are now often delivered by email and e-readers (or whatever is the more modern-day equivalent by the time you read this). This has affected the entire publishing and related industries.

Professions are changing. Most artists now work at a computer keyboard instead of a drawing board. Their jobs did not exist 10 years ago. Accountants are no longer needed to do compounded-growth rates and other complex calculations. Their jobs changed a while back. Salespeople are being replaced by computers and the UPC codes you see on packages. Musicians are being replaced by electronic synthesizers, which can replicate virtually every instrument.

Whether you are talking about manufacturing or hospital technology, artists or accountants, salespeople or teachers—virtually every industry and profession has or will be affected. There are no secure jobs because the jobs themselves are changing. If you think your industry or profession is not being affected, think again.

The Good Old Days—People Were Stuck

I remember the *good old days*—the days of one employer and one career. It used to be that when you found a job, you had found a home. You expected to get in there, do what the organization wanted, learn to play the game, rise through the ranks, and eventually retire. People had secure jobs with large, stable employers.

People may have had job security, but the downside is that they were often stuck. Changing jobs was frowned upon. For every satisfied person, there was someone stifled, who knew he or she had made a dreadful mistake.

Today, many of us might fear losing our jobs—even from week to week—but no one— absolutely no one—needs to feel stifled, deadened, or stuck in a career they no longer find satisfying. *Everyone has an opportunity to do something that is better.*

When we do our volunteer work with young adults who have aged out of foster care, the goal is to get them thinking about a career path and not just another hourly job. We all cheer when Ron, who went through the assessment exercises in this book, lands a job working with fifth graders and quit his job at McDonald's. Royal got his first real job with UPS, then got a job filling the fuel tanks at an airport. When we told him there was a shortage of airline mechanics and the possibility of earning almost $100,000 a year if he made it into management, he met with the mechanics at the airport and they told him the best schools to go to to learn how to be a mechanic. He is on his way. Charlene, a communications major and college graduate, was working in a cell phone store and then got a job selling cars. Since her goal was to work in film editing, she jumped at the chance to talk to a customer who worked at a TV station. She now works there as a film editor despite the very long commute. She knows she is on her career path.

If these people, who grew up with so much hardship, can figure out a career path, and persist until they get on it, then so can you.

Today, many of the people pushed out of organizations after 20 years are actually relieved to get out of jobs they'd found deadening. Some decide to think about what they really want to do and make the second phase of their lives much more fulfilling than the first.

In this book you will learn how to take more control of your life, how to plan for your own future and not be at the mercy of others, and how to keep your eye on your career goals. Many people who are laid off say, "This will never happen to me again. I will never again be caught off guard and unprepared."

A New Definition of Job Hunting

Job hunting in our changing economy is a continuous process and requires a new definition. As I mentioned earlier, **job hunting now means continually becoming aware of market conditions both inside and outside of our present organizations, and continually learning what we have to offer—to both markets.** This definition means we must develop new attitudes about our work lives, and new skills for doing well in a changing economy.

Today's economy requires job hunters to be more proactive, more sophisticated, and more

willing to go through brick walls to get what they want. Employers no longer plan your career for you. You must look after yourself, and know what you want and how to get it.

Understanding How the Job-Hunting Market Works

Fewer than 6% of all jobs are filled through search firms. Fewer than 6% of all jobs are filled through ads. People get jobs in other ways, which we will teach you, but the process starts with the assessment exercises in this book. Knowing why things work the way they do will give you flexibility and control over your job hunt. Knowing how the hiring system works will help you understand why things go right and why they go wrong—why certain things work and others don't. Then you can modify the system to fit your own needs, temperament, and the workings of the job market you are interested in.

It is overly simplistic to say that only one job-hunting system works. The job-selection process is more complicated than that. Employers can do what they want. You need to understand the process from their point-of-view. Then you can plan your own job hunt, in your own industry. You will learn how to compete in this market.

Always remember, the best jobs don't necessarily go to the most qualified people, but to the people who are the best job hunters. You'll increase your chances of finding the job you want by using a methodical job-hunting approach.

Even if you have worked for the same employer for many years, learn how to job hunt in a changing economy. At first it will seem strange. It's a new skill, but one you can use for the rest of your life. For a while you may feel as though things will never be the same. And they won't. No job is secure. At the same time, we now know that no one has to be locked into one job, one boss, one employer. Skilled job hunters have a real ability to plan their careers.

If you haven't the strength to impose your own terms upon life, then you must accept the terms it offers you.

T. S. ELIOT, *THE CONFIDENTIAL CLERK*

The Only Port in This Storm: You

They cannot offer you job security. They cannot offer you loyalty in exchange for your own loyalty. The rules have changed very quickly, and they expect you to adapt very quickly.

If you don't plan your own path through all of this, you will continue to be thrown around by the turbulence. The better you understand yourself—your motivations, skills, and interests—the more solid your foundation will be.

In our world of revolving bosses—whether you are on payroll or not—you will come across a shallow, rough person who does not understand your value. But if you have done the exercises in this book—especially the Seven Stories—you will understand your own value, and your self-esteem is more likely to remain intact. You will keep yourself on course and continue to follow your plan.

The better you are at plotting out your own future, the more you will get out of each of your jobs or assignments. Each one will fit in with your long-term vision, and you will not get so ruffled by corporate politics and pettiness. You will be following your own vision.

They say we will all adapt to this new world, and I am sure we will. I must admit that Five O'Clock Clubbers are a heartier and more resilient bunch than I am sometimes. Every week, I see people land great new jobs and assignments in this tumultuous new world. They have created their own career paths, have let go of the old fields they loved and worked in for so long, and are having fun—sometimes even more fun—in the new fields. Like these other Five O'Clock Clubbers, you can do it too. You will have help from The Five O'Clock Club coach who heads your small group. You can read more about The Five O'Clock Club at the end of this book. And you can learn even more by listening to our lectures on audio.

Changes Mean New Opportunities

The world is changing. What's hot today is not tomorrow. You can use these changes to your advantage. You can choose to head your career in the direction that's right for you.

You can impose your own terms upon life. You don't have to accept the terms it offers you. Read on, and see what others have done.

Alice said nothing: she had sat down with her face in her hands, wondering if anything would ever happen in a natural way again.

LEWIS CARROLL, *ALICE IN WONDERLAND*

The Five O'Clock Club®

How to Change Careers

If an idea, I realized, were really a valuable one, there must be some way of realizing it.

ELIZABETH BLACKWELL
(THE FIRST WOMAN TO EARN A MEDICAL DEGREE)

Ted had spent 10 years in marketing and finance with a large cosmetics company. His dream was to work in the casino industry. He selected two job targets: one aimed at the cosmetics industry, and one aimed at his dream.

All things being equal, finding a job similar to your old one is quicker. A career change will probably take more time. What's more, the job-hunting techniques are different for both.

Let's take Ted's case. The casino industry was small, focused in Atlantic City and Las Vegas. Everyone knew everyone else. The industry had its special jargon and personality. What chance did Ted have of breaking in?

Ted had another obstacle. His marketing and finance background made him difficult to categorize. His hard-won business skills became a problem.

It's Not Easy to Categorize Job Hunters

The easier it is to categorize you, the easier it is for others to see where you fit in their organizations, and for you to find a job. Search firms, for example, generally will not handle career changers. They can more easily market those who want to stay in the same function in the same industry. Search firms that handled the casino industry would not handle Ted.

When a large American steel company began closing plants in the early 1980s, it offered to train the displaced steelworkers for new jobs. But the training never "took"; the workers drifted into unemployment and odd jobs instead. Psychologists came in to find out why, and found the steelworkers suffering from acute identity crises." How could I do anything else?" asked the workers." I am a lathe operator."

PETER SENGE, *THE FIFTH DISCIPLINE*
(CROWN PUBLISHING GROUP)

You Must Offer Proof of Your Interest and Competence

Civility is not a sign of weakness, and sincerity is always subject to proof.

JOHN F. KENNEDY
INAUGURAL ADDRESS, JANUARY 20, 1961

Many job changers essentially say to a prospective employer, "Give me a chance. You won't be sorry." They expect the employer to hire them on faith, and that's unrealistic. The employer has a lot to lose. First, you may lose interest in the new area after you are hired. Second, you may know so little about the new area that it turns out not to be what you had imagined. Third, you may not bring enough knowledge and skill to the job and fail—even though your desire may be sincere.

The hiring manager should not have to take those risks. It is the job hunter's obligation to prove that he or she is truly interested and capable.

Ruth made a great mistake when he gave up pitching. Working once a week, he might have lasted a long time and become a great star.

TRIS SPEAKER, MANAGER OF THE CLEVELAND INDIANS, COMMENTING ON BABE RUTH'S PLANS TO CHANGE FROM A PITCHER TO AN OUTFIELDER, SPRING 1921

How You as a Career Changer Can Prove Your Interest and Capability

- Read the industry's trade journals.
- Get to know the people in that industry or field.
- Join its organizations; attend the meetings.
- Be persistent.
- Show how your skills can be transferred.
- Write proposals.
- Be persistent.
- Take relevant courses, part-time jobs, or do volunteer work related to the new industry or skill area.
- Be persistent!

Ted, as a career changer, had to offer proof to make up for his lack of experience. One proof was that he had read the industry's trade newspapers for more than 10 years. When he met people in his search, he could truthfully tell them that he had followed their careers. He could also say he had hope for himself because he knew that so many of them had come from outside the industry.

Another proof of his interest was that he had sought out so many casino management people in Atlantic City and Las Vegas. After a while, he ran into people he had met on previous occasions. Employers want people who are sincerely interested in their industry, their company, and the function the new hire will fill. Sincerity and persistence count, but they are usually not enough.

Another proof Ted offered was that he figured out how to apply his experience to the casino industry and its problems. Writing proposals to show how you would handle the job is one way to prove you are knowledgeable and interested in an area new to you. Some people prove their interest by taking courses, finding part-time jobs, or doing volunteer work to learn the new area and build marketable skills.

Ted initially decided to "wing it," and took trips to Atlantic City and Las Vegas hoping someone would hire him on the spot. That didn't work and took two months and some money. Then he began a serious job hunt—following the system which will be explained in the pages that follow. He felt he was doing fine, but the hunt was taking many months and he was not sure it would result in an offer.

After searching in the casino industry for six months, Ted began a campaign in his old field—the cosmetics industry. Predictably, he landed a job there quickly. Ted took this as a sign that he didn't have a chance in the new field. He lost sight of the fact that a career change is more difficult and takes longer.

Ted accepted the cosmetics position, but his friends encouraged him to continue his pursuit of a career in the casino industry—a small industry with relatively few openings compared with the larger cosmetics industry.

Shortly after he accepted the new position, someone from Las Vegas called him for an interview, and he got the job of his dreams. His efforts paid off because he had done a thorough campaign in the casino industry. It just took time.

Ted was not unusual in giving up on a career change. It can take a long time, and sometimes the pressure to get a paycheck will force people to take inappropriate jobs. That's life. Sometimes we have to do things we don't want to. There's nothing wrong with that.

What *is* wrong is forgetting that you had a dream. What is wrong is expecting people to hire you on faith and hope, when what they deserve is proof that you're sincere and that hiring you has a good chance of working. *What is wrong is underestimating the effort it takes to make a career change.*

In the future, most people will have to change careers. Your future may hold an involuntary career change, as new technologies make old skills obsolete. Those same new technologies open up new career fields for those who are prepared— and ready to change. Know what you're up against. Don't take shortcuts. And don't give up too early. Major career changes are normal today and may prove desirable or essential tomorrow.

Job Hunting versus Career Planning

Most people say their main fault is a lack of discipline. On deeper thought, I believe that is not the case. The basic problem is that their priorities have not become deeply planted in their hearts and minds.

STEPHEN R. COVEY,
THE SEVEN HABITS OF HIGHLY EFFECTIVE PEOPLE

*Afoot and light-hearted
I take to the open road,
Healthy, free, the world before me,
The long brown path before me,
leading wherever I choose.*

WALT WHITMAN, *COMPLETE POETRY AND COLLECTED PROSE*
(LIBRARY CLASSICS OF THE UNITED STATES)

You are probably reading this because you want a job. But you will most likely have to find another job after that one, and maybe after that. After all, the average American has been in his or her job only four years. To make smoother transitions, learn to plan ahead.

If you have a vision and keep it in mind, you can continually *position* yourself for your long-range goal by taking jobs and assignments that lead you there. Then your next job will be more than just a job. It will be a stepping stone on the way to something bigger and better.

When faced with a choice, **select the job that fits best with your Fifteen- or Forty-Year Vision—the job that positions you best for the long term.**

It takes less than an hour to make up a rudimentary Forty-Year Vision. But it is perhaps the single most important criterion for selecting jobs. Do the exercise quickly. Later, you can refine it and test it against reality. Do the Forty-Year Vision using the worksheet in this book. This is exactly what helped the people in the following case studies. **All of the people described are real people and what happened to them is true.**

CASE STUDY Bill
Bypassing the Ideal Offer

For most of his working life, Bill had been a controller in a bank. He was proud of the progress he had made, given his modest education. Now he was almost 50 years old. It was the logical time to become a chief financial officer (CFO), the next step up, ideally in a company near home, since his family life was very important to him. At just this point, he lost his job.

Following The Five O'Clock Club method, Bill got three job offers:

1. as CFO for a bank only 10 minutes from home —the job of his dreams.
2. as controller for a quickly growing bank in a neighboring area—still a long commute.
3. as controller for the health-care division of an insurance company 200 miles from home.

Bill wisely selected the job that would put him in the strongest position for the long term, and would look best in his next job search.

He selected job #3 because it would allow him to include two new industries on his résumé. Health care was growing, and insurance would broaden his financial-services experience.

Bill wanted to hedge his bets, and not uproot his family. So he got an apartment close to the new company, and went home on weekends. After a year and a half, the company was taken over, an unpredictable event. The new management brought in their own people. He was out.

But this time, Bill was not worried. Since he now had valuable new experience on his résumé, he was sought after. He was offered and took a key post in a consulting firm that served the health-care and financial industries.

CASE STUDY Charlotte
Positioning over Money

Charlotte, a marketing manager, received three offers:
1. with a credit-card company in a staff marketing position dealing with international issues.
2. with a major music company as head of marketing for the classical-music division.
3. with a nonprofit research organization as head of marketing.

The first two positions paid about the same, let's say $90,000. The position with the not-for-profit offered $75,000, and there was no room for moving the salary higher.

How did Charlotte decide which position to take? The music company was not a good fit for her: She was not compatible with the people, and she would probably have failed in that job. The credit-card job would have been easy but boring, and she would not have learned anything new.

Charlotte selected the not-for-profit position, the lowest-paid job. In her Forty-Year Vision, she saw herself as the head of a not-for-profit someday. Since she was only 35, she did not now need a position with a not-for-profit. But she felt good when she interviewed there. So she took the job

that best fit with her long-term vision.

Charlotte loved the people, and her position put her in contact with some of the most powerful business people in America. Top management listened to her ideas, and she had an impact on the organization.

After one-and-a-half years, there was a reorganization. Charlotte was made manager of a larger department. She received a pay increase to match her new responsibilities, which brought her salary higher than the salaries of the other two job offers. But, best of all, Charlotte's job was a good fit for her, and made sense in light of her Forty-Year Vision.

CASE STUDY Harry
Stuck in a Lower-Level Job

Harry was a window-washer for the casinos, earning an excellent hourly salary. The pay was high because the building was slanted, making the job more dangerous.

Harry did a great job, and was responsible and well liked. He was offered a supervisory position that could lead to other casino jobs. But the base pay was less than his current pay including overtime, and allowed for no overtime pay. Harry decided he could not afford to make the move and stayed as a window-washer paid by the hour. Today, several years later, he still cleans windows.

There's nothing wrong with washing windows, or any other occupation. But if you make this kind of choice based on short-term gain, be aware that you may be closing off certain options for your future.

Sometimes we have to make short-term sacrifices to get ahead—if indeed we want to get ahead.

A man may not achieve everything he has dreamed, but he will never achieve anything great without having dreamed it first.

WILLIAM JAMES

Selecting the Right Offer

Doing the exercises will give you some perspective when choosing among job offers. I hope that you will attempt to get 6 to 10 job possibilities in the works (knowing that five will fall away through no fault of your own). Then most likely you will wind up with three offers at approximately the same time.

If you have three offers, the one to choose is the one that positions you best for the long run.

People Who Have Written Goals Do Better

Money is not the only measure of success. When you have a clear, long-term goal, it can affect everything: your hobbies and interests, what you read, the people to whom you are attracted. Those who have a vision do better at reaching their goals, no matter what those goals are. A vision gives you hope and direction. It lets you see that you have plenty of time—no matter how young or how old you are. When you write it down, it means that you take it seriously and can begin to work on it. If you don't write it down, it may be fleeting and perhaps nothing will happen.

CASE STUDY Bill Clinton: A Clear Vision

Bill Clinton is a good example of the power of having a vision. A small-town boy, Bill decided in his teens that he wanted to become president. He developed his vision, and worked his entire life to make that dream come true.

CASE STUDY Bruce: Plenty of Time

Bruce—young, gifted, and black—was doing little to advance his career. Like many aspiring actors, he worked at odd jobs to survive and auditioned for parts when he could.

But, in fact, Bruce spent little time auditioning or improving his craft because he was too busy trying to make ends meet. What's more, he had recently been devastated by a girlfriend.

How We Respond to Life's Difficulties
THE MOST IMPORTANT FACTOR IN SUCCESS IN LIFE

Most of us have read books that have affected us. Beyond Shakespeare and the *Bible*, which both taught me a lot about human nature, the most important book in my life has been George Valliant's *Adaptation to Life*, the forty-year study of 268 male Harvard graduates. The study analyzed who succeeded, who didn't, and why. Because of the homogeneity of the group, the study proved that "the relatively broad socioeconomic differences among the subjects upon college entrance had no correlation" with later success. Participants born to economic privilege did not do better than those from relatively poor backgrounds, such as those on need-based scholarships.

What a hopeful thought—for myself, as well as for those we work with—that the luck of the draw in how we were born is not so relevant to our future success. Everyone has a chance.

> **How we were born is not so relevant to our future success**

Vaillant concluded that family circumstances are not the major determinant of future success. The study showed that <u>everyone has major setbacks, but *how we respond to life's difficulties* is the most important factor in success in life.</u> A broken love affair may lead one man to write great poetry and another to commit suicide.

The study also observed that maturation continued over the span of a person's life. **<u>We stop growing when our human losses are no longer replaced.</u>** The study proved that it is "sustained relationships with people, not traumatic events, that mold character." **Without love, it is hard to grow.**

So I know that there is hope for each of us depending on our responses and our attitudes. **Think long-term about your situation.** Do whatever you can right now to keep your body and soul together, and build for the future—regardless of how things may seem right now.

Using The Five O'Clock Club assessment, Bruce realized he was going nowhere. His first reaction was to attempt to do everything at once: quit his part-time jobs, become a film and stage director, and patch things up with his girlfriend. With the help of the Fifteen- and Forty-Year Visions, Bruce discovered that his current girlfriend was not right for him in the long run, and that he had plenty of time left in his life to act, direct, and raise a family.

Because of his vision, Bruce knew what to do next to get ahead. He was prompted to look for a good agent (just like a job hunt), and take other steps for his career. Six months later, Bruce landed a role in *Hamlet* on Broadway. Then he went on tour with another play. In later years, he did commercials.

The psychic task which a person can and must set for himself is not to feel secure, but to be able to tolerate insecurity, without panic and undue fear.

ERICH FROMM, *THE SANE SOCIETY*

CASE STUDY Sophie
Making Life Changes First

Sophie, age 22, had a low-level office job, wanted a better one, and did the assessment.

She did her Forty-Year Vision, but was depressed by it. Like many who feel stuck, Sophie imagined the same uninspiring situation from year to year. It seemed her life would never change.

With encouragement and help, she did the exercise again, and let her dreams come out, no matter how implausible they seemed. She saw herself eventually in a different kind of life. Although she initially did the exercise because she wanted to change jobs, she saw she needed to change other things first.

She moved away from a bad situation at home, got her own apartment, broke up with the destructive boyfriend she had been seeing for

eight years, and enrolled in night school. It took her two years to take these first steps.

She is now working toward her long-term goal of becoming a teacher and educational filmmaker. She says that she is off the treadmill and effortlessly making progress.

CASE STUDY Dave
A New Life at Sixty-Two

After Dave had worked for his organization for more than 25 years, it eliminated his job. He still had a lot of energy and a lot to offer, and he wanted to work. But he was depressed by his prospects until he did his Fifteen- and Forty-Year Visions.

His dream for his new life included: working two days a week developing new business for a small organization, volunteering on the board of a not-for-profit, heading a state commission, and consulting for an international not-for-profit. Instead of slowing down, Dave became busier and happier than he had been in his old job. He was able to quickly implement most of his vision.

I don't think in terms of failure. I think of things as not the right time or something that's outside of my capabilities. I don't feel like anyone outside of me should be setting limitations. People should be encouraged to shoot for the moon.

ISABEL WILKERSON, *THE NEW YORK TIMES*, Nov. 29, 1992

CASE STUDY Bob
Sticking with His Vision

Bob was feeling restless about his career. This prompted him to do a Forty-Year Vision. He wanted to end up at age 80 having done something significant for the community, and having earned a good living doing it. At age 43, he was offered a substantial promotion at his current job—but it was at odds with his community-service goal. After much soul-searching, Bob turned down the promotion, and took steps to implement his plan. He ended up starting his own not-for-profit that eventually would impact communities across America.

CASE STUDY Karen
Our Values Change over Time

Karen had been a high-powered executive, earning more than $300,000 a year. When she took time off to have her first baby, she was surprised by how much she loved taking care of her daughter. After Karen had stayed at home for two years, her husband lost his job. She had to look for work.

At first, her vision was to *have it all*. She assumed she needed another $300,000-a-year job to keep up their lifestyle, yet she also wanted time with her child. The assessment helped her see that she had never really enjoyed the grueling hours she had to work before, and she now imagined a better balance between work and family.

Karen received three offers: one for $300,000; one for $200,000, which required a lot of travel; and one for $125,000, which she knew fit into her Forty-Year Vision. Although she was at first embarrassed by having taken a lower-level position, she grew to love it and her new lifestyle.

Over time, our values change. As her daughter grows older, Karen may decide again that a higher-powered job is fine for her.

Men experience value changes, too—easing up a little when they want to spend time with the kids, for example, and focusing more on their careers at other times.

CASE STUDY Hank
Thinking Too Small

Hank, a senior executive who lost his job, chose a new field just because it was lucrative. But the assessment showed it would not position him well for the job *after* that one.

Instead, Hank became a senior executive with a major organization in his old field. The

quick route to financial success no longer appealed to him. He took a surer road that would position him well for the future. In fact, the job he took paid well enough to make his family very comfortable.

Thinking Big; Thinking Small

A Fifteen- or Forty-Year Vision gives you perspective. Without one, you may think too small or too big. Writing it down makes you more reasonable, more thoughtful, and more serious. **Having a vision also makes you less concerned about the progress of others because you know** *where you are going.*

CASE STUDY Jim
Objective versus Subjective

Jim had to choose between two job offers, one paying $350,000 and another at $500,000. The thought process is the same regardless of salary. To prove it, let's pretend the positions were paying $35,000 and $50,000. Which should he take?

Jim's wife wanted him to take the $50,000 job. It paid more and had a better title.

Jim liked the people at the $35,000 job, and they appreciated him and listened to his suggestions. But they could pay no more than $35,000. He delayed the start date while we talked, and listed the pros and cons of each position. He still could not decide. After all, $15,000 is a big difference.

Finally, I said to Jim: "I'm going to make it easy for you. The $35,000-a-year job no longer exists. Let's not talk about it. You will take the $50,000 a year job, have a very nice commute, make your wife happy, have a title you can be proud of, and make $50,000."

Jim sat in silence. Then he said: "The thought of going there depresses me. I think the job is not doable. They may be offering me an impossible job."

Sometimes objective thinking alone is not enough. The exercise helped Jim find out what his gut was telling him. During the interview process, things had turned him off about the $50,000 organization—but not enough to turn down the extra $15,000. It wasn't logical.

When Jim finally made up his mind to take the "$35,000" job, he was so happy, he bought presents for everyone. Even his wife was pleased. He had made the right choice.

Consider Objective and Subjective Information

If you tend to pay too much attention to subjective information, balance it by asking: "What is the logical thing for me to do regardless of how I feel?"
If you tend to be too objective, ask: "I know the logical thing to do, but how do I really feel about it?"

For most of us, it is easier to think about how to get what we want than to know what exactly we should want.

ROBERT N. BELLAH ET AL., *HABITS OF THE HEART*

CASE STUDY Dean
Expect to Be Paid Fairly

Dean had been making $60,000. He lost his job and uncovered two choices: one at $75,000 and one at $100,000. He asked to meet with me.

Dean was not worth $100,000 at this stage in his career, and I told him so. In addition, that organization was not a good fit for him.

The $75,000 job seemed just right for Dean. He had an engineering degree, and the work dealt with high-tech products.

Yet he took the $100,000 position. Within four months, he was fired.

Dean met with me again to discuss two more possibilities: another position for $100,000 and one at a much lower salary. Since he had most recently been making $100,000, interviewers thought perhaps he was worth it. Again, he opted for the $100,000 position—he liked making that kind of money. Again he could not live up to that salary, and again he was fired.

Life Skills, Not Just Job-Hunting Skills

A vision helps people see ahead, and realize that they can not only advance in their careers but also change their life circumstances—such as who their friends are and where they live.

Your career is not separate from your life. If you dream of living in a better place, you have to earn more money. If you would like to be with better types of people, you need to **become a better type of person yourself.**

The Forty-Year Vision cannot be done in a vacuum. Research is the key to *achieving your vision*. Without research, it is difficult to imagine what might be out there, or to imagine dream situations. Be sure to read the two chapters on research in this book.

Whatever your level, to get ahead you need:

- **exposure** to other possibilities and other dreams;
- **hard facts** about those possibilities and dreams (through networking and research);
- the **skills** required in today's job market;
- **job-search training** to help you get the work for which you are qualified.

Targeting the Jobs of the Future

*The time is not far off when you will be answering
your television set and watching your telephone.*

RAYMOND SMITH, CHAIRMAN AND CHIEF EXECUTIVE OF THE
BELL ATLANTIC CORPORATION, *THE NEW YORK TIMES*,
FEBRUARY 21, 1993

The Times Are Changing

Ten years from now, half the working population will be in jobs that do not exist today. Positions and industries will disappear almost completely—edged out by technological advances, new industries or global competition. When was the last time you saw a typewriter repairman? Or even a typewriter? There are few TV or radio repair jobs either. They have been replaced by new jobs.

Some industries retrench—or downsize—slowly and trick us into thinking they are solid and dependable. At the turn of the last century, there were literally thousands of piano manufacturers. A few still remain, but that industry was affected by new industries: movies, TV, radio, and other forms of home entertainment—most recently, the Internet, CD-ROMs, IPODS, IPADS, Kindles, Nooks, and video game systems.

In 1900, most people probably thought: "But we'll always need pianos." People today think the same way about the industries they are in. Even when they read in the newspaper or on the Internet that their industry is being affected by economic or social changes, most people are in denial and do nothing about the threat they are under.

*All our lives we are engaged in the process of
accommodating ourselves to our surroundings; living
is nothing else than this process of accommodation.
When we fail a little, we are stupid. When we flagrantly fail, we are mad. A life will be successful
or not, according as the power of accommodation is
equal to or unequal to the strain of fusing and adjusting internal and external changes.*

SAMUEL BUTLER, *THE WAY OF ALL FLESH*
(PENGUIN BOOKS, LIMITED)

Temporary Setbacks

Some industries and occupations ebb and flow with supply and demand. When there is a shortage in a well-paid field, such as nursing, engineering, or law, school enrollments increase, creating an excess. Then people stop entering these fields, creating a shortage. So, sometimes it's easy to get jobs and sometimes it isn't.

The overall economy may also temporarily affect a field or industry. Real estate and construction, for example, may suffer in a down economy and pick up in a strong one.

Ahead of the Market

When the Berlin Wall came down in 1989, there was a rush of companies wanting to capitalize on the potential market in Eastern Europe. Given all they were reading in the papers, job hunters thought it would be a good market for them to explore as well. They were ahead of the market. It took a few years before the market caught up with the concept. Now many people are employed in Eastern Europe or in servicing that market.

The same may be true for the area that you are in or are trying to get into: The market may not be there because it has not yet developed.

Certain medical and personal care jobs will grow by 50% or more as the baby boomer population ages and their needs increase. And let's not forget the impact of healthcare reform on various industries. It's too new and in too much flux for us to understand the impact. Biotech, health care, and related areas (gyms, nutritionists, physical fitness instructors) are also expected to grow. Americans now take it as their right that they should have anything that makes them healthier. Such industries make up a significant part of the GNP, and are projected to grow strongly.

The Bureau of Labor Statistics says we'll also need more actuaries and statisticians, translators and pest control technicians, market research analysts and environmental control specialists.

On the other hand, do give some consideration to the occupations that are expected to decline considerably. This is not the time to decide to work for the Post Office, although some areas will be harder hit than others. Postal Service mail sorters, processors and processing machine operators increasingly are being replaced by more efficient mail sorting machines, and their numbers are projected to decline by more than 50% by 2020.

The printing industry and everything associated with it will continue to be hard hit. Even those who work in desktop publishing will not be needed as much because new software has made it easier for non-experts to develop the publications. Textile repair and the manufacturing industries continue to move jobs overseas.

But don't pick a field simply because it is growing or stay away from it solely because it is declining. The field and industry you target needs to be a good match for you. Part of the answer is in you: what you find out about yourself when you do the exercises in this book. The other part of the answer is "out there" – what you find out as you conduct Internet and library research and talk to people.

If you succeed in judging yourself rightly, then you are indeed a man of true wisdom.

ANTOINE DE SAINT-EXUPÉRY, *THE LITTLE PRINCE*

What about *Your* Industry or Profession?

Is your dream industry or field growing, permanently retrenching, or in a temporary decline because of supply and demand or other economic conditions? If you are lucky, your employer is ahead of the market, and the industry will pick up later. Often, you can find out just by reading your organization's annual report and other information it gives out to the public.

Most people in permanently retrenching industries, including the leaders, incorrectly think the decline is temporary. You have to decide for yourself. You could perhaps gain insight and objectivity by researching what those outside your industry have to say.

It has been predicted that if things continue as they are going, there will soon be a great divide in America, with technologically and internationally aware workers making fine salaries, while the unaware and unskilled earn dramatically lower wages. (Even high-level executives can be unaware and unskilled, and thus face reductions in their salaries as they become less useful.) If this does come to pass, the best a career coach can do is to encourage people to try to be on the winning side of that divide.

Today's workers need to forget jobs completely and look instead for work that needs doing—and then set themselves up as the best way to get that work done.

WILLIAM BRIDGES, *JOBSHIFT: HOW TO PROSPER IN A WORKPLACE WITHOUT JOBS*

CASE STUDY Debbie
Hedging Her Bets for the Future

Debbie had been an account manager in advertising for 15 exciting years. She loved learning everything she could about her shampoo or detergent account, or whatever she was assigned. Debbie was reluctant to change industries despite some negatives: She had a long commute. (Those who want to stay in a retrenching industry often must commute long distances or relocate.) And her job was not as much fun as it used to be. (Companies that survive in retrenching industries tend to experience greater pressure on their bottom line; thus employees have to work longer hours with smaller rewards.) She decided to stay on, but took proactive steps to better ensure her future in two ways:

1. She asked to be assigned to an account that relied on new media, including social media, home shopping and the Internet as well as other non-traditional methods. She knew that if she learned these methods, she could work on the corporate side for an organization that valued her knowledge of these new techniques.
2. In addition, she wanted to work on an account that was in a growing industry, such as healthcare or a related area.

Debbie continues to hold her own as her colleagues get squeezed out of advertising. Some are forced to commute longer distances or relocate just so they can stay in the industry. Although many have lost their jobs, or work for half what they used to, there are still enough people making good money to create the illusion that things are the same as they were. Debbie has hedged her bets: She can either stay in the industry or be valuable outside.

You can be like Debbie: you can position yourself for the future by gaining new experience on the job you are now in, or by doing volunteer work or taking a course to learn the new skills you need to remain competitive.

Retrenching Markets Are All Alike

When an industry retrenches, the results are predictable. A retrenching market, by definition, has more job hunters than jobs. The more that market retrenches, the worse it gets.

Those who want to stay in the field have increasingly longer searches as more people chase fewer jobs. They will also tend to stay in their new jobs for less time as companies in the retrenching industry continue to downsize or go out of business.

Profit margins get squeezed as companies compete for a slice of a shrinking pie. Those companies become less enjoyable to work for because there is less investment in training and development, research, internal communications, and the like. Of course, salaries are cut.

Many young people are enticed into glamour fields, regardless of the practicality, or into fields their parents or friends are in, regardless of the fit for them personally, despite the projections for those fields. Yes, you should pursue your dreams, but check them out a little first.

Most people target only their current industries, fields, or professions at the start of their search. They consider other targets only after they have difficulty getting another job in their present field. They would probably have found something faster if they had looked in other fields from the beginning.

Those in retrenching industries who also target new industries have a shorter search time.

> **The new fields are new to everyone. An outsider has a chance of becoming an insider.**

One doesn't discover new lands without consenting to lose sight of the shore for a very long time.

André Gide

The Attributes of a High-Growth Industry

By definition, growth industries must hire from outside: They don't have enough people inside the industry. The new industry attracts new competitors—many of whom will fail—and there is a shake-out. But if the industry is still growing, those who got in early are the most knowledgeable and valuable, and can command larger salaries. If the industry does not continue to grow, new entrants create a surplus of labor and salaries decrease.

As long as the industry continues to grow, there is an open window: Those outside the industry can get in. As the industry stabilizes, there will be plenty of experienced people, companies will want only those with direct experience, and the window will close.

> **HMOs, cellular technology, for-profit schools—and the Internet—were essentially nonexistent industries just 20 years ago.**

Expanding Your Search Geographically; Targeting Small Companies

Studies show that more jobs are created in the suburbs than in major metropolitan areas, and there is greater job creation in the new suburbs than in the old suburbs. Oops! It's good to know the facts, because you can conduct your search accordingly. If you have been ignoring the suburbs, think about them.

Job growth has been in smaller companies. Large companies do most of the downsizing. In New York City, for example, **there are 193,000 companies. Only 270 of them employ 1,000 people or more.** James Brown, an economist for the New York State Department of Labor specializing in the New York City labor market, advised members of the mid-Manhattan Five O'Clock Club to look to the other 192,730 companies—those that employ fewer than 1,000 employees.

Think about your geographic area, and think about the companies you are targeting. Most job hunters naturally think about the big companies that are in the news, but perhaps you should think about the new *hidden job market*: the suburbs, and companies with fewer than 1,000 employees.

All our lives we are engaged in the process of accommodating ourselves to our surroundings; living is nothing else than this process of accommodation. When we fail a little, we are stupid. When we flagrantly fail, we are mad. A life will be successful or not, according as the power of accommodation is equal to or unequal to the strain of fusing and adjusting internal and external chances.

SAMUEL BUTLER, THE WAY OF ALL FLESH

The Bad News Is Good News—If You Are FLEXIBLE

Virtually every industry and field has been and will continue to be affected by technological changes and global competition. Whether you are in education, work for the Post Office, or sell books, your field will continue to be affected. As Alice said about Wonderland: It takes all the running you can do to stay in the same place.

The good news is that many fields are much easier to enter today than they were in times when careers were more stable. There is room for you if you target properly and stay flexible. If you continue to learn in the field you are now in, and get to know the areas you are pursuing, you will be able to make changes as the world changes.

If your current industry or profession is retrenching (and you expect to be working more than 5 or 10 more years), it makes sense to investigate some of the growing fields.

Even if you end up back in your old retrenching industry, the time you have spent exploring a new industry is not wasted, because you will probably have to search again.

For workers, there are dark spots, but the overall picture is still far brighter than commonly believed. Real wages are starting to turn up, after years of decline. The old factory jobs are disappearing, but new jobs in other industries are being generated at an unprecedented rate. Rather than becoming a nation of hamburger flippers, we are becoming a nation of schoolteachers, computer programmers, and health-care managers. About 11 million new jobs have been created since 1989, and of those, approximately two-thirds are managerial and professional positions. There is a tremendous surge in creativity and new opportunities, ranging from new forms of entertainment to cheap global communications.

MICHAEL MANDEL, *THE HIGH-RISK SOCIETY* (TIME BUSINESS)

Determining a career direction and making progress in your career takes constant attention. The efforts you put into your education (perhaps training as opposed to only thinking about degrees), into career development, into salary negotiation, into networking, into targeting a meaningful job, have never had such a strong chance of bearing good fruit! After all, it is so easy to become discouraged that those who refuse to become discouraged and who attend the small-group strategy sessions weekly, are more likely to make progress.

There is guidance for each of us, and by lowly listening, we shall hear the right word.

RALPH WALDO EMERSON

Getting More Sophisticated

Whether you are relatively new to the labor force or have been working a while, think past the obvious and think more deeply about the changes that are occurring.

Listed below are a few of the industries business experts project will grow in the near future. Try to discover other areas that may be affected by these or how your own job may be affected by growth in these areas. Each is huge and chang-

ing, and can be better defined by your investigation through networking, as well as Internet and library research.

Here is the list of some of the industries expected to grow:

- Health care and biotech, or anything having to do with them. Health care is considered a sure bet because of the aging population, the advances being made in medical technology and medical record-keeping, and the impact of healthcare reform.
- Anything high-tech, or the high-tech aspect of whatever field or industry you are in.
- The international aspect of the field/industry you are considering.
- The environmental area; waste management.
- Safety and security (especially since the September 11th attack on the United States and, unfortunately, the continuing threats in everyday life).
- The constantly changing areas of telecommunications, the new media, and global communications (social media, movie studios, TV networks, cable companies, computer companies, consumer-electronics companies, and publishers).
- Education in the broadest sense (as opposed to the traditional classroom), including computer-assisted instruction. (Researchers have found that people who are illiterate learn to read better with computer-assisted instruction than they do in a classroom.)
- Because all of us will have to keep up-to-date in more areas in order to do our jobs well, technology will play an important part in our continuing education. Further, with America lagging so far behind other countries educationally, both the for-profit and not-for-profit sectors are working hard to revamp our educational system.
- Alternative means of distributing goods.

Instead of retail stores, think not only about direct mail but also about purchasing by TV—or the Internet (think of the impact Amazon is having).

- Anything serving the aging population, both products and services.

In studying the preceding list, think of how you can combine different industries to come up with areas to pursue. For example: Combine the aging population with education, or the aging population with telecommunications, or health care with education, and so on. The more you research, the more sophisticated your thoughts will get.

If you combine education with the new media, you will be thinking like many experts. Students in schools are learning from interactive multimedia presentations on computers—presentations that will be as exciting as computer games and MTV combined, and almost as up-to-date as the morning news (most textbooks are years out of date). Teachers will do what computers cannot do: facilitate the groups, encourage, reinforce learning.

A computer-based approach can be used to train and update the knowledge of the U.S.'s workers: Employees can learn when they have the time and at their own pace, rather than having large numbers of workers leave their jobs to learn in a classroom situation.

When you read predictions that there will be a huge growth in a certain industry, say, home health-care workers, personal and home care aides, and medical assistants, medical secretaries, radiology technologists and technicians, and psychologists, you may think: "I don't want to be any of those." Think more creatively. Companies will have to spring up to supply and train those workers. (Some of the training could be done on multimedia.) People will be needed to manage the companies, regulate the care given, coach patients on how to select and manage such workers, and so on. If you read about the tremendous growth in the temporary help business, you may become a temporary worker yourself, or you could

go to work running one of the temporary help companies.

Potential job growth varies by geographic area. For example, while the fastest growing areas in Massachusetts were in IT, education and healthcare, it is unfortunate that the job growth was centered in Boston and the outlying areas suffered. In other geographic areas, the job growth (or at least the job possibilities because there is less competition) is in the suburbs.

Think about the field you are interested in, and how it is being affected by technology and the global marketplace. Virtually every job and industry—whether it is publishing, entertainment, manufacturing, or financial services—is being impacted. If you are not aware, you will be blindsided.

Your Age: How Much Longer Do You Want to Work?

If you want to work only two more years, it may not be worth investing the time to learn a new area. (This is assuming you can get a job in your old area if it is retrenching.)

If you want to work another 10 years, learn new things—if only to keep up with what is happening in your present field.

The trouble with the future is that it usually arrives before we're ready for it.

ARNOLD H. GLASOW

Some Areas Are Safer Bets

The rate of change is so fast that technologies you read about may never reach the mainstream or may be replaced with new developments. However, some areas are safer bets than others. Hard skills are more marketable than soft skills. For example, a person who wants to get a job as a general writer will have more difficulty than someone who can bring more to the party—such as some specialization or computer skills.

When there is no vision, the people perish.

OLD TESTAMENT, PROVERBS 29:18

Figure It Out

It's your job to figure out how your dream industry or field is being impacted by technology, global competition, and the market in general. Think where you fit into the future. Do research.

We are now on the ground floor of many industries, and at an exciting time for those who choose to take advantage of the revolutionary changes that are taking place.

So, once again, remember the definition of job hunting that The Five O'Clock Club developed:

Job hunting in a changing economy means continuously becoming aware of market conditions inside, as well as outside your present organization, and learning more about what you have to offer.

A New Way of Thinking

Any assignment (or job) you get is a temporary one. You're doing work, but you don't have a permanent job. It's like an actor who lands a part. He or she does not really know how long it may last. Furthermore, actors tend to worry about whether or not a role will typecast them and potentially cause them to lose future roles. Or they may intentionally decide to be typecast, hoping it will increase their chances going forward. Actors understand that they will most likely have to land another role after this one, and they constantly think about how a certain role will position them going forward. And so must you. Your next job is only a temporary assignment.

Work today is not just doing; it is, more than ever, thinking. Today's organization needs thinking, flexible, proactive workers. It wants creative problem solvers, workers smart and skilled enough to move with new technologies and with the ever-changing competitive environment. It needs workers accustomed to collaborating with co-workers, to participating in quality circles, to dealing with people high and low. Communication skills and people skills have become parts of the necessary repertoire of the modern worker.

HEDRICK SMITH, *RETHINKING AMERICA* (AVON BOOKS)

Learning to Track Trends and Move into a New Market

The factory of the future will have only two employees, a man and a dog. The man will be there to feed the dog. The dog will be there to keep the man from touching the equipment.

WARREN BENNIS

You are not stuck in your present field or industry just because that's where you have your experience. You do not have to take a pay cut or start at the bottom to get into a new field. Trade off what you already know. Learn the new area. Become an insider. In this volatile market, where jobs are disappearing every day, new jobs are appearing. Select a field that will position you for the long run. The people in our stories are picking up skills and experience that will be transferable to other jobs—and they will be extremely marketable. Remember, 58% of those in the Five O'Clock Club program decide to change careers.

Virtually every industry is in turmoil. Read what experts write about the industries that interest you. Then think about—or research—the industry you are in now. What are the trends? What outside forces are affecting your industry? How might you be affected? How can you prepare for the future?

If you are targeting other industries, research them to see how you fit in with their new directions. This research and planning will keep you more prepared—and more stable—in this unstable world.

Within the next decades education will change more than it has changed since the modern school was created by the printed book over three hundred years ago. An economy in which knowledge is becoming the true capital and the premier wealth-producing resource makes new and stringent demands on the schools for education performance and educational responsibility.... How we learn and how we teach are changing drastically and fast— the result, in part, of new theoretical understanding of the learning process, in part of new technology.

PETER DRUCKER, *THE NEW REALITIES* (ROUTLEDGE)

The Growth of the Internet

A few years ago, the pace of technological change started to pick up: There was a confluence of technological work in various arenas that began to bear fruit.

You may know that the Internet itself was envisioned in 1945—more than half a century ago—by Vannevar Bush, an electrical engineer. Hypertext, the basis for interactivity on the Internet, was developed in 1965! The World Wide Web was created in 1989 using hypertext. HTML, the *hypertext markup language*, was developed in 1990. Yet, interactive business applications on desktop computers were in relatively wide commercial use by 1980.

> **Here's one way to look at it:**
> Radio ➡ TV ➡ Computers ➡
> Internet ➡ ?

The long-accepted concept of computer-based interactivity, combined relatively recently with HTML and URLs, laid the groundwork for the surge we are experiencing today.

In the mid-1990s, we told concerned Five O'Clock Clubbers who were targeting Internet-related companies that even if the Internet didn't make it, their new skills would be transferable to whatever interactive technologies took its place.

Clearly, *interactive* was here to stay: Computer interactivity had been popular in business applications for over 20 years! But the Internet was not just another interactive medium, such as ATMs, interactive kiosks, and telephones, or even CD-ROMs. The Internet was an international infrastructure for commerce and ideas, an intelligent medium that made people smarter and proactive. It was a core medium that would change everything.

The Same Development Pattern in Other Industries

The development of the Internet—a long gestation period followed by a *sudden* appearance on the market—was paralleled by developments in a number of unrelated industries, and the results added to the cataclysm. Probably half of the jobs that exist today did not exist 10 years ago:

- HMOs, alternative medicine and health-care reform have changed the face of **healthcare**. Hospitals have been merging or shutting down while new hospitals are being built. The aging population, the increase in elective surgery, and (perhaps as of this writing) the increase in the number of Americans with health insurance, have changed that trend and encouraged them to offer services that attract patients who can afford to pay or have the government pay for them. More hospitals are specializing—in eye and ear, heart, cancer, and so on—to increase profitability, putting a squeeze on general hospitals that have to handle the less profitable business.

- Still, employers—and the country— have had to find ways to cut health care costs and innovations abound. Hospitals are spending money on technology to streamline operations, including launching electronic patient-record systems. Insurance companies have added help lines, hoping to reduce the number of actual doctor visits.

- But good help is hard to find. Some private-practice doctors left the profession because of rising malpractice insurance ($35,000+ per year) and the restrictive fees paid by HMOs and Medicare, and went into pharmaceutical sales or medical research. The nursing shortage continues, with bonuses and other lures becoming common. On the other hand, some employers were becoming more demanding by hiring nurses who have a B.S. and not just an Associates degree.

- **Telecom**, with cellular phones that can take photographs and access the Internet with an international reach, looks nothing like it did only a few years ago.

- **Education** will be permanently changed by for-profit schools, the erosion of tenure, and the technological advances that are impacting the industry—with or without the approval of powerful unions.

- **Retail** no longer necessarily means going into a store or even talking to a person. Alternative distribution methods have been in the works for decades—through direct mail and other means—and now through the Internet. People don't need stores to buy computers, travel agents to arrange travel, or stockbrokers to purchase stocks. Automobiles are *sold* over the Internet, a new direct-marketing approach: Showrooms are there so you can kick the tires. But the marketing approaches keep evolving. The direct-mail industry was badly hurt by the Internet. But by 2004, popular Internet sites, such as Ebay and Amazon, mailed millions of glossy catalogues to homes to promote their websites. Internet companies were using direct mail!

- The **entertainment** industry has morphed in unpredictable ways, and media growth is being driven by technology, not programming. For example, 20 years ago, there were three broadcast networks and 20 cable channels. DVDs did not exist. Today, there are six broadcast networks, 300 cable channels (perhaps going to a 600+ channel universe), and PCs in virtually every home, as well as DVD players and VCRs. There's "on demand" on your TV, TIVO so you can record the TV shows you want to see later and fast forward past the commercials, and computer websites where you can see the latest TV show or movie. A large number of families have installed video game consoles attached to their TV sets.
- Cell phones, PDAs, iPods and iPads are all part of the entertainment arena. Traditional marketing approaches are becoming less efficient. And, as of this writing, content is the entertainment king, allowing companies to exploit content over multiple media. Pirated software, music, and movies have plagued those industries, and new technology may be the primary answer because legislation does not seem to be working. As of this writing, the music industry is testing the sale of new releases as digital only—no CD, just the digital music. This is after hundreds of record stores closed, while those that remained have devoted more shelf space to DVDs and video games, leaving less space for CDs.

- Movie theaters look nothing like their old-time counterparts. Instead of the good old days where people listened to an organist, saw two cartoons and a double feature, we now sit through paid advertisements, have more comfortable chairs, stadium seating, and a broader variety of refreshments—almost a meal.
- The **publishing** industry (books, magazines) continues to be under pressure, now competing with the Internet, video games, and DVDs. And Amazon.com is now selling used books— some just a few days old—which further undercuts traditional publishing. E-books sales on Amazon now exceed the sales of printed books.
- The **advertising** industry continues to evolve. It's been decades since the industry relied on the three major networks for its revenue. The latest trends: implanting marketing messages in video games, movies, and TV shows as well as various forms of product placement. In addition, some print advertising is starting to look like editorials.

Who could have dreamed of today's situation just five years ago? But these changes created open windows in the new areas while traditional fields retrenched and revamped.

Risk vs. Security

Should those looking for jobs or consulting assignments focus on the "stable" industries— such as banking ("I've been in banking for 15 years—obviously, I should find another job in banking"), hospitals, the traditional telephone companies, and the old retail? Some should.

But in retrospect—we're almost far enough removed to be able to look back on these *old* industries—the answer for many is *no*. Those looking for another job or assignment cannot necessarily find stability by staying in the same field or industry: Those areas have changed.

> **Are you more likely to find stability in the old, retrenching industries, or in the uncertain industries of the future?**

Professions Also Get Outmoded Overnight

Strangely enough, this is the past that somebody in the future is longing to go back to.

ASHLEIGH BRILLIANT

It used to be that once a person had found a profession, that was their source of stability. That is absolutely no longer the case: Professions change overnight. Ask physicians or attorneys about their early visions of those professions and you will quickly hear how their fields have dramatically changed. Physicians in their fifties and sixties say they are lucky to have been part of the golden age of medicine—when doctors could see whomever they wanted, recommend whatever they felt was in their patients' best interests, get referrals from other physicians, and earn good money. Now, nothing is the same.

Fifteen years ago, we rarely saw an attorney at The Five O'Clock Club, and until five years ago, we had no physicians. Now, we have plenty of both—and computer programmers as well. Their professions have changed—quickly.

In this high-risk society, each person's main asset will be his or her willingness and ability to take intelligent risks. Those people best able to cope with uncertainty... will fare better in the long run than those who cling to security.

MICHAEL MANDEL, *THE HIGH-RISK SOCIETY*

The High-Risk Society

In 1996, Michael Mandel wrote in *The High-Risk Society* that the times are good, but prosperity has come at a high price: more intense, more pervasive economic uncertainty than Americans have suffered at any time in the past 50 years.

Mr. Mandel pointed out that prosperity and security no longer go hand in hand. "Today, the very forces behind economic turbulence are also the world's greatest engines of growth. As a result, success hinges on your willingness to embrace risk—rather than flee from it."

Those who keep up and see where the future is heading—in both their professions and their industries—can benefit from the changes that are going to take place anyway.

Now, we all expect new developments and we expect uncertainty. We expect our fields and industries to change. This time, we're ready.

Our eyes are open now. We keep up-to-date. We stay in touch. We're thinking about our next move even before we start a new position. We know that we have to take charge of our careers, and that doesn't seem so bad anymore. We've got perspective.

God bless you as you face the uncertain future. It's better than trying to stay in the nonexistent past.

The essence of the high-risk society is choice: the choice between embracing uncertainty and running from it.

MICHAEL MANDEL, *THE HIGH-RISK SOCIETY*
(TIME BUSINESS)

When to See a Coach Privately

Just as you have a doctor to help you with medical problems (or to prevent problems), consider developing a relationship with a coach who gets to know you over the long term. Speak to your coach when you have specific problems, such as those listed below, or for a *checkup* to make sure everything is okay. Schedule a private session to:

- Negotiate your severance package (get what you deserve and need)

- Solve present job problems (do a better job of managing up, down, and across)
- Determine your career path (plan now; avoid the rush)

And when you are job hunting, to:

- Prepare your résumé
- Plan your marketing campaign
- Practice for an important interview
- Plan your salary negotiation

If you need help, visit the coaching section of our website: www.fiveoclockclub.com.

When you become a member, we will refer you to two Five O'Clock Club-certified coaches. You can choose one to help you with your job search and career planning.

The line between the self-employed condition and working for an "employer" has become unclear: Communications technology and flextime arrangements allow official, full-time employees to telecommute and to do their forty hours a week without leaving home. At the same time, self-employed people may get contracts that not only require them to perform the tasks that used to be done by a jobholder, but also give them an in-house office, membership on a task force within the organization, and even a discount at the employee store.

WILLIAM BRIDGES, *JOBSHIFT: HOW TO PROSPER IN A WORKPLACE WITHOUT JOBS* (ADDISON-WESLEY)

Case Studies:
Targeting the Future

While your basic emotional temperament may not change much during your lifetime, you can make significant day-to-day adjustments in the way you perceive events and respond to them. When you face an emotionally trying situation, guard against exaggerating or over-generalizing, and focus instead on your specific options for taking direct action. Avoid putting yourself down by doing something that will exercise your good traits. And seek the company of others, whether it's to gather more rational views on the situation or simply to change your mood.

JACK MAGUIRE, *CARE AND FEEDING OF THE BRAIN*
(DOUBLEDAY RELIGIOUS PUBLISHING GROUP)

What about Your Field, Industry, or Geographic Area?

A job target is a clearly selected geographic area, an industry or organization size, and a function or position within that industry. An accountant, for example, may target a certain industry (such as telecommunications or hospitals), or may see himself in the accounting function and may not care which industry he is in but prefer instead to focus on *organization size*. This means he wants to target a small, medium, or large organization, regardless of industry.

Examine your targets to see how each is doing. Perhaps, for example, your industry is okay, but large organizations are not doing well, while smaller organizations are hiring. In this case, target smaller organizations.

What changes are taking place in your in-

dustry or function? If you think your industry or function will continue to retrench, *find a new horse to ride*: an industry or function that is on a growth curve, or one that will give you transferable skills.

The person who fears to try is thus enslaved.

LEONARD E. READ

CASE STUDY Ed
The Benefit of Targeting

Ed and Steve were both administrative managers in the retail industry. Both had lost their jobs. Each had spent 20 years—their entire working lives—in retail. Both wanted to work in health care.

Steve actually had hands-on health-care experience. A few years earlier, his organization had lent him to a major hospital to serve as the interim administrative head for a full year. He loved that assignment, did very well at it, and swore he would get a job like that again someday.

But Steve decided to be *practical*: "All my contacts are in retail, and I need a job *now*. It's true I would like to move into a growth area, but I don't have time to learn a new industry. I have no choice but to focus on the retail industry."

Ed, on the other hand, targeted health care, and had retail as a separate target. Ed joined health-care associations that dealt with administration, read all the health-care administration trade magazines, and became knowledgeable about the industry. He met with lots of people, largely through the associations. He was even willing to take a temp job doing data entry in the administrative area of hospitals so he could see what was happening from the inside. His ego did not get in the way.

A job came up: exactly the same hospital job Steve had worked in for a full year. Both Ed and Steve heard about the job, and interviewed extensively.

Who got the job? Ed did—because he sounded more believable, more committed to the industry. Even though he had never held a job in that industry, Ed had *proven* by all his activities that he was sincerely interested in health care.

Steve sounded like all the other job hunters: He wanted this job just because there happened to be an opening.

He had nothing to talk about except the fact that he had held that job before and that they had liked him. Of course, he tried to maximize that experience. But what was noticed was that he had given no recent indication that he was committed to hospital work—he had not interviewed at other hospitals, etc.

This story is a vivid example of the benefits of thoroughly targeting an industry. It is also encouraging proof that people can enter new industries with no prior experience.

Progress might have been all right once,
But it has gone on too long.

Ogden Nash

"People in That Industry Won't Let Me In."

Job hunters always say it's hard to change from one industry to another. "Hiring managers don't believe I want to get into that field." I don't believe those job hunters either because they never read anything about the field, and don't know anyone in the field who would serve as a

reality check for them. How do you prove to the hiring managers that you are truly interested? As we say in the chapter *How to Change Careers:*

- Read the industry's trade journals.
- Get to know people in that industry or field.
- Join its organizations; attend its meetings.
- Be persistent.
- Write proposals.
- Be persistent.
- Take relevant courses, part-time jobs, or do volunteer work related to the new industry or skill area.
- Be persistent.

If you want to get into an industry or field, learn about it.

It's Time to Take Control of Your Own Career

If you succeed in judging yourself rightly, then you are indeed a man of true wisdom.

Antoine de Saint-Exupéry, *The Little Prince*

Get in the habit of reading the news or searching the Internet and noticing what news may affect the industry or field you are in. Learn about some of the industries of the future.

Even if all you want is a job right now, instead of a career, do the exercises in the next section. Be sure to include at least the Seven Stories Exercise, Interests, Values, and Forty-Year Vision. They won't take a long time to do, and they will shorten the length of your search.

Illness strikes men when they are exposed to change.

Herodotus, Greek historian

Case Study Scott
What Should I Be when I Grow Up?

Scott is 38, a lawyer with a varied background. He had worked for the DA's office and a stock exchange, and wrote for a magazine. With his diverse past, he didn't know what to do next.

I know only one way to figure out what a person should be, and it's to use the methodology in this book. So that's what I did with Scott—a shortened version of the exercises.

Seven Stories Exercise

First, we did the Seven Stories Exercise. I said: "Tell me something you've done that you really enjoyed doing, know you did well, and felt a sense of accomplishment about. It doesn't matter what other people thought, how old you were, whether or not you earned money doing it. You may want to start with: 'There was the time when I. ..'"

Scott said: "There was the time when I argued my first case before a jury."

I asked him to tell me the details and what he enjoyed about it.

"I liked being independent, I was calling the shots. I had to plan the whole thing myself..."

I asked for another story.

Scott said: "I wrote an exposé for a magazine."

I asked Scott to tell me more. He said he enjoyed the same things: being independent, calling the shots, etc. Seemingly, the only time Scott enjoyed a bureaucratic environment was when he broke away from it.

Scott thought that he had a scattered background, and that everything was different. To my mind, those two stories were alike, so I had enough to go on. (If the stories had been in conflict, I would have asked him for as many as seven stories.)

Values Exercise

"Scott, tell me the things that are important to you." He replied, "Money is important, and independence."

Interests Exercise

"Scott, what are your interests?" Languages were very important to him; he had command of a few. The international area was central to his interests.

Scott's exercise results will serve as a template. He can make sure that his next job will allow him to be independent, to earn the money he wants, to enjoy the international area, and so on.

The Forty-Year Vision

Then I guided him through an abbreviated version of the Forty-Year Vision. I don't know how to help people unless I know where they are heading. If all I know is their past, their future will be more of the same. We spent only five minutes on this exercise.

I start with the present to get people grounded in the present. If I simply ask: "What do you want to be?" it doesn't work. They have nothing to base it on.

"Tell me what your life is like right now. What is your relationship with your family, however you define family? Where do you live? What is it physically like? What are your hobbies and interests? How is your health? What do you do for exercise? How would you describe the job you have right now? And tell me anything else you want to about your life today."

Next, I asked Scott to tell me about his life at age 43. Then I asked about his life at age 53. In part, he said:

"I am living in the suburbs. I have a wife and four kids. The oldest is sixteen; the youngest is nine. (It is helpful to put down how old your kids are at each stage so you feel yourself getting older.) I have a small consulting firm, with perhaps four employees who do research and support me in what I am doing. I do a lot of business in Europe. Whatever I am doing is 'at the center of the world'—I feel I'm on top of the important things that are happening."

From my point of view, there were no conflicts in the results of his exercises. They all showed him in an independent situation.

Scott seemed to me to be the stereotypical entrepreneur. I do think he should have his own business, but not right now. Having people work for him sounded right because he seemed disorganized. As he himself suggested, one person could keep him in line and clean up after him. His business might have to do with international business, and also with high-tech. He wants to be at the center of what's happening.

Scott needs to focus on something that is a growth area and also satisfies his other needs. There are lots of areas that could fulfill him. The danger is that he may spend 20 years never selecting something to focus on. If a person like Scott is always exploring, it may be best to just arbitrarily pick something, because there is no one correct answer. Other people who are in a rut may need to spend more time exploring.

Scott happens to have contacts in the telecommunications industry. If he can get into the telecommunications field, he should try to learn what he can, and develop a business plan while he is there.

Scott now has a vision. He can follow the vision, or not. If he continues to try out every field he comes across, he will be in constant turmoil. He will simply go from job to job, wind up in his sixties with a lot of experiences but no career, and never reach his dream.

It's the same for you. Figure out the things you enjoy doing and also do well. Do your Forty-Year Vision. These exercises will serve as your anchor as well as your guide. You won't get as irritated in your next job, because you'll know what you're getting out of it. You will keep up your research and your knowledge of the field. You will gain the skills you need to go forward.

When I examined myself and my methods of thought, I came to the conclusion that the gift of fantasy has meant more to me than my talent for absorbing positive knowledge.

ALBERT EINSTEIN

Retraining Is for Everybody—Even Executives

When people talk about retraining in the United States, they are usually talking about lower-level workers who don't have computer skills. Retraining is necessary at all levels. Do research to learn the terminology of the industry you want to enter so you can be an insider, not an outsider.

By definition, new industries must hire people from outside the industry. If a job hunter studies the field, and develops a sincere interest in it, he or she has a good chance of being hired.

Careful research is a critical component, and will become a central part of every sophisticated person's job search.

If you just think off the top of your head about the areas you should be targeting, your ideas will probably be superficial—and outdated.

Change is happening at an increasingly faster rate. Industries disappear, and new ones spring up quickly. Instead of simply hunting for the next job, think about your long-range career.

You can *pick the right horse to ride* into your future rather than hanging on for dear life in a declining market. If you pick the right horse, you'll have a much easier ride.

Achieving Stability in a Changing World

How can you keep yourself stable in a constantly changing economy? If the world is being battered, and organizations are being battered, and many CEOs cannot keep their jobs, what are you going to do?

The benefit of doing the following exercises is that they give you confidence and a sense of stability in a changing world. You will learn to know yourself and become sure of exactly what you can take with you wherever you go.

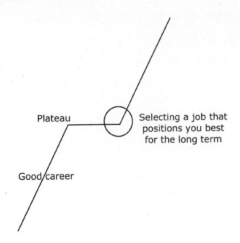

Plateau

Selecting a job that
positions you best
for the long term

Good/career

*One doesn't discover new lands without consenting to
lose sight of the shore for a very long time.*

ANDRÉ GIDE

The Result of Assessment Is Job Targets

If you go through an assessment with a career
coach or vocational testing center, and do not
wind up with tentative job targets, the assessment has not helped you very much. You must go
one more step, and decide what to *do* with this
information.

The Result of Assessment Is Power

The more you know about yourself, the more
power you have to envision a job that will suit
you. The exercises give you power.

People find it hard to believe that I went
through a period of about 30 years when I was
painfully shy. In graduate school, I was afraid
when they took roll because I obsessed about
whether I should answer "here" or "present."

When I had to give a presentation, the best I
could do was read the key words from my index
cards. (Today, my throat is actually hoarse from
all the public speaking I do.) I will be forever
grateful for the kindness of strangers who told me
I did well when I knew I was awful.

The only thing that ultimately saved me was
doing the Seven Stories Exercise. When I was
little, I led groups of kids in the neighborhood,
and I did it well. It gave me strength to know that
I was inherently a group leader regardless of how
I was behaving now. (I was in my thirties at the
time.)

The Seven Stories Exercise grounds you, and
the Forty-Year Vision guides you. When people
said: "Would you like to lead groups?" I said to
myself, "Well, I led groups when I was 10. Maybe
I can do it again." The transition was painful, and
took many years, but my Seven Stories Exercise
kept me going. And my Forty-Year Vision let me
know there was plenty of time in which to do it.

*Enjoy yourself. If you can't enjoy yourself,
enjoy somebody else.*

JACK SCHAEFER

I was going to buy a copy of The Power of Positive
Thinking, *and then I thought: What the hell good
would that do?*

RONNIE SHAKES

The person who fears to try is thus enslaved.

LEONARD E. READ

The Five O'Clock Club®

What Longevity Means to Your Career

Dr. Lydia Bronte, *The Longevity Factor*

*When I was fifty, I thought my life was over...
Little did I know that the best years of my life
were still ahead of me.*

EVELYN NEF, 80-YEAR-OLD PSYCHOTHERAPIST
WHO TRAINED IN HER 60S

In every era there have been a few people who lived to be unusually old, but who kept work-ing—and were still good at what they did. We all know that Pablo Picasso and Marc Chagall continued to paint until their deaths at 92 and 97, respectively; and that classical cellist Pablo Casals remained a master musician until his death at 96, despite arthritis.

Usually we rationalize the accomplishments of people like these by calling them exceptions—implying that perhaps their genius was also responsible for their lasting productivity.

But we won't be able to dismiss such late-life achievements as rarities much longer. One of the most astonishing changes that has ever taken place in human life occurred during the twentieth century, although it went relatively unnoticed until a few years ago: People are living a lot longer.

> **The average life expectancy today in the United States is 29 years longer than it was in 1900. These years have been added to middle age, not old age.**

Recently we have begun to focus upon one aspect of this change—aging—because of the growing numbers of older people in our society. The big news, however, is not aging. It is longevity. And as it turns out, although we tend to confuse them, they are two quite different things.

Galloping Longevity

How many times do you say to yourself, "If only I had more time"? Chances are that you'll have it: up to 30 years' worth of extra time, and maybe more. Longevity has increased during the last 100 years more dramatically than at any other time in recorded human history.

In less than 100 years, the length of adult life has doubled. We've gone from an average life expectancy of 47 to one of 76, and still climbing.

Something that happens over the span of one century may seem ploddingly slow in terms of an individual's day-to-day experience. By ordinary statistical standards, however, this change has taken place with the speed of a moon rocket.

Consider: From A.D. 1 to A.D. 1900, human beings gained about 1½ years of average life expectancy per century. By contrast, from 1900 to 1994, we added 29 years—almost three decades— to average life expectancy.

This is a stunning change. What is even more stunning is that it is continuing; in both 1993 and 1994, average life expectancy gained one year in the United States. **We are nearing the point where we may add as much average life expectancy every year as former generations added in an entire century!**

The extra time starts to click in at around the age of 50. And to make it even better, even though you will live to an older chronological age, for reasons scientists don't yet understand, that extra time for most is not time spent in old age.

The Second Middle Age

As lifetimes have lengthened, the physical aging process has been slowed down or postponed. The three extra decades gained through longevity have really been added to the **middle** of our lives. It amounts to a *second middle age* between the end of the old-style *first middle age*, 35 to 50, and the age at which we become physically old, which varies according to the individual.

The Long Careers Study

From 1987 to 1993, I conducted detailed life-history interviews with 150 people who continued to be active and to work during the second middle age and beyond the age of 65. Their ages ranged between 65 and 102, with the majority in their 70s and 80s. These long-lived Americans can be considered the pathfinder generation for those of us in our 30s, 40s, and 50s.

We have had an image of adult life based on the lives of our parents and grandparents, assuming a relatively short lifetime. Relying on this outdated notion is a little like trying to drive across the United States using a road map that was printed in 1930: The highway system isn't the same and even the landscape is different. Today we need a new map when thinking about adult life.

The Long Careers Study suggests that in order to make good use of this new life stage, all of us need to change radically the way we think about work.

There's no question that the length of your life has a connection to your career. The more you know now, the better you will be able to plan ahead for your work life. If you've followed The Five O'Clock Club's suggestion and made a Forty-

Year Vision, you may live to see every aspect of it come true—even if you're 50 right now.

New Horizons in Growth

As a result of this study, I am convinced that the developmental patterns of a long lifetime are different in many respects from those of a short lifetime. And the patterns of a long career are different from those of a short one.

Americans have a widespread belief that youth and the "first middle age" are the most creative periods of one's life and career.

For many years we have been told that the most vigorous and productive period is between 30 and 45. This idea was publicized around 1950 by Harvey Lehman, a scientist who calculated creative output in scientists, philosophers, artists, writers, and musicians—without, however, taking into account the possibility that the automatic ceiling of a short lifetime might have skewed the results.

The examples cited below are drawn from the careers of well-known people because of their recognition value. But the patterns hold true for average people too.

If you can feel growth and development, you don't feel old. It's when you feel you can't learn anything or do anything new that it's the end of the road.

SHIRLEY BRUSSELL, FOUNDER OF OPERATION ABLE AT AGE 55 (AT AGE 80, WAS STILL ITS EXECUTIVE DIRECTOR)

Multiple Career Peaks

The Long Careers Study participants showed astonishing differences in their periods of high achievement. Some of them did have early peaks of achievement, while others blossomed later or several times. For example: Dr. Linus Pauling made a discovery in his early 30s for which he subsequently won a Nobel Prize; Dr. Jonas Salk invented the polio vaccine in his late 30s to early 40s.

However, most of the people who had early peaks subsequently went on to have second and third peaks later in life. Pauling, for example, went on to make other scientific discoveries, and then in his late 40s took 10 years to go around the world speaking on behalf of world peace, an effort for which he won a second Nobel Prize.

Next, Pauling began his path-breaking research on human nutrition and vitamins. Ultimately, he played a key role both in educating the public about the value of vitamin and mineral supplements and in persuading government agencies to acknowledge the importance of nutrition to health and to sponsor more research on the subject.

Early Sustained Peaks

The exceptions to the multiple-peak pattern were people who stayed in the same career and turned an early peak into a lifelong high plateau, like science fiction writer Isaac Asimov. Beginning with his first successes in his early 30s, Asimov built a career that helped shape the genre itself, developing science fiction into one of the most popular forms of contemporary literature. His productivity continued unabated until shortly before his death of heart failure at 72.

The Age-50 Gateway

There was another group of participants who began an extraordinary period of productivity at about the age of 50. **Almost half of the study participants had a major career peak after age 50.**

This was a completely unexpected finding. In this pattern, the individual seems to be serving a kind of apprenticeship during the first 30 years of working life—accumulating experience in a way that leads to a massive upward shift in achievement around 50.

Culinary expert Julia Child, who died at age 91, is a striking example. Forced to abandon her first career because she married a fellow civil servant, Paul Child, she searched for several years to find another field. Finally she discovered French cooking by chance, when her husband was assigned to France as a USIA officer.

Starting at about the age of 35, Child trained as a chef, founded her own cooking school, and worked on a cookbook, *Mastering the Art of French Cooking*. In 1960, when Child was almost 50, the couple moved back to the United States, where the book was published. A chance publicity appearance on television led to her famous TV series.

A slightly different pattern was that of John W. Gardner, who was president of Carnegie Corporation of New York. When he was in his late 40s, he was stimulated by the discussions of an education commission of which he was a member. Gardner started writing down his ideas. He eventually developed them into a small book, *Excellence: Can We Be Excellent and Equal Too?* Decades later, the book still forms the basis for many popular business books by Tom Peters and others.

Gardner went on to make another leap by leaving his comfortable Carnegie position in his 50s to become administrative assistant of the Department of Health, Education and Welfare in Washington, DC. Next he founded two public-interest organizations. He made his most recent career change at 79 when he accepted a professorship at the Stanford University Business School. Even in his early 80s, he taught students more than half a century younger than he was.

The Age-65 Gateway

About one-third of the participants had major career peaks after age 65; 5 percent had their **highest** peak of achievement after age 65.

Most of these people found their real vocation later in life. They had no intention or expectation of becoming prominent; they were simply following their own developmental pattern.

Take, for example, Maggie Kuhn, who had a stable and respectable career as a church organizer. What changed her life was her mandatory retirement at the age of 65. Several other women she knew were also forced out of their careers.

Kuhn and her friends were furious at the discrimination they had experienced. They felt that if they had been men, they undoubtedly would have been offered several more years of full-time work, or consulting contracts. But as women they were simply ushered out unceremoniously.

They decided to form a discussion group to figure out what to do with the rest of their lives. By a series of fortuitous circumstances, their little association ended up becoming the Gray Panthers, a nationwide activist organization.

You can't retire from life—or from work, in a true sense. Work is something you do because you have internal needs. I can no more help working than I can help breathing.

MAX LERNER, AUTHOR, COLUMNIST, TEACHER, LECTURER, ACTIVE UNTIL HIS DEATH AT AGE 89

The Long Growth Curve

Finally, there was a group of people who had long growth curves. This means that they moved upward at a relatively steady pace throughout the first 30 or 40 years of their work lives. The progression ended in a pinnacle of achievement after age 50 or 65.

The late Norman Cousins, for example, served for decades as the well-known and greatly loved editor of *The Saturday Review of Literature*. In his 50s, he had an almost-fatal illness that stimulated him to write a book, *Anatomy of an Illness* (1979). Its tremendous popularity led him to a major career change at the age of 64: He became an adjunct professor of medicine at the UCLA Medical School.

Until his death at the age of 76, Cousins helped design experiments on the relationship of the mind to physical health. His brilliant work with his medical colleagues at UCLA laid a solid scientific foundation for mind-body health research.

Cousins' career had a steady ascent, with new periods of growth triggered by his response

to experience. This proactive stance toward one's own life was displayed by most of the study participants.

Maturity is the ability to postpone gratification.

ATTRIBUTED TO SIGMUND FREUD

Progressive Patterns

Finally, there were other types of progressions in the careers of some study participants. Many participants progressed from being employees, to becoming managers or administrators, to becoming entrepreneurs. This pattern suggests increased learning about administrative functions, and the growing desire to shape the course of an organization, culminating in the creation of one's own organization.

Another progression was a change in geographical order of magnitude: moving from local concerns, to state or regional, then to national and finally to an international level of interest. Esther Peterson, former advisor on consumer affairs to Presidents Johnson and Carter, started her career as a local union organizer, moved up to state and regional positions, worked on a national level, and until age 87 was still the Consumer's Union's international representative to the U.N.

What about the Future?

In a long-lived society, inevitably more people will make career changes during the course of a lifetime, simply because they have more time available in which they can master and grow beyond a given job or career. Of course, not everyone will have multiple careers; some will still stay in the same career all their lives.

A cause for real concern is the paradox that at a time when human beings are living longer than ever—and remaining youthful and in good health—American corporations and businesses are going in the opposite direction. They are downsizing and early-retiring people out of the workforce in their 50s or even their late 40s.

This is a dysfunctional trend in a society where there are so many people who may want to continue working even beyond the conventional retirement age, and who have much skill, experience, and knowledge to contribute.

It also raises the question of how effective a company can be if a large segment of our population is over 50, while the majority of the company's employees are under 50. A workforce that is predominantly younger may not understand or be able to serve effectively the needs of a mature consumer group.

It seems to me that there must be some correction in the negative attitude of corporations toward maturity if companies wish to remain viable. The research of University of Pennsylvania psychologist Frank Landy has shown that mature workers play roles that are different from those of younger workers, and that **a workforce with a broad spectrum of ages functions better than a workforce with a narrow age spectrum**.

Another related change is the disappearance of the longstanding "psychological contract" of loyalty between the worker and the corporation, which for so long was a foundation for American work life.

For the most part, **the people in the Long Careers Study who were able to continue doing work that they loved at older ages had made themselves independent**. Their identity as workers did not depend on a company but on their own skills and expertise. Frequently they had an individual practice—as a lawyer, artist, doctor, writer, etc.—or they formed their own business.

In a long-lived society, until the prevailing age prejudice has diminished or disappeared, every one of us should have as a goal to achieve the kind of professional, psychological, and financial independence that will enable us to continue working for as long (or short) a time as we choose.

Then perhaps we will be able to say—as Norman Cousins remarked when he was in his early 70s—"I find that now I'm using everything I've ever learned—all of it together at the same time, and more effectively than I could ever have done at any earlier time in my life."

Lydia Bronte, Ph.D., is the author of The Longevity Factor: The New Reality of Long Careers and How They Are Leading to Richer Lives, Harper/Collins. This piece originally appeared in The Five O'Clock News. Although her book was written in 1993, its emphasis on the importance of finding engaging, satisfying work is even more relevant today. For more on this topic, read The Five O'Clock Club's *Achieving the Good Life After 50* by Renée Lee Rosenberg.

The
Five
O'Clock
Club®

PART TWO

Deciding What You Want

START BY UNDERSTANDING YOURSELF

The
Five
O'Clock
Club®

How to Find Your Place in the World

You are a child of the universe no less than the trees and the stars; you have a right to be here. And whether or not it is clear to you, no doubt the universe is unfolding as it should.

DESIDERATA

Change as Opportunity

Don't expect to hold on to the way things have worked for you in the past. Get on with the new way the world is operating. You cannot stop the changes, but you *can* choose the way you will respond. You can see change as a threat to resist—or an opportunity to move forward.

Change represents danger to you when you choose to resist it. While your energy goes into trying to keep your situation the same, you will become more dissatisfied as you see others taking advantage of changes.

You can use change to your advantage if you decide to see it as a source of opportunity. Then, it won't be so threatening. You will reduce your chances of being run over. You will be running your own life.

To look at change as a source of opportunity, become more aware of the changes taking place around you—the events that can affect you and your job. Decide which are best for you and how to take advantage of those that interest you. The pace of change in today's economy can be

overwhelming—unless you can assess changes more objectively. In doing so, you will have more control *over the way you respond.*

An Internal Reference Point

How can you make the most of changes? How can you decide which ones bode well for you and which ones bode ill? You need a stable, internal point of reference—a clear picture of what you need to feel satisfied with your job and with your life. You can measure a changing situation against your list of the *elements* you require, to decide if a change is in your favor or not. You can perhaps alter the situation to suit you, or get out of there at the earliest point.

To feel in control and actually to be in control of your life, make choices based on your inner direction. With so many changes swirling around, the only stabilizing point must be inside of you. Nothing outside can be your anchor. This book has exercises to help you determine your inner direction.

We can help one another find out the meaning of life.... But in the last analysis, each is responsible for "finding himself."

THOMAS MERTON, *NO MAN IS AN ISLAND*

A Career Coach Cannot Decide for You

Let's be practical about it: A career coach cannot possibly know all the options out there for you. There are so many choices and the world is changing so fast, how *could* one person know the answer that is right for you? And when things change again, as they will, will you expect a career coach to tell you what to do then?

What you do with your life is *your* decision. A coach cannot decide for you, but can only help you decide. Blaming someone else for your lack of progress can be a reflection of your attitude about life. Do you basically feel you control what happens to you? Or do you feel what happens is essentially in the hands of others? When you blame others, you give up your power. You are saying that someone else is deciding what will happen to you. When you do not blame others, you have more power: You are taking control over your own life.

Those who take responsibility for their own lives do better than those who expect others to solve their problems.

Accepting responsibility means, generally, not blaming others for your situation. You accept that your choices have gotten you where you are. You are in control. You can make new choices to head your life where you want.

Nobody owns a job, nobody owns a market, nobody owns a product. Somebody out there can always take it away from you.

RONALD E. COMPTON, PRESIDENT/CHAIRMAN, AETNA, AS QUOTED IN THE NEW YORK TIMES, MARCH 1, 1992

Why Use a Career Coach?

In this changing marketplace, increasingly we all have to be out there selling ourselves. This is causing people a great deal of understandable stress. Most of us would rather just do our jobs and trust that we will be treated fairly. Since we cannot depend on this, some people have made a

career coach a normal part of their lives—as normal as having a regular tune-up on your car or an annual physical. They go to their coach not only when they are conducting a job search or when they have problems, but perhaps once or twice a year for a checkup.

An important component of the career assessment process is to help clients accept themselves: their strengths as well as what does not come naturally to them.

BARRY LUSTIG, DIRECTOR OF THE PROFESSIONAL DEVELOPMENT INSTITUTE, FEDERATION EMPLOYMENT AND GUIDANCE SERVICES, NY

Clients working with a career coach learn what works for them personally and what does not, come to better understand the kinds of environments in which they should be working (bosses, corporate cultures, pace, etc.), learn how to be more effective in their work relationships (bosses, peers, subordinates, clients), learn how to balance their lives more effectively, and also lay the groundwork for the next career move they may have to make. They talk about their long-term career goals and the steps they need to take to reach them—or perhaps simply to stay even. They make sure they are doing what they must to develop their careers as the economy changes, such as getting specific experience, taking courses, or joining organizations.

Over time, your coach gets to know you, just as your family doctor gets to know you, and can warn you against things that may cause you problems, or advise you about things you could be doing next. Just as a family doctor would want to give you a complete physical if you are to become his patient, so, too, your coach would want to give you an assessment to find out as much as possible about you. I tell clients that if I don't know enough about them, it is as if they were someone on the street coming up to me to ask advice. I need to know something about them so I can be a real coach.

If you decide to use a private coach, use someone who charges by the hour. Do not pay a huge up-front fee. After you have worked with the coach a number of times, assess your relationship with that person. There should be a good personality fit between you and your coach. For example, some coaches are very intense, while others have a softer approach. If the relationship is not good, or if the meetings damage your sense of self-worth, go to someone else.

For your part, make sure you are willing to make the necessary commitment. If you go only for one hour to have the coach handle an emergency you are facing, do not expect that coach to come to know very much about you. If you decide to use a coach, you are likely to learn more about the wonderful person you are, so you can figure out how you fit into this changing world. You will have increased self-esteem and increased effectiveness.

The field cannot well be seen from within the field.
RALPH WALDO EMERSON

Develop a Vision; Make a Commitment

Take a stand. Decide where you want to head, and go for it. You'll be happier because you'll have a goal and you'll work toward it. Work will no longer be work, but an activity that brings pleasure, pride, and a sense of accomplishment, and that carries out your vision.

When you know yourself and make a commitment, things become clearer. You act more decisively, have less stress, and cope better with the progress of your career and the changes around you. Negative things will not bother you as much. The direction will not be coming from someone else, but from inside you.

Without commitment, we are wanderers without roots in a rapidly changing world. We feel a lack of meaning in our lives.

Commitment means accepting that you are responsible for your own career direction.

It means choosing what you want to do in this changing society without losing your inner bearings.

For I know the plans I have for you, declares the Lord,
plans to prosper you and not to harm you,
plans to give you a hope and a future.

JEREMIAH 29:11

Looking for Where You Fit In

We each fit in. What you're looking for is where you fit in. As you learn more about what is inside you, as well as what is outside, you will progressively change your situation to suit yourself better, and so you will also fit better into the world.

To grow with the world, know what you want and what you want to offer. Knowing yourself, in the context of career development, means knowing how you prefer to operate, what you like to do, and what you can do well. Knowing what you want to offer means stepping outside yourself to see what the world values. Take what you want to offer and market it.

Don't be *too* specific about what you want. If you are open to new opportunities, surprising things can happen. A large number of jobs are created with a certain person in mind. A job created with you in mind would probably be more satisfying than one in which you would have to mold yourself to fit a rigid job description. You would enjoy your job more and do better because you would be doing what you want.

What are the chances of having a job created to suit you? If you don't know what would suit you, chances are slim. Having definite ideas increases your chances of finding such a job, or even of changing your present job to better suit your goals. Opportunities come along all the time. You won't recognize them unless you know what you are looking for.

We change the world and the world changes us. As we grow, we are developing ourselves—in

45

relation to the world. We are each trying to know what we want and how to get it, while we are also trying to understand and fit into a changing world. It is a lifelong process, but a happy one. It is a process of seeing change as an opportunity while accepting the limitations of the world.

You can never enslave somebody who knows who he is.

ALEX HALEY

Cartoon Courtesy © Jerry King

"You've both been at this company for the same amount of time, but deciding who gets the promotion was relatively easy."

CASE STUDY Henry
Aiming Too Low

Henry, an executive of about 45, had just been fired, and I was asked to be his coach. Henry said he already had a clear idea of what he wanted to do next—something that was quite in demand—loan workouts (when loans go bad, he would try to salvage them). Henry could certainly get a job like that, and quickly, but I felt as though I didn't know him at all, so I asked if we could

do a few exercises. If I understood him better, I would be in a better position to coach him.

In his Seven Stories (an exercise you will do in this book), Henry stated that he was proud that he had grown up in a tiny Midwestern town (there were only 60 people in his entire high school), had gotten into Harvard, and graduated very high in his class.

Where was that little boy now? What had caused him to settle for a loan workout position that would have been right for lots of *other* people? I told Henry that I thought he could do better than that. I asked him to aim to find a job that would make him so proud it would wind up on his future Seven Stories list.

Within two-and-a-half months, Henry had landed a job that was better than anything he had ever dreamed possible. At an excellent salary, he became a very senior executive in a major corporation. Henry was so proud, he beamed. He was there for many years and did very well.

When written in Chinese, the word crisis is composed of two characters—one represents danger and the other represents opportunity.

JOHN F. KENNEDY, ADDRESS, UNITED NEGRO COLLEGE FUND CONVOCATION, APRIL 12, 1959

You Need Information—Out in the World

You need information about yourself and about the changing world of work. Find an optimal fit by matching what you learn about yourself against what you learn about the world.

If you're like most people, at least part of your career plan was decided by someone else. If that decision was not best for you, something has to change. You must either change to fit the job, or you must change the job to fit you. If you have often changed yourself to suit the job you were in, you may not know what you want. Soon we will help you figure out what you would enjoy doing in a job.

You cannot find out about yourself in a vacuum. Go out and test your ideas about yourself against what others think of you. That's the only healthy way. With more knowledge about the world, and with a clearer sense of our place in it, options will appear that we never noticed before.

It is the first of all problems for a man to find out what kind of work he is to do in this universe.

THOMAS CARLYLE, *SARTOR RESARTUS*

The Steps to Finding Your Place

The basic steps to finding your place are covered in greater detail in the other chapters in this section. Spend as much or as little time as you want on each. The process can go on forever. Do what you want now, and do more later.

Step 1: Determine what you want. Develop a long-term view of yourself—a guiding light that can see you through a number of jobs. In fact, you could develop a view that will see you through your entire life.

Step 2: Decide what you want to offer. Notice that I say what you want to offer—not what you have to offer. You may be tempted to offer what you have been offering all along. Although a pragmatic choice may see you through a job transition, it is more important to decide what you want to offer. If you offer things you do not want to do, you increase your chances of doing things you do not want to do.

I looked at an administrative assistant's résumé. It mentioned heavy phone work as one of her duties. When I asked her if she liked phone work, she responded, "I hate phone work." I advised her to remove it from her résumé, or someone would say, "That's just what we need: someone who can do heavy phone work."

Of course, every job has parts you don't like. In fact, you may decide to offer such an aspect as one of your strong skills until you develop yourself in the areas on which you want to focus. That's often a good approach.

I'll use my own life as an example. I started out in computers as a way of working my way through school. After learning so much about them, I have always used computers to my advantage even though working with them was not central on my list of life goals. Sometimes the fact that I knew computers gave me an edge over other job hunters. While I didn't want working with computers to be a central part of my job, the skill has been a handy one to offer.

In this step you will develop a menu of everything you have to offer, and then you can decide to offer what you want.

Step 3: A combination of the results of Steps 1 and 2. You'll do best in a job that relies on some of your strengths and experiences, but also provides you with some growth toward your goals. Bring something to the job. This book will help you select a job target that considers both.

Having gifts that differ according to the grace given to us, let us use them.

ROMANS 12:6

CASE STUDY Aaron
Knowing Where He Wants to End Up

Aaron has been in corporate marketing for eight years. Through the Seven Stories Exercise and his Forty-Year Vision (which you will see in the next chapter), he developed a long-term view of himself: the head of a 500-person public-sector-related agency or organization, such as the World Wildlife Fund.

Now that he knows where he wants to end up, he can work backward to figure out how he could get there. To head up such a large organization, he has two choices: He can start it from scratch, or he can take over an existing organization. Aaron decided that five years from now, he would prefer to become the head of an existing 50-person organization and expand it to a 500-person organization.

But how can he go from where he is now to becoming the head of a 50-person organization? What he has to offer is his corporate marketing background. Therefore, his next logical step is to try to get a marketing job in a not-for-profit organization that is similar to the one he would eventually like to head up. That way, his next job will be one that positions him well for the moves after that, and increases his chance of getting where he wants to go.

The earth is a medium-sized planet orbiting around an average star in the outer suburbs of an ordinary spiral galaxy, which is itself only one of about a million million galaxies in the observable universe.

STEPHEN M. HAWKING, *A BRIEF HISTORY OF TIME*

The Benefits of Knowing What You Want

As I have stressed so far, you are responsible for your own career development. Decide what you want, rather than hoping someone will think about it for you. The next chapter will get you started.

Now, I can look at you, Mr. Loomis, and see you a man who done forgot his song. Forgot how to sing it. A fellow forget that and he forget who he is. Forget how he's supposed to mark down life.

AUGUST WILSON, *JOE TURNER'S COME AND GONE*

America has entered the age of the contingent or temporary worker, of the consultant or subcontractor, of the just-in-time work force—fluid, flexible, disposable. This is the future. Its message is this: You are on your own. For good (sometimes) and ill (often), the workers of the future will constantly have to sell their skills, invent new relationships with employers who must, themselves, change and adapt constantly in order to survive in a ruthless global market.

LANCE MORROW, "THE TEMPING OF AMERICA," *TIME*, 1993

God grant me the serenity to accept the things I cannot change, the courage to change the things I can, and the wisdom to know the difference.

"SERENITY PRAYER"

Alice: "Will you tell me please, which way I ought to go from here?"
Cat: "That depends a good deal on where you want to get to."
Alice: "I don't care much where—so long as I get somewhere."
Cat: "Oh, you're sure to do that if only you walk long enough."

LEWIS CARROLL, *ALICE IN WONDERLAND* (CAMBRIDGE UNIVERSITY PRESS)

The
Five
O'Clock
Club®

How to Decide What You Want

What seems different in yourself;
that's the rare thing you possess.
The one thing that gives each of us his worth,
and that's just what we try to suppress.
And we claim to love life.

ANDRÉ GIDE

Looking Ahead—A Career Instead of a Job

If you don't decide where you want to go, you may wind up drifting from one organization to another whenever you're dissatisfied, with pretty much the same job each time. Even if you decide that you want to continue doing what you're doing right now, that's a goal in itself and may be difficult to achieve.

The first step in career management is goal setting. There are a lot of processes involved in the goal-setting area. But the one considered most central is that by which a person examines his or her past accomplishments, looking at the strongest and most enjoyable skills.

This process is not only the one favored by coaches, it is also the one most often used by successful people. In reading the biographies of such people, I see again and again how they established their goals by identifying those things they enjoy doing and also do well. This process of identifying your *enjoyable accomplishments* is the most important one you can go through.

What Successful People Do

When Steven Jobs, the founder of Apple Computers, was fired by John Sculley, the man he had brought in to run the company, he felt as though he had lost everything. Apple had been his life. Now he had lost not only his job, but his company. People no longer felt the need to return his phone calls. He did what a lot of us would do. He got depressed. But then:

Confused about what to do next...he [Jobs] put himself
through an exercise that management psychologists
employ with clients unsure about their life goals. It
was a little thing, really. It was just a list. A list of all
the things that mattered most to Jobs during his
ten years at Apple." Three things jumped
off that piece of paper, three things that were
really important to me," says Jobs.

MICHAEL MEYER, *THE ALEXANDER COMPLEX*
(MACMILLAN PUBLISHERS)

Let me listen to me and not to them.

GERTRUDE STEIN

The exercise Steven Jobs went through is essentially what you will do in the *Seven Stories Exercise*. The threads that ran through his stories formed the impetus for his next great drive: the formation of NeXT computers. If the *Seven Stories Exercise* is good enough for Steven Jobs, maybe it's good enough for you.

"Successful managers," says Charles Garfield, head of Performance Services, Inc., in Berkeley, California, "go with their preferences." They search for work that is important to them, and when they find it they pursue it with a passion.

Lester Korn, chairman of Korn, Ferry, notes in his book *The Success Profile*: "Few executives know, or can know, exactly what they aspire to until they have been in the work force for a couple of years. It takes that long to learn enough about yourself to know what you can do well and what will make you happy. The trick is to merge the two into a goal, then set off in pursuit of it."

Targeting a Great Career will help you decide what you want to do in your next job as well as in the long run. You will become clearer about the experiences you have enjoyed most and may like to repeat. You will also examine your interests and values, and look at past positions to analyze what satisfied you and what did not. In addition, you will look farther ahead (through your Forty-Year Vision) to see if some driving dream may influence what you will want to do in the short term. I did my Forty-Year Vision about 25 years ago, and the vision I had of my future still drives me today.

Knowing where you would like to wind up broadens the kinds of jobs you would be interested in today.

Look at it this way:

A B   C

The line represents your life. Right now, you are at A. Your next job is B. If you look only at your past to decide what to do next, your next job is limited by what you have already done. For example, if you have been in finance and accounting for the past 15 years, and you base your next move on your past, your next job is likely to be in finance or accounting.

If you know that at C you would like to wind up as vice president of finance and administration, new possibilities open up. Think of all the areas you would manage:

Finance	Human Resources
Operations	Accounting
Administration	Computers

Experience in any one of these would advance your career in the right direction. For example, you may decide to get some computer experience.

Without the benefit of a Forty-Year Vision, a move to computers might look like the start of a career in computers, but you know it's just one more assignment that leads to your long-term goal. You'll keep your vision in mind and take jobs and assignments that will continually position you for the long run. For example, in the computer area, you may focus on personnel or administrative systems, two areas that fit your goal. Then your computer job will be more than a job. You will work hard for your employer, but you will also know why you are there—you are using your job as a stepping-stone to something bigger and better.

Make no little plans; they have no magic to stir men's blood and probably themselves will not be realized. Make big plans; aim high in hope and work.

Daniel Burnham

Happy in Your Work

People are happy when they are working toward their goals. When they get diverted—or don't know what their goals are—they are unhappy. Many people are unhappy in their jobs because they don't know where they are going.

People without goals are more irked by petty daily problems than are those with goals.

To control your life, know where you are going, and be ready for your next move—in case the ax falls on you. When you take that next job, continue to manage your career. Companies rarely build career paths for their employees any more. Make your own way. There are plenty of jobs for those who are willing to learn and to change with the times.

The
Five
O'Clock
Club®

Deciding What You Want:
Selecting Your Job Targets

It may sound surprising when I say, on the basis of my own clinical experience as well as that of my psychological and psychiatric colleagues," that the chief problem of people in the middle decade of the twentieth century is emptiness." By that I mean not only that many people do not know what they want; they often do not have any clear idea of what they feel.

ROLLO MAY, *MAN'S SEARCH FOR HIMSELF*
(W.W. NORTON & COMPANY)

Studies have shown that up to 85 percent of all American workers are unhappy in their jobs. They feel that they would be happier elsewhere, but they don't know where. After going through an evaluation process (assessment), many decide that their present situation is not so bad after all, and that no change is required. Some may find that a small change is all that is needed. On the other hand, some may want to make a major career change.

The exercises in this book will help you assess your work life so that you can better understand the situations in which you perform your best and are happiest. And, since we will all have to change jobs—and probably even careers—more often in the future, we should get to know ourselves better.

Assessment is helpful even if you do not want to change jobs. You will learn more about the way you operate and how to improve the situation where you are currently working.

In the Nazi death camps where Victor Frankl learned the principle of proactivity, he also learned the importance of purpose, of meaning in life. The essence of "logotherapy," the philosophy he later developed and taught, is that many so-called mental and emotional illnesses are really symptoms of an underlying sense of meaninglessness or emptiness. Logotherapy eliminates the emptiness by helping the individual to detect his unique meaning, his mission in life. Once you have that sense of mission, you have the essence of your own proactivity. You have the vision and the values that direct your life. You have the basic direction from which you set long- and short-term goals.

STEPHEN R. COVEY, *THE SEVEN HABITS OF HIGHLY EFFECTIVE PEOPLE* (CBS CORPORATION)

Getting Started

The following exercises help you identify the aspects of your jobs that have been satisfying and dissatisfying. You will know which parts need to be changed and which parts need to stay the same.

You may do certain exercises and skip others. But don't skip the Seven Stories Exercise, and try to do the Fifteen- or Forty-Year Vision. If you have had problems with bosses, you need to discover what those problems were and analyze them. Or perhaps examining your values may be an issue at this time. Your insights about yourself from the Seven Stories Exercise will be the primary source for your accomplishment statements, help you interview better, and serve as a template for selecting the right job.

After you do the exercises, brainstorm a number of possible job targets. Then research each target to find out what the job possibilities are for someone like you.

This book will guide you through the entire process.

To have a great purpose to work for, a purpose larger than ourselves, is one of the secrets of making life significant; for then the meaning and worth of the individual overflow his personal borders, and survive his death.

WILL DURANT

Consider Your History

If you have enjoyed certain jobs, attempt to understand exactly what about them you enjoyed. This will increase your chances of replicating the enjoyable aspects.

For example, an accounting manager will probably not be happy in just any accounting-management job. If what he really enjoyed was helping the business manager make the business profitable, and if this thread of helping reappears in his enjoyable experiences (Seven Stories Exercise), then he would be unhappy in a job where he was *not* helping.

If, however, his enjoyment repeatedly came from resolving messy situations, then he needs a job that has messes to be resolved and the promise of more messes to come.

Furthermore, if he wants to do again those things he enjoyed, he can state them in the summary on his résumé. For instance:

Accounting Manager
Serve as right hand to Business Manager, consistently improving organization's profitability.
or

Accounting Manager
A troubleshooter and turnaround manager.

"Johnson, if you're going to have negative thoughts, I suggest you get rid of that thought balloon."

The Results of Assessment: Job Targets—*Then* a Résumé

A job target contains three elements:

- industry or organization size (small, medium, or large organization);
- position or function; and
- geographic location.

If a change is required, a change in any one of these may be enough.

Geographic Location

Let's take Joseph, for example. Joseph had been in trusts and estates for 25 years, and had taken early retirement. He didn't know what he wanted to do next, but he knew that it had to be *completely different.*

Joseph did all of the exercises in this section. I also gave him a personality test, and did *confidential phone calls* on his behalf—a process by which I called people who knew him well and asked them about him. I assured them that I would compile the results and not tell him who said what.

Based on all of this information, we developed a number of targets for him to investigate. We also developed a résumé that positioned him for these new targets.

Joseph conducted a campaign to get interviews in each of his three target areas. However, once he clearly looked at these new fields, his old field began to look more appealing. (This happened to me years ago when I desperately wanted museum work—until I actually looked into it and found it wasn't for me.)

Joseph decided to stay in his old field—but on the West Coast rather than the East—because he is bothered by the climate in the East and because many of his old friends had moved West. This change in location would get him out of the old rut and give him a new lease on life. But it was a relatively minor change compared with what he originally had in mind.

Industry or Organization Size

Many unhappy people may be in essentially the right position but in the wrong industry. A minor adjustment may be all that is needed.

A person could be a lawyer, but it makes a great deal of difference whether that person is a lawyer in a corporation, in a stuffy law firm, or in a not-for-profit organization. A change in industry may end the dissatisfaction.

By the same token, moving from a large organization to a small one—or vice versa—could increase your satisfaction.

Position or Function

On the other hand, a new field may be what is called for. My own career is a case in point. I had a successful career in computers, advertising, and the financial end of business, with a respect-

able amount of prestige and money. However, when I did the Seven Stories Exercise (to identify those things I enjoyed doing and also did well), I discovered that only one of my stories related to my work life. The message was clear: My true enjoyment was coming from those things I was doing on the outside, such as running The Five O'Clock Club and other entrepreneurial ventures. I had a choice to make:

- I could stay in the lucrative field I was in, and continue to do on the side those things that gave me the most satisfaction; or
- I could move my career in the direction of those things I found most satisfying.

Being risk averse, I was reluctant to give up the 20-plus years I had invested in a business career for a profession that might prove to be financially or otherwise unsatisfying. I decided to hedge my bets. I took a job as the chief financial officer of a major outplacement firm, and also headed up one of their career coaching offices. That way, I could slide into the new career, or go back into the old one if I was unhappy.

Many major career changes are made this way. A person *somehow* gets some experience in the new field while holding on to the old one. In general, it is relatively easy to get experience in the new field if you really want it.

. . . and then I decided that to turn your life around you had to start from the inside.

ETHAN CANIN, *EMPEROR OF THE AIR*

Looking Ahead—A Career Instead of a Job

Assessment will help you decide what you want to do in your next job as well as in the long run. You will become clearer about the kind of boss you work best with and about all the other things that are important to you in a job.

Through your Forty-Year Vision, you will have the opportunity to look ahead to see whether there is some hidden dream that may dramatically influence what you will want to do in both the short and long run. I did my own Forty-Year Vision many, many years ago, and the idea I had about my future still drives me today, even though that vision was actually rather vague at the time. Knowing where you would like to wind up in 10, 20, 30, or 40 years can broaden your ideas about the kinds of jobs you would be interested in today.

The Forty-Year Vision is a powerful exercise. It will help you think long term and put things into perspective.

The Seven Stories Exercise is equally powerful. Without it, many job hunters develop stilted descriptions of what they have accomplished. But the exercise frees you up to brag a little, and express things very differently. The results will add life to your résumé and your interviews, and also dramatically increase your self-confidence.

No Easy Way

It would be nice if you could simply take a test that would tell you what you should be. Unfortunately, there is no such sure-fire test. But fortunately, in today's rapidly changing world, we are allowed to be many things: we can be a doctor, a lawyer, and an Indian chief. We have an abundance of choices.

A man is what he thinks about all day long.
RALPH WALDO EMERSON

A Clear Direction

People are happy when they are working toward their goals. When they get diverted from their goals, they are unhappy. Businesses are the

same. When they get diverted from their goals (for instance, because of major litigation or a threatened hostile takeover), they too are unhappy. Life has a way of sneaking up and distracting both individuals and businesses. Many people are unhappy in their jobs because they don't know where they are going.

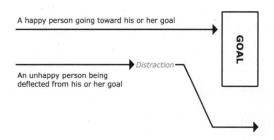

People without goals are more irked by petty problems on their jobs. Those with goals are less bothered because they have bigger plans. To control your life, you have to know where you are going, and be ready for your next move—in case the ax falls on you.

Even after you take that next job, continue to manage your career. Organizations rarely build career paths for their employees any more. Make your own way.

I've never been poor, only broke. Being poor is a frame of mind. Being broke is only a temporary situation.
MIKE TODD

Don't just wish things were different. Figure out exactly what you want, then look for ways to make that happen. Whatever you believe, you achieve. With this law, you create both what you want and what you don't want.

KARIN IRELAND, *THE JOB SURVIVAL INSTRUCTION BOOK*

The Five O'Clock Club®

Exercises to Analyze Your Past and Present: The Seven Stories Exercise

The direction of change to seek is not in our four dimensions: it is getting deeper into what you are, where you are, like turning up the volume on the amplifier.

THADDEUS GOLAS, *LAZY MAN'S GUIDE TO ENLIGHTENMENT*

In this exercise, you will examine your accomplishments, looking at your strongest and most enjoyable skills. The core of most coaching exercises is some version of the Seven Stories exercise. A coach may give you lots of tests and exercises, but this one requires *work* on your part and will yield the most important results. An interest or personality test is not enough.

There is no easy way. Remember, busy executives take the time to complete this exercise— if it's good enough for them, it's good enough for you.

Do not skip the Seven Stories Exercise. It will provide you with information for your career direction, your résumé, and your interviews. After you do the exercise, brainstorm about a number of possible job targets. Then research each target to find out what the job possibilities are for someone like you.

If you're like most people, you have never taken the time to sort out the things you're good at and also are motivated to accomplish. As a result, you probably don't use these talents as completely or as effectively as you could. Too often, we do things to please someone else or to survive in a job. Then we get stuck in a rut—that is, we're *always* trying to please someone else or *always* trying to survive in a job. We lose sight of

what could satisfy us, and work becomes drudgery rather than fun. When we become so enmeshed in survival or in trying to please others, it may be difficult to figure out what we would rather be doing.

When you uncover your enjoyable skills, you'll be better able to identify jobs that allow you to use them, and recognize other jobs that don't quite fit the bill. *Enjoyable skills* are patterns that run through our lives. Since they are skills from which we get satisfaction, we'll find ways to do them even if we don't get to do them at work. We still might not know what these skills are—for us, they're just something we do, and we take them for granted.

Tracking down these patterns takes some thought. The payoff is that our enjoyable skills do not change. They run throughout our lives and indicate what will keep us motivated for the rest of our lives.

Look at Donald Trump. He knows that he enjoys – and is good at – real estate and self-promotion, and that's what he concentrates on. Now remember that you may have 3 to 5 different careers throughout your life – not 3 to 5 jobs, but 3 to 5 *careers*. Still, you can identify commonalities in those careers—aspects that you must have that will make you happier and more successful. In my case, for example, whether I was a computer programmer, a chief financial officer or a career coach, I've always found a way to teach others and often ran small groups – even in my childhood!

You too will find commonalities in your accomplishments, and these may be indicators of the elements you need in a job to be happier and more successful. Let's take one more example. An accountant whose enjoyable accomplishments involve helping the business head and giving advice would probably not be happy sitting in a corner crunching numbers and getting the numbers to balance. If what motivates him is the helping part, then he must be in a job where he is helping – perhaps giving advice to clients. Chances are, this person enjoyed helping people even when he was very young and this is a pattern that runs through many of his accomplishments.

One's prime is elusive....You must be on the alert to recognize your prime at whatever time of life it may occur.

MURIEL SPARK, *THE PRIME OF MISS JEAN BRODIE*

The Seven Stories Approach: Background

This technique for identifying what people do well and enjoy doing has its roots in the work of Bernard Haldane, who, in his job with the U.S. government in the 1940s, helped military personnel transition their skills to civilian life. Its overwhelming success in this area won the attention of Harvard Business School where it went on to become a significant part of its Manual for Alumni Placement. Haldane's work is being carried on today all over the world through DependableStrenghts.org. They have brought Haldane's method to places as diverse as South Africa and China, to colleges and universities and in their work with young people.

The Seven Stories (or enjoyable accomplishments) approach, now quite common, was taught to me by George Hafner, who used to work for Bernard Haldane.

The exercise is this: Make a list of all the enjoyable accomplishments of your life, those things you enjoyed doing *and also* did well. List at least 25 enjoyable accomplishments from all

parts of your life: work, from your youth, your school years, your early career up to the present. Don't forget volunteer work, your hobbies and your personal life. Other people may have gotten credit or under-appreciated what you did. Or the result may not have been a roaring success. For example, perhaps you were assigned to develop a new product and take it to market. Let's say you worked on this project for two years, loved every minute of it, but it failed in the market. It doesn't matter. What matters is that you enjoyed doing it and did it well.

Examine those episodes that gave you a sense of accomplishment. Episodes from your childhood are important, too, because they took place when you were less influenced by trying to please others.

You are asked to name 25 accomplishments so you will not be too judgmental—just list anything that occurs to you. Expect this exercise to take you four or five days. Most people carry around a piece of paper so they can jot things down as they occur to them. When you have 25, select the seven that are most important to you by however you define important. Then rank them: List the most important first, and so on.

Starting with your first story, write a paragraph about each accomplishment. Then find out what your accomplishments have in common. If you are having trouble doing the exercises, ask a friend to help you talk them through. Friends tend to be more objective and will probably point out strengths you never realized.

You will probably be surprised. For example, you may be especially good interacting with people, but it's something you've always done and therefore take for granted. This may be a thread that runs through your life and may be one of your enjoyable skills. It *may* be that you'll be unhappy in a job that doesn't allow you to deal with people.

When I did the Seven Stories Exercise, one of the first stories I listed was from when I was 10 years old, when I wrote a play to be put on by the kids in the neighborhood. I rehearsed everyone, sold tickets to the adults for two cents apiece, and served cookies and milk with the proceeds. You might say that my direction as a *general manager*—running the whole show, thinking things up, getting everybody working together— was set in the fourth grade. I saw these traits over and over again in each of my stories.

After I saw those threads running through my life, it became easy for me to see what elements a job must have to satisfy me. When I interviewed for a job, I could find out in short order whether it addressed my enjoyable skills. If it didn't, I wouldn't be as happy as I could be, even though I may decide to take the job as an interim step toward a long-term goal. The fact is, people won't do as well in the long run in jobs that don't satisfy their enjoyable skills.

Sometimes I don't pay attention to my own enjoyable skills, and I wind up doing things I regret. For example, in high school I scored the highest in the state in math. I was as surprised as everyone else, but I felt I finally had some direction in my life. I felt I had to use it to do something constructive. When I went to college, I majored in math. I almost flunked because I was bored with it. The fact is that I didn't enjoy math, I was simply good at it.

There are lots of things we're good at, but they may not be the same things we really enjoy. The trick is to find those things we are good at, enjoy doing, and feel a sense of accomplishment from doing.

To sum up: Discovering your enjoyable skills is the first step in career planning. I was a general manager when I was 10, but I didn't realize it. I'm a general manager now, and I love it. In between, I've done some things that have helped me toward my long-range goals, and other things that have not helped at all.

It is important to realize that the Seven Stories Exercise will *not* tell you exactly which job you should have, but the *elements* to look for in a job that you will find satisfying. You'll have a range of jobs to consider, and you'll know the elements the jobs must have to keep you happy. Once you've selected a few job categories that might satisfy you, talk to people in those fields to find out if a particular job is really what you want, and the job possibilities for someone with your experience. That's one way to test if your aspirations are realistic.

After you have narrowed your choices down to a few fields with some job possibilities that will satisfy your enjoyable skills, the next step is to figure out how to get there. That topic will be covered in our book *Shortcut Your Job Search*.

. . . be patient toward all that is unsolved in your heart and try to love the questions themselves like locked rooms and like books that are written in a foreign tongue.

Rainer Maria Rilke, *Letters to a Young Poet*

A Demonstration of the Seven Stories Exercise

To get clients started, I sometimes walk them through two or three of their achievement stories, and tell them the patterns I see. They can then go off and think of the seven or eight accomplishments they enjoyed the most and also performed well. This final list is ranked and analyzed in depth to get a more accurate picture of the person's enjoyable skills. I spend the most time analyzing those accomplishments a client sees as most important. Some accomplishments are more obvious than others. But all stories can be analyzed.

Here is Suzanne, as an example: "When I was nine years old, I was living with my three sisters. There was a fire in our house and our cat had hidden under the bed. We were all outside, but I decided to run back in and save the cat. And I did it."

No matter what the story is, I probe a little by asking these two questions: What gave you the sense of accomplishment? and What about that made you proud? These questions give me a quick fix on the person.

Cartoon Courtesy © Jerry King

"I realize I'm only 3 years old, but have 21 years of experience."

The full exercise is a little more involved than this. Suzanne said at first: "I was proud because I did what I thought was right." I probed a little, and she added: "I had a sense of accomplishment because I was able to make an instant decision under pressure. I was proud because I overcame my fear."

I asked Suzanne for a second story; I wanted to see what patterns might emerge when we put the two together: "Ten years ago, I was laid off from a large company where I had worked for nine years.

I soon got a job as an administrative assistant in a Wall Street company. I loved the excitement and loved that job. Six weeks later, a position opened up on the trading floor, but I didn't get it at first. I eventually was one of three finalists, and they tried to discourage me from taking the job. I wanted to be given a chance. So I sold myself because I was determined to get that job. I went back for three interviews, said all the right things, and eventually got it."

What was the accomplishment? What made her proud?

- "I fought to win."
- "I was able to sell myself. I was able to overcome their objections."
- "I was interviewed by three people at once. I amazed myself by saying, 'I know I can do this job.'"
- "I determined who the real decision maker was, and said things that would make him want to hire me."
- "I loved that job—loved the energy, the upness, the fun."

Here it was, 10 years later, and that job still stood out as a highlight in her life. Since then she'd been miserable and bored, and that's why she came to me.

Normally after a client tells two stories, we can quickly name the patterns we see in both stories. What were Suzanne's patterns?

Suzanne showed that she was good at making decisions in tense situations—both when saving the cat and when interviewing for that job. She showed a good intuitive sense (such as when she determined who the decision maker was and how to win him over). She's decisive and likes fast-paced, energetic situations. She likes it when she overcomes her own fears as well as the objections of others.

We needed more than two stories to see if these patterns ran throughout Suzanne's life and to see what other patterns might emerge. After the full exercise, Suzanne felt for sure that she wanted excitement in her jobs, a sense of urgency—that she wanted to be in a position where she had a chance to be decisive and operate intuitively. Those are the conditions she enjoys and under which she operates the best.

Armed with this information, Suzanne can confidently say in an interview that she thrives on excitement, high pressure, and quick decision making. And, she'll probably make more money than she would in safe jobs. She can move her life in a different direction—whenever she is ready.

Pay attention to those stories that were most important to you. The elements in these stories may be worth repeating. If none of your enjoyable accomplishments were work related, it may take great courage to eventually move into a field where you will be happier. Or you may decide to continue to have your enjoyment outside of work.

People have to be ready to change. Fifteen years ago, when I first examined my own enjoyable skills, I saw possibilities I was not ready to handle. Although I suffered from extreme shyness, my stories—especially those that occurred when I was young—gave me hope. As I emerged from my shyness, I was eventually able to act on what my stories said was true about me.

People sometimes take immediate steps after learning what their enjoyable skills are. Or sometimes this new knowledge can work inside them until they are ready to take action—maybe 10 years later. All the while internal changes can be happening, and people can eventually blossom.

If one advances confidently in the direction of his dreams, and endeavors to live the life which he has imagined, he will meet with success unexpected in common hours.

HENRY DAVID THOREAU

Enjoyable skills—Your Anchor in a Changing World

Your enjoyable skills are your anchor in a world of uncertainty. The world will change, but your enjoyable skills remain constant.

Write them down. Save the list. Over the years, refer to them to make sure you are still on target—doing things that you do well and are motivated to do. As you refer to them, they will influence your life. Five years from now, an opportunity may present itself. In reviewing your list, you will have every confidence that this opportunity is right for you. After all, you have been doing these things since you were a child, you know that you enjoy them, and you do them well!

Knowing our patterns gives us a sense of stability and helps us understand what we have done so far. It also gives us the freedom to try new things regardless of risk or of what others may say, because we can be absolutely sure that this is the way we are. Knowing your patterns gives you both security and flexibility—and you need both to cope in this changing world.

Now think about your own stories. Write down everything that occurs to you.

The Ugly Duckling was so happy and in some way he was glad that he had experienced so much hardship and misery; for now he could fully appreciate his tremendous luck and the great beauty that greeted him.... And he rustled his feathers, held his long neck high, and with deep emotion he said: "I never dreamt of so much happiness, when I was the Ugly Duckling!"

HANS CHRISTIAN ANDERSON, *THE UGLY DUCKLING*

The Seven Stories Exercise® Worksheet

This exercise is an opportunity to examine the most satisfying experiences of your life and to discover those skills you will want to use as you go forward. You will be looking at the times when you feel you did something particularly well that you also enjoyed doing. Compete this sentence: "There was a time when I…" List enjoyable accomplishments from all parts of your life: from your youth, your school years, your early career up to the present. Don't forget volunteer work, your hobbies and your personal life. Other people may have gotten credit or under-appreciated what you did. Or the result may not have been a roaring success. None of that matters. **What matters is that you enjoyed doing it and did it well.**

This exercise usually takes a few days to complete. Many people review different life phases in order to capture the full scope of these experiences. Most carry around a piece of paper to jot down ideas as they think of them.

List anything that occurs to you, however insignificant. When I did my own Seven Stories Exercise, I remembered the time when I was 10 years old and led a group of kids in the neighborhood, enjoyed it, and did it well.

When you have 25, select the seven that are most important to you by however you define important. Then rank them: List the most important first, and so on. Starting with your first story, write a paragraph about each accomplishment. Then find out what your accomplishments have in common. If you are having trouble doing the exercises, ask a friend to help you talk them through. Friends tend to be more objective and will probably point out strengths you never realized.

Section I

Briefly outline below *all* the work/personal/life experiences that meet the above definition. Come up with at least 20. We ask for 20 stories so you won't be too selective. Just write down anything that occurs to you, no matter how insignificant it may seem. **Try to think of concrete examples, situations, and tasks, not generalized skills or abilities**. It may be helpful if you say to yourself, **"There was the time when I . . ."** You may start with, for example, "Threw a fiftieth birthday party for my father," "Wrote a press release that resulted in extensive media coverage," and "Came in third in the Nassau bike race."

Don't just write that you enjoy "cooking." That's an activity, not an accomplishment. An accomplishment occurs at a specific time. You may wind up with many cooking accomplishments, for example. But if you simply write "cooking," "writing" or "managing," you will have a hard time thinking of 20 enjoyable accomplishments.

RIGHT

- Got extensive media coverage for new product launch.
- Delivered speech to get German business.
- Coordinated blood drive for division.
- Came in third in Nassau Bike Race.
- Made basket in second grade.

WRONG

- Writing press releases.
- Delivering speeches.
- Coordinating.
- Cycling.
- Working on projects alone.

1. _____
2. _____
3. _____
4. _____
5. _____
6. _____
7. _____
8. _____
9. _____
10. _____
11. _____
12. _____
13. _____
14. _____
15. _____
16. _____
17. _____
18. _____
19. _____
20. _____
21. _____
22. _____
23. _____
24. _____
25. _____

Section II

Choose the seven experiences from the above that you enjoyed the most and felt the most sense of accomplishment about. (Be sure to include non-job-related experiences also.) Then rank them. Then, for each accomplishment, describe what you did. Be specific, listing each step in detail. Notice the role you played and your relationship with others, the subject matter, the skills you used, and so on. Use a separate sheet of paper for each.

If your highest-ranking accomplishments also happen to be work related, you may want them to appear prominently on your résumé. After all, those were things that you enjoyed and did well. And those are probably experiences you will want to repeat again in your new job.

Here's how you might begin:

Experience #1: Planned product launch that resulted in 450 letters of intent from 1,500 participants.

a. Worked with president and product managers to discuss product potential and details.
b. Developed promotional plan.
c. Conducted five-week direct-mail campaign prior to conference to create aura of excitement about product.
d. Trained all product demonstrators to make sure they each presented product in same way.
e. Had great product booth built; rented best suite to entertain prospects; conducted campaign at conference by having teasers put under everyone's door every day of conference. Most people wanted to come to our booth.

—and so on—

Analyzing Your Seven Stories

Now it is time to analyze your stories. You are trying to look for the threads that run through them so that you will know the things you do well that also give you satisfaction. Some of the questions below sound similar. That's okay. They are a catalyst to make you think more deeply about the experience. The questions don't have any hidden psychological significance.

If your accomplishments happen to be mostly work related, this exercise will form the basis for your *positioning* or summary statement in your résumé, and also for your Two-Minute Pitch.

If these accomplishments are mostly not work related, they will still give you some idea of how you may want to slant your résumé, and they may give you an idea of how you will want your career to go in the long run.

For now, simply go through each story without trying to force it to come out any particular way. Just think hard about yourself. And be as honest as you can. When you have completed this analysis, the words in the next exercise may help you think of additional things. **Do this page first.**

Story #1. _____

What was the *accomplishment?* _____

_____

What about it did you *enjoy most?* _____

_____

What did you *do best?* _____

_____

What *motivated you to do this?* _____

_____

What about it *made you proud?* _____

_____

What *prompted you to do this?* _____

_____

What *enjoyable skills did you demonstrate?* _____

_____

What was the *subject matter?* (e.g., music, mechanics, tress, budgets, etc.) _____

_____

Story #2. _____
The accomplishment? _____
Enjoyed most? _____
Did best? _____
A motivator? _____
Made you proud? _____
Prompted you to do this? _____
Enjoyable skills demonstrated? _____
Subject matter? _____

Story #3._____

The accomplishment? _____

Enjoyed most? _____

Did best? _____

A motivator? _____

Made you proud? _____

Prompted you to do this? _____

Enjoyable skills demonstrated? _____

Subject matter?

Story #4._____

The accomplishment? _____

Enjoyed most? _____

Did best? _____

A motivator? _____

Made you proud? _____

Prompted you to do this? _____

Enjoyable skills demonstrated? _____

Subject matter?

Story #5._____

The accomplishment? _____

Enjoyed most? _____

Did best? _____

A motivator? _____

Made you proud? _____

Prompted you to do this? _____

Enjoyable skills demonstrated? _____

Subject matter? _____

Story #6._____

The accomplishment? _____

Enjoyed most? _____

Did best? _____

A motivator? _____

Made you proud? _____

Prompted you to do this? _____

Enjoyable skills demonstrated? _____

Subject matter? _____

Story #7._____

The accomplishment? _____

Enjoyed most? _____

Did best? _____

A motivator? _____

Made you proud? _____

Prompted you to do this? _____

Enjoyable skills demonstrated? _____

Subject matter? _____

We are here to be excited from youth to old age, to have an insatiable curiosity about the world. ...We are also here to help others by practicing a friendly attitude. And every person is born for a purpose. Everyone has a God-given potential, in essence, built into them. And if we are to live life to its fullest, we must realize that potential.

NORMAN VINCENT PEALE, *THE POWER OF POSITIVE THINKING* (SIMON AND SCHUSTER)

Skills from Your Seven Stories

The numbers across the top represent each of your seven stories. Start with Story #1 and check off all of your specialized skills that appear in that story. When you've checked off the skills for all seven stories, total them.

Story #	1	2	3	4	5	6	7	Total
Administration								
Advising/Consulting								
Analytical								
Artistic Ability								
Budgetary								
Client Relations								
Communication								
Community Relations								
Contract Negotiation								
Control								
Coordination								
Creativity								
Decisiveness								
Design								
Development								
Financial								
Foresight								
Frugality								
Fund Raising								
Human Relations								
Information Mgmt.								
Imagination								
Individualism								
Initiative								
Inventiveness								
Leadership								
Liaison								
Logic								
Management								
Marketing								
Mathematical								
Mechanical								
Motivational								
Negotiation								
Observation								
Organization								
Other Talents								

Story #	1	2	3	4	5	6	7	Total
Operations Mgmt.								
Org. Design/Devel.								
Ownership								
Perceptiveness								
Perseverance								
Planning								
Policy Making								
Practicality								
Presentation								
Problem Solving								
Procedures Design								
Production								
Program Concept								
Program Design								
Project Management								
Promotion								
Public Relations								
Public Speaking								
Quality Assessment								
Research								
Resourcefulness								
Sales Ability								
Service								
Showmanship								
Speaking								
Staff Dev./Mgmt.								
Strategic Planning								
Stress Tolerance								
Systems								
Teamwork								
Tenacity								
Training								
Travel								
Troubleshooting								
Writing								
Other Talents								

Note: Job hunters enjoy exercises like this because they are simple. **But your experiences are more complex than the words on this page. These words alone do not reflect the richness of what you have to offer. So combine these words with the more in-depth answers you came up with on the preceding page, and continue to analyze your stories throughout your life. You will find deeper and deeper answers about yourself.**

Top six or seven specialized skills, based on which had the most checkmarks:

1. _____
2. _____
3. _____
4. _____
5. _____
6. _____
7. _____

Your Current Work-Related Values

What is important to you? Your values change as you grow and change, so they need to be reassessed continually. At various stages in your career, you may value money, or leisure time, or independence on the job, or working for something you believe in. See what is important to you now. This will help you not be upset if, for instance, a job provides you with the freedom you wanted, but not the kind of money your friends are making.

Sometimes we are not aware of our own values. It may be that, at this stage of your life, time with your family is most important to you. For some people, money or power is most important, but they may be reluctant to admit it—even to themselves.

Values are the driving force behind what we do. It is important to truthfully understand what we value in order to increase our chances of getting what we want.

Look at the list of values below. Think of each in terms of your overall career objectives. Rate the degree of importance you would assign to each for yourself, using this scale:

1—Not at all important in my choice of job   3—Reasonably important
2—Not very but somewhat important   4—Very important

Add other values that don't appear on the list or substitute wording you are more comfortable with.

___ chance to advance
___ work on frontiers of knowledge
___ have authority (responsibility)
___ help society
___ help others
___ meet challenges
___ work for something I believe in
___ public contact
___ enjoyable colleagues
___ competition
___ ease (freedom from worry)
___ influence people
___ enjoyable work tasks
___ work alone
___ be an expert
___ personal growth and development
___ independence

___ artistic or other creativity
___ learning
___ location of workplace
___ tranquility
___ money earned
___ change and variety
___ have time for personal life
___ fast pace
___ power
___ adventure/risk taking
___ prestige
___ moral fulfillment
___ recognition from superiors, society, peers
___ security (stability)
___ physical work environment
___ chance to make impact
___ clear expectations and procedures

Of those you marked "4," circle the five **most** important to you today:

- If forced to compromise on any of these, which one would you give up? _____
- Which one would you be most reluctant to give up? ___

Describe in 10 or 20 words what you want most in your life and/or career.

Your health is bound to be affected if, day after day, you say the opposite of what you feel,
if you grovel before what you dislike and rejoice at what brings you nothing but misfortune.

BORIS PASTERNAK, DR. ZHIVAGO

Other Exercises: Interests, Satisfiers, and Bosses

Case Study Laura
Using Her Special Interests

For many people, interests should stay as interests—things they do on the side. For others, their interests may be a clue to the kinds of jobs they should do next or in the long run. Laura had food as her special interest. She had spent her life as a marketing manager in cosmetics, but she assured me that food was *very* important to her.

We redid her résumé to downplay the cosmetics background. Next, Laura visited a well-known specialty food store. She spoke to the store manager, a junior person, asked about the way the company was organized, and found that there were three partners, one of whom was the president. Laura said to the store manager, "Please give my résumé to the president, and I will call him in a few days." We prepared for her meeting with the president, in which she would find out the company's long-term plans, and so on. At the meeting, he said he wanted to increase revenues from $4 million to $40 million. Laura and I met again to decide how she could help the business grow through her marketing efforts, and to decide what kind of compensation she would want, including equity in the company. She met with the president again, and got the job!

It was the Interests exercise that prompted her to get into that field. Remember, all you need to do is make a list of your interests. Laura simply wrote food. Other people list 20 things. Here is the exercise:

Interests Exercise

List all the things you really like to do. List anything that makes you feel good and gives you satisfaction. List those areas where you have developed a relatively in-depth knowledge or expertise. For ideas, think back over your day, your week, the seasons of the year, places, people, work, courses, roles, leisure time, family, etc. These areas need not be work related. Think of how you spend your discretionary time.

If you cannot think of what your interests may be, think about the books you read, the magazines you subscribe to, the section of the newspaper you turn to first. Think about the knowledge you've built up simply because you're interested in a particular subject. Think about the volunteer work you do—what are the recurring assignments you tend to get and enjoy? Think about your hobbies—are there one or two you have become so involved in that you have built up a lot of expertise/information in those areas? What are the things you find yourself doing—and enjoying—all the time, things you don't have to do?

Your interests may be a clue to what you would like in a job. Rob was a partner in a law firm, but loved everything about wine. He left the law firm to become general counsel in a wine company. Most people's interests should stay as interests, but you never know until you think about it.

Satisfiers and Dissatisfiers Exercise

Simply list every job you have ever had. List what was satisfying and dissatisfying about each job. Some people are surprised to find that they were sometimes most satisfied by the vacation, pay, title, and other perks, but were not satisfied with the job itself.

Bosses Exercise

Simply examine those bosses you have had a good relationship with and those you have not, and determine what you need in your future relationship with bosses. If you have had a lot of problems with bosses, discuss this with your coach.

My illness helped me to see that what was missing in a society is what was missing in me: a little heart, a lot of brotherhood. The 80s were about acquiring wealth, power, prestige. I acquired more . . . than most. But you can acquire all you want and still feel empty....I don't know who will lead us through the 90s, but they must be made to speak to this spiritual vacuum at the heart of American society, this tumor of the soul.

LEE ATWATER, FORMERLY OF THE REPUBLICAN NATIONAL COMMITTEE, SHORTLY BEFORE HE DIED, *LIFE*, FEB. 1991

Your Special Interests

For many people, interests should stay as interests—things they do on the side. For others, their interests may be a clue to the kinds of jobs they should do next or in the long run. Only you can decide whether your interests should become part of your work life.

List all the things you really like to do—anything that makes you feel good and gives you satisfaction. List those areas in which you have developed a relatively in-depth knowledge or expertise. For ideas, think of your day, your week, the seasons of the year, places, people, work, courses, roles, leisure time, friends, family, etc. Think of how you spend your discretionary time.

- Think about the books you read, the magazines you subscribe to, the section of the newspaper you turn to first.
- Think about knowledge you've built up simply because you're interested in it.
- Think about the volunteer work you do—what are the recurring assignments you tend to get and enjoy?
- Think about your hobbies—are there one or two you have become so involved in that you have built up a lot of expertise/information in those areas?
- What are the things you find yourself doing all the time and enjoying, even though you don't have to do them?

Satisfiers and Dissatisfiers in Past Jobs

Wherever I went, I couldn't help noticing, the place fell apart. Not that I was ever a big enough wheel in the machine to precipitate its destruction on my own. But that they let me—and other drifters like me —in the door at all was an early warning signal. Alarm bells should have rung.

MICHAEL LEWIS, *LIAR'S POKER*

For each job you have held in the past, describe as fully as possible the factors that made the job especially exciting or rewarding (satisfiers) and those that made the job especially boring or frustrating (dissatisfiers). **Be as specific as possible** (See the example below, which shows that sometimes the satisfiers can be the perks, while the dissatisfiers can be the job itself.)

JOB	SATISFIERS	DISSATISFIERS
VP of Mfg., ABC Co.	1. Status—large office, staff of 23, Exec. Dining room 2. Fringes—four weeks' vacation, travel allowance, time for outside activities	1. Manage—cold and aloof, too little structure and feedback, no organizational credibility 2. Limited promotional opportunities—none laterally, only straight line
JOB	SATISFIERS	DISSATISFIERS

Your Relationship with Bosses

1. Make a list of all the bosses you have ever had in work situations. Use a very broad definition. They don't have to have been bosses in the strictest sense of the word. Include bosses from part-time jobs, summer jobs, and even professors with whom you worked closely in your student days.

_____   _____
_____   _____
_____   _____
_____   _____
_____   _____

2. Divide the names from above into three lists: those people with whom you had no problems, those with whom you had some problems, and those with whom you had severe problems.

NO PROBLEMS	**SOME PROBLEMS**	**SEVERE PROBLEMS**
_____	_____	_____
_____	_____	_____
_____	_____	_____
_____	_____	_____

3. Look for factors that might help explain why you had some problems or severe problems with some bosses and not with others (or why you have never had problems). For example, consider:
  • the type of people involved: age, sex, personality, etc.
  • the structure of your relationship with the people: how much and what type of power they had over you.
  • the broader contexts: the kind of work involved, the type of organizations involved, etc.

Think about it. Do you see any patterns...

...regarding the type of people?

_____
_____

...regarding the structure of the relationship?

_____
_____

...regarding the contexts?

_____
_____

This exercise is based on lectures given by John P. Kotter in his classes in power dynamics at the Harvard Business School.

Natural talent, intelligence, a wonderful education—none of these guarantees success. Something else is needed: the sensitivity to understand what other people want and the willingness to give it to them. Worldly success depends on pleasing others. No one is going to win fame, recognition, or advancement just because he or she thinks it's deserved. Someone else has to think so too.

Looking into Your Future

Your motivated abilities tell you the elements you need to make you happy, your Values exercise tells you the values that are important to you right now, and the Interests exercise may give you a clue to other fields or industries to explore. But none of them gives you a feel for the *scope* of what may lie ahead.

Dreams and goals can be great driving forces in our lives. We feel satisfied when we are working toward them—even if we never reach them. People who have dreams or goals do better than people who don't.

Setting goals will make a difference in your life, and this makes sense. Every day we make dozens of choices. People with dreams make choices that advance them in the right direction. People without dreams also make choices—but their choices are strictly present oriented, with little thought of the future. When you are aware of your current situation, and you also know where you want to go, a natural tension leads you forward faster.

When you find a believable dream that excites you, don't forget it. In the heat of our day-to-day living, our dreams slip out of our minds. Happy people keep an eye on the future as well as the present.

Freeing-Up Exercises

Here are a few exercises to inspire you and move you forward, add meaning to your everyday life, and give it some long-term purpose.

It's okay if you never reach your dreams. In fact, it can be better to have some dreams that you will probably never reach, so long as you enjoy the process of trying to reach them. For example, a real estate developer may dream of owning all the real estate in Phoenix. He may wind up owning much more than if he did not have that dream. If he enjoys the process of acquiring real estate, that's all that matters.

Rev. Martin Luther King, Jr. had a dream, and it drove his life. Is your dream driving your life? Consider how you would be remembered if your life ended right now. Does the way you are living your life accurately reflect your dream and driving purpose? You may have some work to do.

Exercise #1—Write Your Obituary

Write out what you would want the newspapers to say about you when you die. Alfred Nobel had a chance to *rewrite* his obituary. The story goes that his cousin, who was also named Alfred, died. The newspapers, hearing of the death of Alfred Nobel, printed the prepared obituary—for the wrong man. Alfred read it the day after his cousin's death. He was upset by what the obituary said because it starkly showed him how he would be remembered: as the well-known inventor of a cheap explosive called dynamite.

Alfred resolved to change his life. Today, he's remembered as the Swedish chemist and inventor who provided for the Nobel Prizes.

Write your obituary, as you want to be remembered after your death. Include parts that are not related to your job. If you don't like the way your life seems to be headed, change it—just as Alfred Nobel did. Write your own obituary, and *then make a list of the things you need to do to get there.*

Exercise #2—Invent a Job

If you could have any job in the world, what would it be? Don't worry about the possibility of ever finding that job—make it up! Invent it. Write it out. It may spark you to think of how to create

Exercise #3—If You Had a Million

If you had a million dollars (or maybe 10 million) but still had to work, what would you do?

When I asked myself this question some time ago, I decided I'd like to continue doing what I was doing at work, but would like to write a book

on job hunting because I felt I had something to say. I did write that book—and I've gone on to write others!

People often erroneously see a lack of money as a stumbling block to their goals. Think about it: Is there some way you could do what you want without a million dollars? Then do it!

Exercise #4—Your Fifteen-Year and Forty-Year Visions

Take a look at this very important exercise, which starts on the next page.

Your Fifteen-Year Vision®
And Your Forty-Year Vision®

In my practice as a psychiatrist, I have found that helping people to develop personal goals has proved to be the most effective way to help them cope with problems.

Ari Kiev, M.D., *A Strategy for Daily Living*

If you could imagine your ideal life five years from now, what would it be like? How would it be different from the way it is now? If you made new friends during the next five years, what would they be like? Where would you be living? What would your hobbies and interests be? How about 10 years from now? Twenty? Thirty? Forty? Think about it!

Some people feel locked in by their present circumstances. Many say it is too late for them. But a lot can happen in five, 10, 20, 30, or 40 years. Reverend King had a dream. His dream helped all of us, but his dream helped him too. He was living according to a vision (which he thought was God's plan for him). *It gave him a purpose in life.* Most successful people have a vision.

A lot can happen to you over the next few decades—and most of what happens is up to you. If you see the rest of your life as boring, I'm sure you will be right. Some people pick the "sensible" route or the one that fits in with how others see them, rather than the one that is best for them.

On the other hand, you can come up with a few scenarios of how your life could unfold. In that case, you will have to do a lot of thinking and a lot of research to figure out which path makes most sense for you and will make you happiest.

When a person finds a vision that is right, the most common reaction is fear. It is often safer to wish a better life than to actually go after it.

I know what that's like. It took me two years of thinking and research to figure out the right path for myself—one that included my motivated abilities (Seven Stories Exercise) as well as the sketchy vision I had for myself. Then it took 10 more years to finally take the plunge and commit to that path—running The Five O'Clock Club. I was 40 years old when I finally took a baby step in the right direction, and I was terrified.

You may be lucky and find it easy to write out your vision of your future. Or you may be more like me: It may take a while and a lot of hard work. You can speed up the process by reviewing your assessment results with a Five O'Clock Club career coach. He or she will guide you along. Remember, when I was struggling, the country didn't have Five O'Clock Club coaches or even these exercises to guide us.

Test your vision and see if that path seems right for you. Plunge in by researching it and meeting with people in the field. If it is what you want, chances are you will find some way to make it happen. If it is not exactly right, you can modify it later—after you have gathered more information and perhaps gotten more experience.

Start with the Present

Write down, in the present tense, the way your life is right now, and the way you see yourself at each of the time frames listed. **This exercise should take no more than one hour**. Allow your unconscious to tell you what you will be doing in the future. Just quickly comment on each of the questions listed on the following page, and then move on to the next. If you kill yourself off too early (say, at age 60), push it 10 more years to see what would have happened if you had lived. Then push it another 10, just for fun.

When you have finished the exercise, ask yourself how you feel about your entire life as you laid it out in your vision. Some people feel depressed when they see on paper how their lives are going, and they cannot think of a way out. But they feel better when a good friend or a Five O'Clock Club coach helps them think of a better future to work toward. If you don't like your vision, you are allowed to change it—it's your life.

Do what you want with it. Pick the kind of life you want.

Start the exercise with the way things are now so you will be realistic about your future. Now, relax and have a good time going through the years. Don't think too hard. Let's see where you wind up. You have plenty of time to get things done.

> **The 15-year mark proves to be the most important for most people. It's far enough away from the present to allow you to dream.**

There are more things in heaven and earth, Horatio, than are dreamt of in your philosophy.

WILLIAM SHAKESPEARE, *HAMLET*

Your Fifteen- and Forty-Year-Vision Worksheet

1. The year is **xxxx** (current year).
   You are _____ years old right now.

- Tell me what your life is like right now. (Say anything you want about your life as it is now.)
- Who are your friends? What do they do for a living?
- What is your relationship with your family, however you define "family"?
- Are you married? Single? Children? (List ages.)
- Where are you living? What does it look like?
- What are your hobbies and interests?
- What do you do for exercise?
- How is your health?
- How do you take care of your spiritual needs?
- What kind of work are you doing?
- What else would you like to note about your life right now?

Year: _____   Your Age _____

_____
_____
_____
_____
_____
_____
_____
_____
_____
_____
_____
_____
_____
_____
_____

Don't worry if you don't like everything about your life right now. Most people do this exercise because they want to improve themselves. They want to change something. What do you want to change? ***Please continue.***

2. The year is **xxxx** (current year + 5).
   You are _____ years old.
   (Add 5 to present age.)

Things are going well for you.
- What is your life like now at this age? (Say anything you want about your life as it is now.)
- Who are your friends? What do they do for a living?
- What is your relationship with your "family"?
- Married? Single? Children? (List their ages now.)
- Where are you living? What does it look like?
- What are your hobbies and interests?
- What do you do for exercise?
- How is your health?
- How do you take care of your spiritual needs?
- What kind of work are you doing?
- What else would you like to note about your life right now?

Year: _____   Your Age _____

_____
_____
_____
_____
_____
_____
_____
_____
_____
_____
_____
_____
_____
_____
_____
_____

3. The year is **xxxx** (current year + 15).
   Year: _____ Your Age _____
   You are _____ years old.
   (Current age plus 15.)

   - What is your life like now at this age? (Say anything you want about your life as it is now.)
   - Who are your friends? What do they do for a living?
   - What is your relationship with your "family"?
   - Married? Single? Children? (List their ages now.)
   - Where are you living? What does it look like?
   - What are your hobbies and interests?
   - What do you do for exercise?
   - How is your health?
   - How do you take care of your spiritual needs?
   - What kind of work are you doing?
   - What else would you like to note about your life right now?

Year: _____   Your Age _____

_____

_____

_____

_____

_____

_____

_____

_____

_____

_____

_____

_____

_____

_____

_____

_____

_____

The 15-year mark is an especially important one. This age is far enough away from the present that people often loosen up a bit. It's so far away that it's not threatening. Imagine your ideal life. What is it like? Why were you put here on this earth? What were you meant to do here? What kind of life were you meant to live? Give it a try and see what you come up with. If you can't think of anything now, try it again in a week or so. On the other hand, **if you got to the 15-year mark, why not keep going?**

4. The year is **xxxx** (current year + 25). You are _____ years old!
   (Current age plus 25.)

Year: _____   Your Age _____
Using a blank piece of paper, answer all of the questions for this stage of your life.

5. The year is **xxxx** (current year + 35). You are _____ years old! (Current age plus 35.)

Repeat.

6. The year is **xxxx** (current year + 45). You are _____ years old! (Current age plus 45.)

Repeat.

7. The year is **xxxx** (current year + 55). You are _____ years old! (Current age plus 55.)

Keep going. How do you feel about your life? You are allowed to change the parts you don't like

(Keep going—don't die until you are past 80!)

You have plenty of time to get done everything you want to do. Imagine wonderful things for yourself. You have plenty of time. Get rid of any "negative programming." For example, if you imagine yourself having poor health because your parents suffered from poor health, see what you can do about that. If you imagine yourself dying early because that runs in your family, see what would have happened had you lived longer. It's your life—your only one. As they say, "This is the real thing. It's not a dress rehearsal."

Your Forty-Year Vision®...Fifteen Years is a Good Start

How to Create Your Future One Step at a Time

David Madison, Ph.D., Director of The Five O'Clock Club
Guild of Career Coaches

When my daughter was a month old, I started writing a daily diary to preserve memories of her growing up. She's now 44 and I haven't missed a day since. Now well past the 16,000-page mark—and with my daughter living in California with her husband and two children—I sometimes wonder why I continue writing it. But someone once sent me a 10-year old photo of friends and I was able to find the occasion, the day, and even the hour in the diary. What a triumph! An even bigger triumph: I was able to tell my daughter what she was doing (building a snowman with me) on the day her husband was born.

Whenever I go digging in the old diaries, I am usually astounded: This happened 15 years ago! The clichés turn out to be so true: "It seems like only yesterday," or "Where did the years go?" It's only when we look ahead that we feel that the future is so far away. Ten or 15 years out seems impossibly far away, but September 2020 and April 2030 will one day be a reality.

And it is so depressing to find out that people coast along for years—in jobs that they don't really like—because they fail to imagine in concrete terms: What can my life be like in 2020 or 2030? On a consulting assignment a few years ago, I worked with 17 people who had been downsized by a small bank. As a way of getting them to see the value of the Forty-Year Vision, I asked them what their dream careers were.

Did they simply want to move to other banks and continue processing financial transactions? Most were emphatic: No! And their aspirations were across the board: One wanted to get into filmmaking; another, physical therapy; another, the hospitality industry; and yet another wanted to teach ballroom dancing.

But guess what: No one had seriously considered trying to make such career moves because it was easier and safer to drift along in their current jobs, month after month, year after year. Their aspirations were just unfocused dreams that never moved beyond the wouldn't-it-be-nice stage, precisely because they had never made any attempt to structure the dream. They had never thought of making serious and realistic plans, and wishing upon a star won't make it happen!

But how is a 15- or 40-year strategy manageable? This won't seem nearly so intimidating or scary if you bear five things in mind:

1. Don't start with the most distant point on the calendar! We're the first to admit that possibilities a few decades from now would be too much to wrap your mind around—at first. The initial notch in the Forty-Year Vision is the five-year mark. And that's totally realistic: What do you want your life and career to be like in five short years? That's only 60 months out. And 10 years out won't seem so farfetched or daunting if the five-year mark has been given some form and content.

On the way to your Forty-Year Vision, make the Fifteen-Year Vision your primary stopping point. This benchmark allows you to do some really creative thinking and wondering. You can develop scenarios that are especially meaningful. Try this test: think back 10 or 15 years. In other words, were there steps you could have taken in the 2000s that would have shaped your life and career for the better today? The answer is probably "yes." There's a lesson here about your future!

2. Don't be fooled by the simple wisdom that we can't predict the future. Of course we can't—but that really doesn't have any bearing on trying to make the future turn out on your terms. Not being able to predict the future doesn't stop you from having kids, buying a 20-year CD to pay for college, or committing to a mortgage. Why let it stop you from seriously plotting your career? Five O'Clock Club career coaches try to overcome the skepticism or even ridicule that some people express when they hear about the Forty-Year Vision. We commonly hear, "I have trouble planning next week. Forty years? Give me a break!" But we're not asking you to predict 40 years out, much less guess the distant future: This is not supposed to be an exercise in crystal-ball gazing. The career coach who urges you to do the Forty-Year Vision is asking you to imagine, fantasize, strategize, as the first steps in trying to create the future on your terms.

There once was a commercial for public television that included the words "If it can be imagined, it can be done." Of course that's TV hype, because it's very true that not everything that can be imagined can be done. But it's also a fact that nothing will be done unless it is imagined. Goals are born in the imagination, and a Fifteen- or Forty-Year Vision is a tool to help get the imagination firing at maximum capacity—and to give you the motivation to do the necessary planning and strategizing.

3. Don't despair because you're too old. Sitting down at the kitchen table on your 50th birthday to write a Forty-Year Vision may strike most people as silly. But don't forget the lament of one senior citizen: "If I had known I was going to live so long, I would have taken better care of myself." Precisely because we can't predict the future, the Forty-Year Vision is a good idea. If you do make it to 85 or 90 or beyond, don't you want those years to be fruitful, exciting, and purposeful? We're living longer, and the age-65 cutoff for productive years has become meaningless! So the 50th or even 60th birthday is as good a time as any to let yourself imagine and plan for a long future—at least give the Fifteen-Year Vision a try!

4. Remember that the Forty-Year Vision is always subject to change. You're not chained down to anything; you're the one in charge. Your vision for the future is a pact you make with yourself. Your career coach will be the first to remind you that it is never written in stone—although having it in writing can be a very powerful tool and guide. As you grow and learn more about yourself and the realistic options you face, the Forty-Year Vision evolves too. Course corrections or even radical changes are part of the process.

5. The Forty-Year Vision is meant to be fun: It's not a term paper; it's not a test. Sure, it's serious business, but let your mind go and imagine all the possibilities you can create. As time goes by and events unfold, you'll need to do reality checks, but try to catch the excitement of imagining all the things you can accomplish.

Whether you choose to walk down memory lane with a diary or home movies, photo albums or scrap books, you know that nothing you do now can change what happened 10 years ago. But your daily routine in 10 or 15 years does depend largely on the visions and strategies you develop now. So give the Forty-Year Vision the benefit of the doubt. It could change your life.

Steve Jobs, the legendary founder of Apple Computer, had his share of ups and downs, but he was known for staying the course. After he was ousted from Apple (by John Sculley, whom he brought in to head the company), Jobs labored for seven years on his new company, NeXT Computers, and then founded Pixar, which made him a billionaire. Later, he sold NeXT to Apple, while serving as a consultant to that company. What is the secret of his success? Here are three quotes that shed light on the Steve jobs success story.

There are very few people who have a vision and stick to it. Steve (Jobs) does.

KEITH BENJAMIN, QUOTED IN *SUCCESS*, JULY/AUGUST, 1996

You need a lot more than vision— you need stubbornness, tenacity, belief, and patience to stay the course.

EDWIN PIXAR, COFOUNDER OF PIXAR, ON STEVE JOBS AS QUOTED IN *THE NEW YORK TIMES MAGAZINE*, JANUARY 12, 1997

Asked what he wants to pass on to his children, Jobs answers: "Just to try to be as good a father to them as my father was to me. I think about that every day of my life."

STEVE LOHR, "CREATING JOBS," *THE NEW YORK TIMES MAGAZINE*, IBID. (STEVE JOBS WAS ADOPTED)

The Five O'Clock Club®

The Value of Having a Long-Term Vision No Matter What Your Age

We are living in a culture that emphasizes immediate gratification, does not value planning, and gives slight consideration to consequences. Hence, far too many people, young and old alike, are saddled with credit card debt and live as if there's no tomorrow. We are urged to live one day at a time, especially in the face of adversity, and that may be all some people can handle. But this is not healthy for most, and one-day-at-a-time does not qualify as a goal.

Many of our favorite clichés are *wrong*. Tomorrow does not take care of itself. Not everyone learns from his or her mistakes. "Following your bliss" does not necessarily make you happier. And sometimes it doesn't "all work out" Instead, many people end up resigned to bad situations and "live with it." They say, "This is what fate had in store for us."

Ironically, Americans are action-oriented and like to think they'll figure things out as they go along. I've even heard very famous people brag that they don't have a plan, which adds to the mystique. But they *do* have a solid strategy, which they follow religiously. They may let someone else figure out their detailed plans, but they are not as haphazard as many would like to pretend.

For example, when I heard a successful children's book author give a speech, I was intrigued by her lack of candor. People in the audience were dying to know to what she attributed her success. She said it was pure luck—that she rarely got out of her pajamas and the money kept pouring in. Yet, she wrote four or five books a year and had

many deals for related items. I believe she was far more *planful* than she let on, and she simply didn't want to tell us any of her secrets.

I once appeared on the radio show of a major, nationally syndicated host. As we were waiting for the show to start, he asked about the contacts I might have at the prominent TV shows I had been on and what I thought of each. Then he bragged that he was lucky because he'd never had to job search in his life! He said things just happened to fall in his path. But that wasn't true: he was using me to network! He was actually job searching *continuously*, although not formally, *and* he had a plan for himself.

Many successful people don't like to admit that they plan. It ruins the aura. But most successful people are always aware and always planning—and modifying their plans depending on what they learn.

People are happy when they are working toward their goals. When they get diverted from their goals, they are unhappy. Businesses are the same. When they get diverted from their goals (for instance, because of major litigation or a threatened hostile takeover), tensions build and morale sinks. Life has a way of sneaking up and distracting both individuals and businesses. Many people are unhappy in their jobs because they don't *know* where they are going.

People without goals are more irked by petty everyday problems. Those with goals are less bothered because they have bigger plans. To control your life, you need at least a *tentative* vision of your future that encompasses your whole life.

Dreams and goals can be great driving forces in our lives. We feel satisfied when we are working toward them—even if we never reach them. People who have dreams or goals do better than people who don't.

Setting goals will make a difference in your life, and this makes sense. Every day we make dozens of choices. People guided by dreams make choices that advance them in the right direction. Dreams are the equivalent of the North Star. People without dreams also make choices—but their choices are strictly present oriented, with little thought of the future and are more likely to have bad consequences. When you are aware of your current situation, and you also know where you want to go, a natural tension (between what you face today and what you're trying to create!) leads you forward faster.

When you find a believable dream that excites you, don't forget it. Write it down. Look at it daily. It's less likely to slip out of your mind in the heat of day-to-day living. Happy people keep an eye on the future as well as on the present.

Lack of Vision and Depression

Herbert Rappaport, Ph.D., conducted extensive studies on the way people thought about time (temporal attitudes). His book, *Marking Time* (Simon and Schuster, 1990), is sub-titled "What our attitudes about time reveal about our personalities and conflicts." Dr. Rappaport asked various people to draw "timelines" of their lives: on a horizontal line representing a life span, make a dot to indicate the "NOW point" of life, noting your age. Then note your age at every significant event before NOW and every significant event after NOW.

In one poignant example, he notes the timelines drawn by two women in their early 70s. One, who was depressed, imagined *only two* significant events in her future. The second was fully engaged in life. She imagined almost as many events *after age 72* as she had before that age, and she noted the end of the line—her death.

"Death for this woman is a motivator rather than a suppressor of goals and objectives. The acceptance of death as a 'punctuation' point in the life cycle signals her to 'crowd' the future with the unfinished business of her life."

Rappaport points out that although the two women are approximately the same age, they view life quite differently. The first woman seems to have little in her future to look forward to. She spoke frequently about aging and was considering moving into a retirement community. The second woman had a sense of urgency and planned to "work until it hurt too much."

Having a vision is important *at every age and stage*. Without a vision, we are on a journey without navigation. We are taking day trips and not heading toward a significant destination.

Since I read his book, I, too, have noticed this temporal difference in individuals. One elderly couple, in their late 80s, still has goals and milestones. They are determined to crowd the years ahead with events. They look forward to the marriages of six of their grandchildren who happened to get engaged at about the same time. They also look forward to the renewal of their wedding vows on their 60th anniversary. And they also picked out the plot where they want to be buried—with great cheeriness.

A second couple, in their early 70s and 15 years younger, said they no longer wanted to have photographs taken of themselves because they weren't going to look any better than they now did! They are cheerful but full of nostalgia for the good old days. Their only anticipated event is the high school graduation of the youngest of their eight grandchildren, which will take place in four years. Otherwise, they plan events one day at a time.

Both couples are aware of their future deaths, but one couple takes great joy in the details of their future. The other has their feet planted firmly in the present and *past*.

When a person focuses mainly on the past, that person is often described as depressed. Depressed people, experts say, often have a hard time thinking about the future. The present and its immediate extension are all there is. Rappaport has an opposing and compelling point of view about depression:

"Typically, it has been reasoned that the patient cannot relate to the future because he is depressed While some individuals clearly become depressed in response to problems such as divorce, death, job loss and natural calamities, there are also individuals who seem to be depressed without a clear precipitating cause…

"Eugene Minkowski (1970), in his profound treatise on temporality and depression, suggested the opposite: 'Could we not, on the contrary, suppose the basic disorder is the distorted attitude toward the future.' The future and its possibilities are for Minkowski and a host of other existential theoreticians the force that energizes us and carries us forward in our lives."

Rappaport and others are suggesting that rather than being unable to relate to the future because he is depressed, **the person has become depressed because he is unable to relate to the future.**

And don't people know this intuitively? When a friend is having a down day, it comes naturally to encourage him or her to think about the future. We say that tomorrow is a new day and the possibility of a bright future is there. "This is just a bump in the road," we say. We all know to *steer the person away from the present and into the future.* "Things will get better." This applies, of course, only to those everyday "depressions" we all experience—not to clinical depression or depressions caused by a chemical imbalance.

An Ability to Move On

One interesting aspect of the Fifteen- and especially the Forty-Year Vision® is how it helps people to overcome being programmed by their past. A woman whose parents both died in their 50s cannot imagine a life for *herself* beyond 50. We urged her to push her imagination a little and see what her life *would* be like if she lives until 80—which is probably what will happen to her if she stops counting on dying at 50!

Some people *overcome* traumatic childhoods and others are *bound* by them. Some people overcome by re-writing the past. They *choose* to remember certain things or interpret the past in a certain way. Others may choose a negative interpretation. One may become proud of one's poverty-stricken roots rather than feel deprived by them. As Alfred Adler (a disciple of Freud) said, "What an individual seeks to *become* determines what he remembers of his *has been*. In this sense, the future determines the past." (R. May, E. Angel, and H.F. Ellenberger, *Existence*, New York, Simon & Schuster, 1958). A Fifteen- or Forty-Year Vision can help a person to create a new future, and re-frame a person's past so that it no longer disables.

People must move on. We are sad not just because of some traumatic experience, but because we feel *tied* to it. It controls us; We can't get over it. One of my aunts in her 90s lost her husband of 70 years. She doesn't want to go out; she says she wants to "spend the evening with Frank." Even at her advanced age, we are trying to help her move on, because the years she has left *can* be brighter.

We must replace lost loved ones—those who are no longer in our lives for various reasons. When my grandmother was in her 80s but still vibrant, she volunteered to rock babies at an orphanage. Those babies perked up the minute she walked into the room. She knew that her efforts were worthwhile, and the babies satisfied her need for the everyday caring of children after her own children and grandchildren were grown. That was her bright future, instead of sitting home thinking about the past.

Her daughter, my now 87-year-old mother, makes hundreds of rosaries for the missions and volunteers at her church, helping others and making friendships at the same time.

Ultimately, man should not ask what the meaning of his life is, but rather he must recognize that it is he who is asked.

VIKTOR E. FRANKL

"We stop growing when our human losses are no longer replaced," wrote George Vaillant in *Adaptation to Life*. "Letting go" and moving on "making the replacement" is a healthy response

When one's life has become unsettled, such as through the death of a loved one, the loss of a job, and other situations, to thrive again one must envision a new future. It takes hard work, and sometimes it takes years to figure out what your new life should be like. But it's the same result at any age: You will have a more satisfying future if you put effort into analyzing yourself and also exploring your options.

Work alone does not do it. Without love for others and from others, it is hard to grow. It is the continuity of those important relationships that keep us going over the decades. If you don't have them, you must make them.

The Impact on Older People of Imagining a Future

We say your vision should push you past age 80 so you can see what can happen if you live that long. People are sometimes emotionally scripted for bad health or unhappiness. But all of us *can* break away from the script and re-write the future—as well as the past. We can re-write the way we see our past. We can decide to have very different lives from those we grew up with or now have. That different life requires a different vision of our future.

No matter what a person's age, the process of imagining a future is difficult and can provoke anxiety. We would all like to "go with the flow" and hope it will all work out. Rappaport noted: "More so than individuals who are in their forties, for example, those who are over sixty have a great deal of trouble extending into the future." Yes, those who are over 60 may feel that imagining a future is wishful thinking. Even some career coaches titter at the thought of a 60-year old doing a Fifteen- or Thirty-Year Vision.

When Rappaport met with older people who were simply living day-to-day, doing what needed to be done and essentially wasting time, he asked them: "If you learned at the beginning of a two-week trip to Alaska that the trip had to be shortened, would you forget about your itinerary and aimlessly wander around your room? Would you pick up and go home, or would you accelerate and get as much done as possible?" The reality of death can make us get more out of the time that we do have, including making our wills and putting our houses in order. We're all going to die. What matters is *what we do with the time we have*. It makes sense to accept our future deaths and *make the most of the time we have*.

When he asked someone over 60: "What would you do if you were told you had a few weeks left to live?," the question helped a person to explore his or her priorities. Rappaport found that, in most cases, people who had been wandering aimlessly became energized and focused on what was important to them.

Most of us *do* have a lot of time left. Being 60, 70, even 80 is not the end of the road. The average life expectancy today in the United States is 29 years longer than it was in 1900. Because of better healthcare, these years have been added to middle age, not old age. You have the time to learn and be productive for many, many years. You could have your greatest life accomplishments after the age of 50 or even older. Why give up now? You have plenty of time to make great progress toward whatever you plan. When Jean Calment of France was asked on her 120th birthday what kind of future she expected, she answered, "A short one— but, guess what—she lived for two more years!

So, the after-retirement years may add up to 30 or more. We have plenty of time to make progress toward our vision of the future. Yet, people "retire" with no thought of how they will spend that time or how they will manage their lives through the decades. People may want to retire to get off the treadmill, but to do *what?* I have met too many retired people who are depressed and at a loss for what to do with their time. If a person was used to a vibrant career, this feeling of dislocation can go on for *decades*.

Often *unplanned* years are full of self-oriented pursuits: shopping, traveling, and keeping physically fit. But many don't *think through* what their lives will actually be like. Some decide that they want to live in an adult community where there are no children around, but later become sad at being around all these old people. They think, "I'll travel or play golf." But 30 years of self-indulgence is a long time. Where is the sense of momentum and purpose?

Self-oriented pursuits are not considered the healthiest for the long haul. If you have been working hard for years and deserve a break, take a break. Cut back. But stay involved with life, especially in pursuits that *help others.*

Rappaport says that one of the common themes he sees among depressed adults in his practice is the deep sense of regret for not "stretching oneself" at different life stages. It is not too late to become deeply immersed in something that matters. Rappaport found that those who engage in meaningful activities are happier than those who engage only in self-indulgent activities.

Yet the evidence at hand suggests that ultimately life does not appear satisfying or socially valuable when approached as an opportunity to be free of responsibility.

HERBERT RAPPAPORT, PH.D.

All of Those Years Ahead

People usually imagine retirement—if they imagine it at all—as one big lump of time. But 50 is *different* from 70, 80 and 90, just as 10 is very different from 30, 40 and 50. Each of the segments over 50 can be envisioned and planned for.

Let's take living arrangements, for example. You may want to continue to live where you do now until age 75, and then move to something smaller—say a two-bedroom apartment instead of a four-bedroom house. Then, at say age 85 or 90, you may have to move to a retirement home, and finally to a nursing home. If you don't like

this vision for yourself, that's okay. Write your own! Where do you want to live geographically? What does your residence look like at each stage? If you live to be 90, your living arrangements will be worked out somehow, by someone. If *you* don't plan them, chances are, you won't be happy with how things work out. In the Fifteen- and Forty-Year Visions, you will plan this for each stage of life ahead.

Now, what about your preoccupations? Are you planning to travel when you retire? Thirty years is a long time to travel. How much time can you actually spend doing that? Many older people are depressed and bored. Life seems to drag. That's because the retirement dream was too vague and not well thought out, i.e., "travel." They're not productive and contributing. More and more people are in great physical health and not as well off emotionally because they're *drifting*. They lack goals.

In the Fifteen- and Forty-Year Visions, we suggest that you push yourself to at least age 80 so you can see what can happen if you live that long. According to Kubler-Ross, while there is life, there is still potential for meaningful behavior. Rappaport, in a study of adults in a retirement community, found that those with an unstructured future ended up being present-centered, which is actually stagnation. For those in their 60s and 70s, there is a link between lack of purpose and death anxiety. Planning for the rest of life and retaining a sense of forward motion are at the core of mental health. "Once we get people over the bias that it is frivolous to [plan] at these ages, there is usually ample time, focus and financial resources to face these critically important issues."

What would you like your pursuits to be? If you are now 60, for example, why not now imagine what your pursuits will be like at age 70 and get started in those pursuits now. This may take a lot of thought and exploration, just as it would for a young person choosing a profession. Would you like to raise dogs, for example? Then join dog-related associations now.

When I retire, which is many years away, I envision myself working with some disadvantaged population, perhaps continuing to teach in prisons. I have already researched the prisons and their educational programs in the geographic area where I plan to live— just to make sure the vision is doable. I also envision having an active role as a grandparent and have had serious discussions with my children about living in the same community. If that doesn't work out, I imagine myself doing something with young adults. I also imagine myself gardening, always my favorite hobby, and cooking more—although I do now cook just about every day. I also imagine myself writing another book, but probably not about careers. Working with young adults and inmates, gardening, cooking, writing books: I can research and plan now for all these activities, to assure that they don't remain pipe dreams, but can have real structure and content.

What kind of future would *you* like to imagine for yourself? You may have to work hard to make it happen, and you can plant the seeds now. The present is an opportunity to plan what we would like to do with the rest of our lives, but ironically that happens only when we accept that there is only so much time. Then we begin to worry that there is not enough time. Time becomes precious, not something to be squandered. We can still play bridge and go to the movies, but they become pastimes—just as they were during our "productive" years, and the foreground of our lives become areas of contribution.

Your Age: How Much Longer Do You Want to Work?

Age puzzles me. I thought it was a quiet time. My seventies were interesting and fairly serene, but my eighties are passionate. I grow more intense as I age.

FLORIDA SCOTT MAXWELL

I started this business at age 40; my brother started his business at age 55. With the Fifteen- and Forty-Year Visions, you realize that you have the time to start and be successful in whatever your pursuits are. Would you like to make an impact on an environmental issue? Your family? Other families? A community issue? Or just on the quality of life? Would you like to learn new things (you still have time to become an expert in something new)? Actually work for a not-for-profit? Do consulting work?

Culinary expert Julia Child, for example, brought joy to millions when she was past 60. She died at age 91, and is a striking example of those who don't really hit their stride until they are older. She was forced to abandon her first career because she married a fellow civil servant, Paul Child. After several years of searching, she discovered French cooking when her husband was assigned to France as a USIA officer. Starting at about the age of 35, Julia trained as a chef, founded her own cooking school, and worked on a cookbook, *Mastering the Art of French Cooking*. In 1960, when she was almost 50, the couple moved back to the United States, where the book was published. A chance publicity appearance on television led to her famous TV series.

At one point, by the way, after a double mastectomy, Julia was convinced that her life was ruined. But after many weeks of grieving and weeping, she snapped out of it. "After all, I could be six feet under," she said, "but I'm not." She resumed her forward motion. She had a new lease on life and decided to make the most of it.

Any why not? At age 40, 50, 60, you will find that you are now using everything you have ever learned in your life and bringing it all together. You don't have the pressure of putting the kids through school. You can afford to take risks. Some fields, such as consulting, often favor the older folks. Who wants a twenty-year-old financial advisor?

The trouble with the future is that it usually arrives before we're ready for it.

ARNOLD H. GLASOW

The Fifteen and Forty-Year Visions®

Our business is about helping people with their careers, but we have always urged our clients to do the Forty-Year Vision—or at least a fifteen-year version of it. You can't consider one part of your life without also considering its impact on the rest of your life: where you want to live, your relationship with your family, and so on.

Write down, in the present tense, the way your life is right now, and the way you see yourself five years from now and fifteen years from now, using the questions below.

When you have finished the exercise, ask yourself how you feel about your life as you laid it out in your vision. Some people feel depressed when they see on paper how their lives are going, and they cannot think of a way out. But they feel better when a good friend or a Five O'Clock Club coach helps them think of a better future to work toward. If you don't like your vision, change it—it's your life.

Start the exercise with the way things are now so you will be realistic about your future. Don't think too hard. See where you wind up. You have plenty of time to get things done.

The fifteen-year mark proves to be the most important for most people. It's far enough away from the present to allow you to dream. You've already seen the questions to ask yourself:

- What is your life like right now? (Say anything you want about your life.)
- Who are your friends? What do they do for a living?
- What is your relationship with your family, however you define "family"?
- Are you married? Single? Children? (List ages.)
- Where are you living? What does it look like?
- What are your hobbies and interests?
- What do you do for exercise?
- How is your health?
- How do you take care of your spiritual needs?
- What kind of work or work-substitute are you doing?
- What else would you like to note about your life right now?

We know that engaging in the Fifteen-Year Vision (at least) has energized many people to turn their lives in exciting new directions.

We are prone to judge success by the index of our salaries or the size of our automobiles, rather than by the quality of our service relationship to humanity.

REV. DR. MARTIN LUTHER KING, JR.

The Old-Fashioned Career Coach

In the old days of career coaching, coaches focused on what was called the "job-person match." They helped clients understand their values, accomplishments and interests—but did not discuss a person's goals or vision for a future. In fact, for some coaches, the entire assessment consisted of having the client write a lengthy autobiography—perhaps 30 or more pages long! Coaches simply helped people straight-line their past. A career change was an after-thought. The focus was to help the person get into an organization that matched his skills, abilities and values, but with an assumption that it would be in the same kind of job.

But Five O'Clock Club research in the early '80s proved that coaches had to help people not only analyze their past, but also *envision their future*, a future that looked at the whole person. We pointed out that coaches who did not do that were doing their clients a disservice. It took a decade to convince coaches—inside and outside the Club—of this necessity. But it makes sense. In the old days, people were stuck in their careers: once you were an accountant, you stayed as an accountant. Today, there is no reason for a person to feel stuck. It's easier to talk about the past than to plan for the future. But a coach can help someone envision a new future, regardless of that person's age. Today, 58% of the people who attend the Club make a career change, moving to a new industry or field. For example, one person went from being a high school science teacher in Canada to pharmaceutical sales in New Jersey.

Another went from accounting to sales to human resources—two major career changes in under eight years. You, too, have a future. Try developing a vision and research it.

The Five O'Clock Club®

The Ideal Scene

*Every great personal victory was preceded
by a personal goal or dream.*

DENNIS R. WEBB

This is another exercise to help you imagine your future. Relax for a while. Arrange a time when you will not be distracted. Set aside about an hour. Sit by yourself, have a cup of tea, take out a pad of paper, and imagine yourself 5, 10, 15, or 20 years from now—at a phase in your life when all is going well. Just pick one of these time frames.

Imagine in very general terms the kind of life you were meant to have. Start writing—it's important to write it down, rather than just thinking about it.

What is your ideal life like? Describe a typical day. What do you do when you get up in the morning? Where are you living? Who are your friends?

If you are working, what is it like there? What kind of people do you work with? How do they dress? What kind of work are they doing? What is the atmosphere (relaxed? frantic?)? What is your role in all of this? Describe it in greater and greater detail.

In addition to describing your work situation, think about the other parts of your life. Remember: we each have 24 hours a day. How do you want to spend your 24 hours? Where are you living? What do you do for exercise? How is your health? What is your social life like? Your family life? What are your hobbies and interests? What do you do for spiritual nourishment? What are you contributing to the world? Describe all of these in as much detail as possible. But don't worry if you are not able to identify seemingly important things, such as the city in which you are living, and the field in which you are working.

Keep on writing—include as many details as you can—and develop a good feel for that life. Work on your Ideal Scene for a while, take a break, and then go back and write some more. Change the parts you don't like, and include all the things you really enjoy doing or see yourself doing at this imaginary time in the future.

---

*For whatever we do, even whatever we do not do
prevents us from doing the opposite. Acts demolish their
alternatives, that is the paradox. So that life is a matter
of choices, each one final and of little consequence,
like dropping stones into the sea. We had children, he
thought; we can never be childless. We were moderate,
we will never know what it is to spill out our lives...*

JAMES SALTER, *LIGHT YEARS* (RANDOM HOUSE, INC.)

CASE STUDY Max
Identifying His Future Career

Max, age 40, is a lawyer. A temporary placement firm sends him on assignments to various organizations. He imagined working in a suburban office of six casually dressed people who were on the phone all day talking excitedly to people all over the world. He had a partner in this business. His own role was one of making contacts with prospective customers. He also saw himself writing about the topic they were engaged in, and becoming relatively well-known within their small segment of the industry.

Max's Ideal Scene may seem general, but it contains a lot of information. It appears that he would like to be in his own small but hectic business, operating on an international level. It would be a niche business where he could develop an expertise and become known to his small marketplace.

The international element was strong in this exercise. It was also evident in his Seven Stories Exercise and his Forty-Year Vision. It was clear that an international focus had to be central in his future.

You Can Develop Multiple Scenarios for Your Future

If you simply do the exercise up to this point, you will have done more than most people. You will have developed one scenario for your future. Some people develop multiple scenarios and think about the various possible futures they could have. Then they decide which they would like best, and which they think is doable.

It all starts with describing an Ideal Scene, but it takes a lot more than that. Writing down the scene makes it more serious, and is the start of a more concrete vision. The written vision and the plan are a lot of work, so you can see why most people do not develop visions—and therefore may tend to drift. But those who write down their visions usually find that they have a lot of fun doing it, and those who keep going realize that their future is, in large part, up to them.

Some people become less self-conscious and braver when they think not of what they would like to do, but what they think God has in mind for them. They try to discern God's plan for them, and it is this that motivates and inspires them. Whatever technique or inspiration you use to develop your vision, you will be better off for having done it.

Difficulty need not foreshadow despair or defeat. Rather achievement can be all the more satisfying because of obstacles surmounted.

William Hastie, *Grace under Pressure*

The Next Step: Define It Better and Research It

Some people are more ambitious, and want to go on to the next step: They want to flesh out their vision and then test it against reality. In Max's case, he had to figure out what kind of international business he could go into that would rely on his skills and support his values. He came up with a few ideas that excited him. Now he needs to investigate the potential for the various ideas, come up with a plan, develop new skills in the areas where he may be lacking, and take other steps toward fulfilling that vision.

You too will need to flesh out your bare-bones idea and then check it against reality. But be aware that other people will almost always tell you that it's not doable. Conduct enough research so that you can decide for yourself.

Then, if you are serious about achieving the kind of life that you have envisioned, think of what you need to do to succeed. Take a few little steps immediately to help you advance toward your goal.

. . . [I]n my foolishness and crude want of learning, everything I didn't know seemed like a promise.

Ethan Canin, *Emperor of the Air*

Encountering Roadblocks

Remember that this is not a sprint; it is a long-distance run. Do not become discouraged the first time you venture out. You will come up against lots of roadblocks along the way. That's life. Say to yourself, "Isn't this interesting? Another roadblock. I'll take a short breather (and perhaps even allow myself to feel a tingle of discouragement for a little while) and then I'll think of how I can get around this barrier."

Ask yourself what you have learned from the experience, because these experiences are here to teach us something. "What is the lesson for me in this setback?" And then get moving again.

What we do is nothing but a drop in the ocean; but if we didn't do it, the ocean would be one drop less.

MOTHER TERESA

My Forty-Year Vision

My own Ideal Scene evolved from the Forty-Year Vision I did well over 30 years ago. I imagined myself at age 80 in a beautiful living space with a housekeeper. I had a strong visual image of someone from the community coming to the door to ask my advice. What this vision meant to me was that I had lived my life in such a way that I had had a great impact on the community—people were asking my advice even when I was old. However, I wasn't poverty stricken because of my devotion to the community.

In my Forty-Year Vision I hadn't yet thought of The Five O'Clock Club or even considered a life in career coaching. But the image that came to me, and which I later developed, served as a template for my ideas and my research. My Seven Stories Exercise told me I had better be working with groups, and perhaps writing and lecturing. My Forty-Year Vision eliminated other interests of mine that would not have helped the community as much as career coaching.

It took many years to develop the concept and the focus of The Five O'Clock Club. For years, I continually used the Seven Stories Exercise and the Forty-Year Vision as my template. If an idea fit in with my vision and abilities, I considered it. If an idea didn't fit, I rejected it. I spent many long hours doing research to select the field I wanted to be in. All of this finally evolved into the concept of The Five O'Clock Club.

As you can see, the Forty-Year Vision is simply a vision of your future. By studying it, along with the Ideal Scene, you can get at unconscious desires you may have. Making your desires conscious increases your chances of being able to do something about them.

First, write out your Ideal Scene. Then in the next section, follow Howard step by step as he uncovers his dream.

Peter Schwartz, *The Art of the Long View* (Random House, Inc.)

In order to make effective decisions, you must articulate them to begin with. Consider, for example, the choice of a career in biotechnology. A scenario-planner would tackle the decision differently. It depends, he or she might argue, on another set of questions: What is the future of the biotechnology industry? (That in turn depends on:) What is the path of development in the biotech industry? (Moreover:) What skills will have enduring value? (And:) Where will be a good place to begin? The hardest questions will be the most important. What is it that interests you about biotechnology in the first place? What sorts of things about yourself might lead you to make a decision with poor results? What could lead you to change your mind?

Scenarios are not predictions. It is simply not possible to predict the future with certainty.

For individuals and small businesses, scenarios are a way to help develop their own gut feeling and assure that they have been comprehensive, both realistic and imaginative, in covering all important bases.

If you look at yourself on the level of historical time, as a tiny but influential part of a century-long process, then at least you can begin to know your own address. You can begin to sense the greater pattern, and feel where you are within it, and your acts take on meaning.

MICHAEL VENTURA, QUOTED BY P. SCHWARTZ

He was, after all, a good father—that is to say, an ineffective man. Real goodness was different, it was irresistible, murderous, it had victims like any other aggression; in short, it conquered.

JAMES SALTER, *LIGHT YEARS*

The Ideal Scene Worksheet

Imagine yourself 5, 10, 15, or 20 years from now—at a phase in your life when all is going well. Just pick one of these time frames. Imagine in very general terms the kind of life you were meant to have. Start writing—it's important to write it down, rather than just think about it.

What is your ideal life like? Describe a typical day. _____

_____

_____

_____

_____

What do you do when you get up in the morning? Where are you living? _____

_____

_____

_____

Who are your friends? _____

_____

_____

_____

If you are working, what is it like there? _____

_____

_____

_____

What kind of people do you work with? How do they dress? _____

_____

What kind of work are *they* doing? _____

_____

What is the atmosphere (relaxed or frantic)? _____

_____

What is your role in all of this? _____

_____

_____

Use another sheet of paper to describe it in greater and greater detail.

In addition to describing your work situation, think about the other parts of your life. How do you want to spend your 24 hours?

Where are you living? _____

_____

What do you do for exercise? _____

_____

How is your health?

_____

What is your social life like? _____

_____

Your family life? _____

_____

What are your hobbies and interests?_____

_____

What do you do for spiritual nourishment? _____

_____

What are you contributing to the world? _____

_____

Describe all of these in as much detail as possible. But don't worry if you are not able to identify seemingly important things, such as the city in which you are living, and the field in which you are working. Keep on writing—include as many details as you can—and develop a good feel for that life. Work on your Ideal Scene for a while, take a break, and then go back and write some more. Change the parts you don't like, and include all the things you really enjoy doing or see yourself doing at this imaginary time in the future. _____

_____

_____

_____

_____

_____

_____

_____

_____

_____

_____

_____

The
Five
O'Clock
Club®

My Ideal Job

Human... life is a succession of choices, which every conscious human being has to make every moment. At times these choices are of decisive importance; and the very quality of these choices will often reveal that person's character and decide his fate. But that fate is by no means prescribed: for he may go beyond his inclinations, inherited as well as acquired ones. The decision and the responsibility is his: for he is a free moral agent, responsible for his actions.

JOHN LUKACS, *A HISTORY OF THE COLD WAR*
(RANDOM HOUSE, INC.)

Throughout this book, you have been actively planning, identifying action steps, determining good-fit work environments, and analyzing the appropriateness of career decisions. Your ultimate goal is to develop a career plan on which you can begin taking action immediately.

Right now, you will do a simple exercise that will help you picture yourself in your Ideal Job. Then you will be able to identify some of the strategies you can use to get there.

Choose a job you love, and you will never have to work a day in your life.

CONFUCIUS

Describing Your Ideal Job

A visualization exercise will help you define your ideal job in specific detail. It only requires you to use your thinking and visualizing skills to complete it.

This can be your current job in its ideal state, another ideal job in the organization, or any other job that would be ideal for you. At this point, you should not be concerned about whether or not this job appears to be realistic or feasible.

Creative visualization is a technique many people use to visualize clearly and specifically the results they want. Research has shown that the more clarity you have around what you are trying to achieve, the more likely you are to achieve it.

In sports, for example, many star athletes have used this technique with great success. Before and during the match, a tennis player pictures himself or herself successfully executing each stroke. Before the race, a slalom skier pictures every twist and turn in the course and exactly how he or she will negotiate each one. Previewing the action in detail, like running a movie in their minds, helps these athletes to achieve far better results than they would be able to achieve otherwise.

But sports is only one area where this technique is effective. You can use it in any context to set yourself up for success.

For example, what if you will soon be attending a meeting, and you feel a little uncomfortable about it. You can preview the meeting in your mind. Imagine the room that you will be in. Think of the people who will be sitting around the table. Who will be there? What are they likely to say? What do you think their key issues will be that have anything to do with you? What is your opinion of those issues?

How are you dressed for this meeting? How do you sit? Perhaps someone brings up a project that you have been working on. What would you say about your project in this meeting? Imagine yourself talking about your project.

If you didn't like the way you spoke about your project in your own mind, replay it and try again. Perhaps you need to informally meet with some of the attendees ahead of time to get a better feel for what may happen in the meeting, and then you can visualize the meeting again—but with more information.

You can use visualization for everything that may come up. You can visualize the next step you plan to take in your project, and the informal meetings you may have. If you have been reluctant to tackle a certain problem, such as working at a computer, you can visualize yourself using certain computer software.

You can use visualization now to start to imagine your own future. There are a couple of ways you can go about this.

You can work with your Career Buddy. Your Career Buddy can slowly read the questions to you while you imagine your Ideal Job, and then you can do the same for your Career Buddy.

Or you can imagine your future all by yourself. You can't rush this exercise. Instead, arrange a time when you will not be distracted. Set aside about half an hour. Relax for a while. First, you'll want to sit comfortably by yourself, and eliminate distractions. Take out a pad of paper.

You'll think about a series of questions. Let the answers come to you and picture the results silently as opposed to giving your responses aloud. At the end of the exercise, you can jot down your answers in this manual. When you are ready, start by getting very comfortable. Now imagine the following:

You see yourself one or two years from now —or further if you want. Some people find it more comfortable to imagine themselves 5 or even 15 years from now because they may want to imagine something very different from what they are doing now. Making big changes takes time, and you want to give yourself the time it really takes to make progress in your career. Very little that is significant happens quickly.

So here you are—1, 2, 5, 10, or even 15 years from now. You are in your ideal job. Everything is going very well. You've managed your career in ways that have brought you personal and professional satisfaction, in terms of what you are doing, with whom, where, and how.

Take a long time to imagine your ideal job, and take a long time to answer the questions below. Do not rush. Make the image as realistic as possible for yourself.

- What do you see?
- How do you feel?
- What are you saying?
- How do you talk about yourself in this ideal job?
- What has happened in your career?
- What are the signs that you are successful?
- In achieving this, what was the first thing you did?
- Who did you use as resources in achieving your goal?
- When did you contact them?
- What was the hardest lesson you learned?
- What was the best lesson you learned?

Now, without speaking to anyone, fill in the worksheet. *Describing Your Ideal Job.* Jot down your answers to the questions asked above in as much detail as you can remember. Use extra paper if you need to. The greater the detail of your description, the more firmly the scene can remain implanted in your mind.

Life is an end in itself, and the only question as to whether it is worth living is whether you have had enough of it.

Oliver Wendell Holmes

Describing Your Ideal Job Worksheet

Thinking back over what you just visualized, answer the following questions as specifically as possible in order to describe your ideal work outcomes. Your answers will help you determine how you will know when you have achieved your goals.

What has happened in your career? _____

_____

What are the signs that you are successful? _____

_____

Looking around you, what do you see? _____

_____

What are you saying? _____

_____

How do you feel? _____

_____

How do you talk about yourself? _____

_____

What was the first step you took? _____

_____

Who did you use as resources in achieving this goal? _____

_____

When did you contact them? _____

_____

What was the hardest lesson you learned in achieving your outcome? _____

_____

What was the best lesson you learned? _____

Even if you did not work with your Career Buddy on this, the two of you may want to discuss these results. Spend some time describing your ideal job and how you got there.

If you are not satisfied right now with your description of your ideal job, that's okay. Some people feel locked in by their present circumstances. Others simply have a hard time using visualization. Try it again in a few days, and see what you come up with. Or ask your Career Buddy to help you. If that still doesn't work, you may have to meet with a career coach.

Visualization can be a highly effective technique for creating a picture of what you want in your career. Once you have begun to see it in your mind's eye, a goal becomes much easier to realize. Knowing what you want sets the stage for achieving it.

Life can only be understood backwards; but it must be lived forwards.

Kierkegaard

The Five O'Clock Club

My Ideal Work Environment

*Dear sir, be patient toward all that is unsolved in your heart and try to love the **questions themselves** like locked rooms and like books that are written in a very foreign tongue. Do not now seek the answers, which cannot be given you because you would not be able to live them. And the point is, to live everything.*

***Live** the questions now. Perhaps you will then gradually, without noticing it, live along some distant day into the answer. Perhaps you do carry within yourself the possibility of shaping and forming as a particularly happy and pure way of living; train yourself to it—but take whatever comes with trust, and if only it comes out of your own will, out of some need of your inmost being, take it upon yourself and hate nothing.*

Rainer Maria Rilke, *Letters to a Young Poet* (trans. M.D. Herter Norton, 1993)

Most of us occasionally think about what would be ideal for us in terms of lifestyle and work environment. The problem is, we may dream about that environment and do nothing to create it!

A motivating work environment can contribute greatly to career effectiveness and job satisfaction. So your next step will be to focus on identifying the work environment where you will be most productive and satisfied. That means getting even more specific about the situation that is ideal for you. Below are some elements you would need to consider in creating your ideal work environment. You will be asked to consider these elements as you complete the worksheet starting on the next page.

Physical surroundings/location—What does this environment look and feel like? Are you in an office or moving from place to place? Is it busy or quiet? Are you working primarily alone or surrounded by people?

People—What kinds of people are you working with? Are they energetic, quiet, creative, highly structured? Do you interact with many people or a few?

Activities—What kinds of activities are you engaged in? Are you working primarily with other people, with equipment, or with information? Are you a manager or an individual contributor?

Style—What type of work, communications, and management styles are prevalent? Are people formal or informal? How do they communicate with each other? How do they dress?

Recognition and rewards—What types of recognition do you receive? Do you get frequent recognition/acknowledgment from peers/superiors? How are you rewarded for good performance?

A little while ago, you pictured yourself in your ideal job. Now, once again, imagine yourself in your ideal job some time in the future. See how many specifics you can come up with about the environment of that job. Complete the My Ideal Work Environment worksheet on the following pages, which looks at the five elements just presented.

Then talk to your Career Buddy. Take five minutes apiece to describe your ideal work environments to each other. Use the notes you took in this workbook, but elaborate even further. Your objective is to make your description as real as possible for your Buddy. Your Buddy, when listening to you, should ask you questions to help you make the picture clear for yourself. And you should do the same for your partner. When working with your Buddy, make sure each of you is focusing on your ideal environment and not your current environment. You should each be as specific as you can.

Assess what is needed to change your present work environment to make it an ideal work environment. If this change is within your control, what can you do about it? If the change is not within your control, remember that your response to the situation is always within your control.

Don't forget what we said earlier about visualizing the results you want to create. The more specific you are about the results you want, the more you are setting yourself up to achieve them.

Additional Ideas

Below is a list of words employees have used to describe their ideal work environments. You may want to add one or two of these to your list.

- Friendly coworkers around me (they say "Good morning")
- Geographic location—near stores
- Painted offices (they care about their environment)
- Large desk space
- My own desk
- Windows
- Resources, such as training materials
- Short commute
- A separation of work time and personal time
- Smart people
- If open space, conference space is private
- Good lighting
- A phone system that meets people's needs
- Personalized space
- Quiet so I can think

My Ideal Work Environment Worksheet

Now that you have identified your ideal job, the next step is to think about the specific elements that make up your ideal work environment. Review the list of questions in each category and jot down your thoughts in the spaces provided.

Physical surroundings/location:

- Are you in an office or are you moving from one place to another?_____

_____

- If you are in an office, describe its appearance. How is it furnished? _____

_____

- Is it a formal or an informal environment?_____

_____

- Are there distractions or is it quiet? _____

_____

- Do you have a place you can go to relax, do necessary paperwork, talk with your coworkers?_____

_____

- Are the processes computerized for control? _____

_____

- Are you isolated or surrounded by people? _____

_____

- How do you get to work—bus, train, car, bicycle, car pool, walk? _____

_____

People:

- What kind of people do you work with (e.g., creative, energetic, technical, or mechanical)?_____

_____

- Do you prefer to work with many people or a few? _____

_____

- Do you socialize with your colleagues outside the work environment? _____

_____

Activities:

- Are you working with other people, with equipment, or with information?_____

_____

- Are you managing or directing people? _____

_____

- Are you reading reports?_____

- Do you attend meetings regularly? _____

- Are you communicating with others?_____

- Are you responsible for complete tasks? Or are you responsible for a piece of a task? _____

- What kinds of activities are most rewarding? Least rewarding? _____

- Do you attend meetings of external professional organizations? _____

- How much do you travel? _____

- Are you a decision maker? _____

- How much freedom do you have to carry out your responsibilities?_____

Style:

- Are people formal or informal in how they relate to each other?_____

- What type of management style is typical? _____

- Do people prefer to communicate mainly through talking or through written communication?___

- What are people wearing?_____

Recognition/Rewards:

- What types of recognition do you receive? _____

- How are you rewarded? _____

- Are monetary rewards based on individual or team performance? _____

- What are your working hours? _____

- Do you have flexible working hours? _____

Case Study: Howard
Developing a Vision

Howard attended a Five O'Clock Club group that specializes in helping people who are not yet in professional-level jobs. He had done the Seven Stories and other exercises, and had tried to do the Forty-Year Vision. Like most people, he had left out important parts, such as what he would be doing for a living. That's okay. I asked him if he would mind doing it in the small discussion group.

At the time, Howard was 35 years old and worked in a lower-level job in the advertising industry. He wanted to advance in his career by getting another job in advertising. Based on our research into the jobs of the future, which showed that his current industry was a shaky choice, we asked him to postpone selecting an industry while we helped him complete his Forty-Year Vision.

Howard was just getting started on his career even though he was 35. You're just getting started too. Regardless of your age, take pen to paper and force yourself to write something. You can always change it later.

Filling in His Forty-Year Vision

Kate: "Howard, you're 35 years old right now. Tell me: Who are your friends and what do they do for a living?"

Howard: "John is a messenger; Keith minds the kids while his wife works; and Greg delivers food."

Kate: "What do you do for a living?"

Howard: "I work in the media department of an advertising agency."

Kate: "Okay. Now, let's go out a few years. You're 40 years old, and you've made a number of new friends in the past five years. Who are these people? What are they doing for a living?"

Howard: "One friend is a medical doctor; another works in finance or for the stock exchange; and a third is in a management position in the advertising industry."

Kate: "That's fine. Now, let's go out further. You're 50 years old, and you have made a lot of new friends. What are they doing for a living?"

Howard: "One is an executive managing 100 to 200 people in a corporation and is very well respected; a second one is in education he's the principal or the administrator of an experimental high school and gets written up in the newspapers all the time; a third is a vice president in finance or banking."

Kate: "Those are important-sounding friends you have, Howard. But who are you and what are you doing that these people are associating with you?"

Howard: "I'm not sure."

Kate: "Well, how much money are you making at age 50 in today's dollars?" Howard: "I'm making $150,000 a year." Kate: "I'm impressed. What are you doing to earn that kind of money, Howard? What kind of place are you working in? Remember, you don't have to be specific about the industry or field you're in. For example, how do you dress for work?"

Howard: "I wear a suit and tie every day. I have a staff of 60 people working for me: six departments, with 10 people in each department."

Kate: "And what are those people doing all day?" Howard: "They're doing paperwork, or computer work."

Kate: "That's great, Howard. We now have a pretty good idea of what you'll be doing in the future. We just need to fill in some details."

I said to the group: "Perhaps Howard won't be making $150,000, but he'll certainly be making a lot by his own standards. And maybe it won't be 60 people, but it will certainly be a good-sized staff. What Howard is talking about here is a concept. The details may be wrong, but the concept is correct."

If I see what I want real good in my mind, I don't notice any pain in getting it.

GEORGE FOREMAN, FORMER HEAVYWEIGHT BOXING CHAMPION OF THE WORLD

Howard: "But I'm not sure if that's what I really want to do."

Kate: "It may not be exactly what you want to

do, Howard, but it's in the right direction and contains the elements you really want. What you just said fits in with your Seven Stories exercise (one story was about your work with computers; another was about an administrative accomplishment). Think about it for next week, but I'll tell you this: You won't decide you want to be a dress designer, like Roxanne here. Nor will you say you want to sell insurance, like Barry. What you will do will be very close to what you just described.

"If you come back next week and say that you've decided to sell ice cream, for example, I'll tell you that you simply became afraid. Fear often keeps people from pursuing their dreams. Over the week, read about the jobs of the future, and let me know the industries you may want to investigate for your future career. It's usually better to pick growth industries rather than declining ones. You stand a better chance of rising with the tide."

The Next Week

When it was Howard's turn in the group the next week, he announced that he had selected health care as the industry he wanted to investigate. That sounded good because it is a growth field and because there will be plenty of need for someone to manage a group of people working on computers.

We brainstormed the areas within health care that Howard could research. He could work in a hospital, an HMO, a health-care association, and so on. He could learn about the field by reading the trade magazines having to do with health care administration, and he could start networking by meeting with someone else in the group who had already worked in a hospital.

Week #3

Howard met with the other person in the group and got a feel for what it was like to work in a hospital. He also got a few names of people he could talk to—people at his level who could give him basic information. He had spent some time in a library reading trade magazines having to do with health-care administration.

Howard needed to do a lot more research before he would be ready to meet with higher-level people—those in a position to hire him.

Week #4

Howard announced to the group that he had done more research, which helped him figure out that he should start in the purchasing area of a hospital, as opposed to the financial area, for example. In previous jobs, he had worked both as a buyer and as a salesman, so he knew both sides of the picture. He would spend some time researching the purchasing aspect of health care. That could be his entry point, and he could make other moves after he got into the field.

A human being certainly would not grow to be seventy or eighty years old if his longevity had no meaning for the species.

C. G. Jung

Week #5

Today Howard is ready to meet with higher-level people in the health-care field. As he networks around, he will learn even more about the field, and select the job and the organization that will position him best for the long run—the situation that fits in best with his Forty-Year Vision.

After Howard gets his next job, he will occasionally come to the group to ask the others to help him think about his career and make moves within the organization. He will be successful in living his vision if he continues to do what needs to be done, never taking his eye off the ball.

If Howard sticks with his vision, he will make good money, and live in the kind of place

in which he wants to live. Like many people who develop written plans, Howard has the opportunity to have his dream come true.

You can either say the universe is totally random and it's just molecules colliding all the time and it's totally chaos and our job is to make sense of that chaos, or you can say sometimes things happen for a reason and your job is to discover the reason. But either way, I do see it meaning an opportunity and that has made all the difference.

CHRISTOPHER REEVE, INTERVIEW WITH BARBARA WALTERS

You Can Do It Too

As I mentioned earlier, the group that Howard attended is a special Five O'Clock Club program that works mostly with adults who are not yet in the professional or managerial ranks, and helps them get into professional-track jobs. For example:

Emlyn, a 35-year-old former babysitter, embarked on and completed a program to become a nurse's aide. This is her first step toward becoming an R.N., her ultimate career goal.

Calvin, who suffers from severe rheumatoid arthritis, hadn't worked in 10 years. Within five weeks of starting with us, he got a job as a consumer advocate with a center for the disabled, and has a full caseload. We are continuing to work with him.

These ambitious, hard-working people did it, and so can you. It's not easy, but what else are you doing with your 24 hours a day? The people who did it followed this motto: "Have a dream. Make a plan. Take a step. Keep on climbing."

You can complain that you haven't gotten lucky breaks, but Howard, Emlyn, and Calvin didn't either.

They made their own breaks, attended a Five O'Clock Club group, and kept plugging ahead despite difficulties. If they can do it, you can do it too.

This is a real test of the wedding vows.
He's my partner. He's my other half, literally.
It's not within the realm of my imagination to
do anything less than what I'm doing.

MRS. CHRISTOPHER REEVE (DANA),
IN THAT SAME INTERVIEW

We live in an age when art and the things of the spirit
come last. The truth still holds, however, that through
dedication and devotion one achieves another kind
of victory. I mean the ability to overcome one's
problems and meet them head on.
"Serve life and you will be sustained." That is a truth
which reveals itself at every turn in the road.
I speak with inner conviction because I have been
through the struggle. What I am trying to emphasize
is that, whatever the nature of the problem, it can only
be tackled creatively. There is no book of "openings,"
as in chess lore, to be studied. To find an opening
one has to make a breach in the wall—and the wall
is almost always in one's own mind. If you have the
vision and the urge to undertake great tasks, then you
will discover in yourself the virtues and the capabilities
required for their accomplishment. When everything
fails, pray! Perhaps only when you have come to the
end of your resources will the light dawn. It is only
when we admit our limitations that we find there
are no limitations.

HENRY MILLER, *BIG SUR AND THE ORANGES*
OF HIERONYMOUS BOSCH (NEW DIRECTIONS PUBLISHING)

Self-Assessment Summary

Summarize the results of all of the exercises. This information will help define the kind of environment that suits you best, and will also help you brainstorm some possible job targets. Finally, it can be used as a checklist against job possibilities. When you are about to receive a job offer, use this list to help you analyze it objectively.

1. **What I need in my relationship with bosses:** _____

2. **Job satisfiers/dissatisfiers:**

   Satisfiers: _____

   Dissatisfiers: _____

3. **Most important work-related values:** _____

4. **Special interests:** _____

5. **Patterns running through the Seven Stories analysis:**

   Main accomplishments: _____

   Enjoyed most; Did best: _____

   Key motivators: _____

   Made you proud: _____

   Enjoyable skills demonstrated: _____

   Subject matter: _____

6. **Top six or seven Specialized Skills:** _____

   _____

   _____

   _____

   _____

   _____

   _____

7. **From Fifteen- or Forty-Year Vision:**

   Where I see myself in the long run: _____

   _____

   What I need to get there: _____

8. **My basic personality and the kinds of work cultures into which it will fit:** _____

   _____

   _____

Take a Breather

The Five O'Clock Club

*For deep in our hearts
We do believe
That we shall overcome someday.*

"WE SHALL OVERCOME"
AFRICAN-AMERICAN FREEDOM SONG

Sometimes we get so caught up in the path we are on that we think we have no choice. We forget what we would rather be doing. It is easy to lose sight of what would make us happy. We forget we have made choices that have brought us to where we are.

Resolve to be thyself and know that he who finds himself loses his misery.

MATTHEW ARNOLD

Approach career planning and job hunting with an open mind—be open to the possibilities available to you. It is only by going out into the world and testing your ideas that the possibilities present themselves. Explore. Don't rush to take a job just because it is something well-known to you.

The purpose of knowledge, and especially historical knowledge, is understanding rather than certainty.

JOHN LUKACS, *A HISTORY OF THE COLD WAR*

Although your enjoyable skills do not change, keep reexamining them so you can see how they fit into various situations in your changing world. You will always fit in because your enjoyable skills adapt themselves to new situations and new possibilities.

How many cares one loses when one decides not to be something but to be someone.

COCO CHANEL

Expect to be surprised. And think of surprise as a pleasant thing, because it adds interest to your life. Every move you make will open a new range of possibilities.

The step you are now taking is one that can alter the direction of your life. If you are aware, it can have as much or as little effect as you want it to have. If it turns out to be a mistake, you can move on.

This is not the last step: It is a transition. The next step is a preparation for the one after that. In the future, it will rarely be possible to say, in concrete terms, "I want to be this for the rest of my life." The past is over and is subject to a new interpretation depending on the situation you are now in and where you want to go from here. It's your story, and it is a story you make up as you go along. You don't know how the story will end, and the ending really doesn't matter. What matters is that you are living your life, enjoying the process of living. It's a journey, not a battle.

You move from obsessing about why me and it's not fair and when will I move again and all of those things into well, what is the potential? And now, four months down the line, I see potential I wasn't capable of seeing...So I really sense being on a journey that's very interesting.

CHRISTOPHER REEVE, INTERVIEW WITH BARBARA WALTERS

To repeat part of a quote we included earlier:

OPTIMISM EMERGES AS THE BEST PREDICTOR TO SUCCESS IN LIFE

"Hope has proven a powerful predictor of outcome in every study we've done so far," said Dr. Charles R. Snyder, a psychologist at the University of Kansas. Having hope means believing you have both the will and the way to accomplish your goals, whatever they may be....It's not enough to just have the wish for something. You need the means, too. On the other hand, all the skills to solve a problem won't help if you don't have the willpower to do it.

DANIEL GOLEMAN, *THE NEW YORK TIMES*, DEC. 24, 1991

The
Five
O'Clock
Club®

PART THREE

How to Select
Your Job Targets

BRAINSTORMING POSSIBLE JOBS

Brainstorming Possible Jobs

But when the family continued to struggle, and when Steve Ross was a teenager, he was summoned to his father's deathbed to learn that his sole inheritance consisted of this advice: There are those who work all day, those who dream all day, and those who spend an hour dreaming before setting to work to fulfill those dreams." Go into the third category," his father said," because there's virtually no competition."

OBITUARY OF STEVEN J. ROSS, CREATOR OF TIME WARNER, *THE NEW YORK TIMES*, DEC. 21, 1992

Use the Brainstorming Possible Jobs worksheet in this section, to help you brainstorm possible jobs that you can then explore.

1. **Across the top of the page**, list the following elements as they apply to you. Use as many columns as you need for each category.

   - Your basic personality
   - Interests
   - Values
   - Specialized skills
   - From the Seven Stories Exercise:
   - the role you played
   - the environment in which you worked
   - the various subject matters in your stories
   - Long-range goals
   - Education
   - Work experience
   - Areas of expertise

   Here is one person's list of column headings across the top:

   - Personality: **outgoing**

   - Interests: **environment, computers, world travel** (three different interests— takes three columns)
   - Values: **a decent wage** so I can support a family
   - Specialized Skills: **computer-based research**
   - From the Seven Stories Exercise:
   being **part of a research group**
   enjoy **Third World countries** (takes two columns)
   Goals from the Forty-Year Vision: **head up not-for-profit organization**
   Education: **masters in public policy**
   Work Experience: **seven years' marketing experience**.

   This takes a total of 11 columns across the top.

CHARLEY: Yeah. He was a happy man with a batch of cement.
LINDA: He was so wonderful with his hands.
BIFF: He had the wrong dreams. All, all, wrong.
HAPPY, almost ready to fight Biff: Don't say that!
BIFF: He never knew who he was.

ARTHUR MILLER, *DEATH OF A SALESMAN* (PENGUIN BOOKS)

2. **Down the side of the page, list possible jobs, fields, or functions** that rely on one or more of these elements. For example, combine marketing with environment, or computers with research and Third World countries.

   At this point, do not eliminate anything. Write down whatever ideas occur to

111

you. Ask your friends and family. Do library research and talk to lots of people. Open your eyes and your mind when you read or walk down the street. Be observant and generate lots of ideas. Write down whatever anyone suggests. A particular suggestion may not be exactly right for you, but may help you think of other things that are right.

3. **Analyze each job possibility**. Check off across the page the elements that apply to the first job. For example, if the job fits your basic personality, put a checkmark in that column. If it uses your education or relies on your work experience, put checkmarks in those columns. If it fits in with your long-range goals, put a checkmark there.

   Do the same for every job listed in the left column.

It is never too late to be what you might have been.

GEORGE ELIOT

4. **Add up the checkmarks for each job, and write the total in the right-hand column**. Any job that relies on only one or two elements is probably not appropriate for you. Pay attention to the ones with the most check-marks. Certain elements are more important to you than others, so you must weight those more heavily. In fact, some elements probably must be present so you will be satisfied, such as a job that meshes with your values.

Those jobs that seem to satisfy your most important elements are the ones you will list as some of the targets to explore on the Preliminary Target Investigation worksheet (see page xxxx). Also list positions that would be logical next steps for you in light of your background.

You must have long-range goals to keep you from being frustrated by short-range failures.

CHARLES C. NOBLE, MAJOR GENERAL

CASE STUDY Agnes
Broadening Her Targets

Agnes has been a marketing/merchandising/promotion executive in the fashion, retail, and banking industries. Her only love was retail, and her dream job was working for one specific, famous fashion house. Perhaps she could actually get a job with that fashion house, but what kind of job could she go for after that? The retail and fashion industries were both retrenching at the time of her search, although she could probably get a job in one of them. She needed more targets, and preferably some targets in growing industries so she would have a more reasonable career path.

In addition to the retail and fashion industries, what other industries could Agnes consider? In the banking industry, where she had been for only three years, some of the products she promoted had been computerized. In combining *computers* with *retail*, we came up with *computerized shopping*, a growing field that is threatening the retail industry. Computerized shopping and related areas were good fields for Agnes to investigate. What about something having to do with debit cards and credit cards or other computer-based systems aimed at retail? Or what about selling herself to banks that were handling the bankrupt retail companies that she was so familiar with? We came up with 20 areas to explore. Agnes's next step is to conduct a Preliminary Target Investigation (which you will read about soon) to determine which fields may be worth pursuing in that they hold some interest for her and there is some possibility of finding a job in them. At this point she has an exciting search lined up—one with lots of fields to explore and one that offers her a future instead of just a job.

I've got peace like a river in a my soul.

AFRICAN-AMERICAN SPIRITUAL

Brainstorming Possible Jobs Worksheet

Assesment Results ➡																Total Check-marks Across
Possible Jobs																

Case Study: Chiron
Finding a Future

Growing up means eliminating what doesn't work for you.

JAN HALPER, PH.D., *QUIET DESPERATION—*
THE TRUTH ABOUT SUCCESSFUL MEN

Chiron is worn out. He is 40 years old, and has had lots of different jobs in his life. Getting jobs has never been a problem. He has just gotten another one, and is afraid that it, too, will go nowhere. His wife is in her early 30s, and they would like to have children, but feel they cannot afford them on Chiron's income, which is approximately $60,000 a year.

In addition to his day job, where he works 30 hours a week, Chiron still has the small business he started on the side—keeping the books for a small company—just in case. He earns very little at this business, which is why he answered the ad for the job he just landed: director of development for a small not-for-profit in the medical field.

My Role as a Coach

Chiron came to see me because his career path had caused him so much stress. He couldn't take the instability. My job was to help him uncover the central things that may be holding him back in his career—the things that may cause him not to live up to his abilities.

To save him money and time in the career-coaching session, I asked Chiron to complete the exercises in this book before we met. I told him that if he could not complete all of them, he should at least complete the Seven Stories.

Chiron was very serious when he came for his session. He hoped he could turn his life around. I will give you some highlights from our sessions.

Every client is different, and every coach is different. But most coaches have similar goals. The purpose of the exercises is to get a sense of the person's career-related issues in an organized, methodical way. The exercises simply help a person talk about those issues. In addition, I try to teach the client the process we are going through so that he or she can think more deeply about the issues and do more self-analysis when I am not around.

Our Initial Session

We reviewed Chiron's Seven Stories Exercise. I will show you how the discussion went. First, I asked him to rank his Seven Stories so that we could work first on the one he ranked number one.

The First Story

Kate: "Chiron, tell me your first accomplishment." Chiron: "I planned and organized a free concert."

Kate: "When did this happen, or how old were you?"

Chiron: "It happened in 2001. I was 25 or 26."

Kate: "Tell me about it."

Chiron: "I came up with the idea and organized the event. This was when people were first upset about the war in Afghanistan, and there had been a lot of protests. I wanted to turn that discontent into something good."

Kate: "So exactly what did you do? What was involved?"

Chiron: "I coordinated with various government offices to get permission for the concert. The government folks liked the idea because it was peaceful. It wasn't a political protest. Everything was donated, and everyone performed for free."

Kate: "How successful was it? For example, how many people attended?"

Chiron: "Twenty to thirty thousand people attended."

Kate: "Good grief! That's a lot of people! What prompted you to do this event? What led up to it?"

Chiron: "I wanted to make a difference. I wanted to do the community a favor."

Kate: "This was your number-one accomplishment. What about it made it number one for you?"

Chiron: "I picked this experience as number one because I was doing good and also having fun."

Kate: "What kind of time frame was involved? How long did the whole project take?"

Chiron: "Two months from start to finish."

Kate: "Even if you've already told me, what about it was most enjoyable for you? What was the most fun?"

Chiron: "Coordinating the folk groups and the other performers and all of the government offices. I also loved working with the press."

Kate: "What about it gave you a sense of accomplishment?"

Chiron: "Creating something out of nothing and having it be a success."

Yet when most companies are confronted with problems, they try simply to fix them. They fail to use a problem or crisis as an opportunity to explore a new way to do business.

JOHN SCULLEY

The Second Story

Kate: "That was great. Let's look at your next accomplishment. What was it?"

Chiron: "I taught myself journalism and got hired as a reporter."

Kate: "When did this happen and how old were you?"

Chiron: "Around 2004. I was 29."

Kate: "So tell me about it."

Chiron: "I went after a job creatively. I targeted one newspaper where I knew there was a job opening. The other people going after the job were all journalism majors. But I figured out how to write a story by studying books on my own. Then I covered some news events as if I were actually writing for the newspaper. I sent the editor the stories and said, 'This is how I would have covered the story if I had been writing for you.' I did this with a few stories, and actually had a lot of fun doing it. After each one, I would call him. I got the job and beat out all those people who had better qualifications."

Kate: "That's a great accomplishment. What led up to your doing it?"

Chiron: "I had spent two sessions working with the Connecticut legislature, and that's what got me interested in being a journalist."

Kate: "You mentioned as your success the fact that you got hired; what about the job itself? You didn't mention that as a success."

Chiron: "I loved the job."

Kate: "What about it did you love?"

Chiron: "I covered a diverse range of subjects: kids and skateboards; arson. Each time, I had to teach myself the subject area."

Kate: "What did you enjoy the most?"

Chiron: "Teaching myself and getting hired and covering a wide range of subjects. I enjoyed doing the research required."

Kate: "Is there anything else you'd like to tell me about this experience?"

Chiron: "Yes. I loved meeting new people."

Kate: "How long did you have this job?"

Chiron: "Only two months. My wife got transferred to a new job in another city. We weighed it and decided to move."

Analysis of the First Two Stories

After I have heard two stories, I give the client some feedback so he or she will see the process I use. Later, the client should be able to do a better job analyzing the stories than I could. After all, he or she was there; I wasn't.

In this case, I gave Chiron my initial impressions, based solely on what he had told me:

"Chiron, it may be that your other stories show things very differently from these first two, but I'll tell you what I've noticed so far, for what it's worth.

"Both of these happened a long time ago—10 to 15 years ago. Part of our quest in going through the assessment process is to come up with goals for you so that your next experience has a better chance of winding up as one of your top seven stories.

"A second thing I noticed is that they were both of short duration. In addition, a lot of the jobs on your résumé were also of relatively short duration.

"This is not necessarily bad. A person can choose to work on short-term things forever, such as people who get involved in fads—like the 'pet rocks' people. They don't expect these fads to last. They expect them to be short-lived. Then they move on to the next thing. Planning fads is their focus, and they become expert at it.

"Other examples are people who run events, or head up special projects. Some people can be very successful working on short-term projects—but they tend to have a specific area of expertise and they tend to intend to have project-oriented work.

"On the other hand, a person can decide to hunker down and remain in something more long-term so that he or she can become somewhat expert at it. That's another way to go.

"So, a person can choose to have a short-term

project orientation, or a longer-term orientation. One is not better than the other. The important point is planning. An opportunistic approach of doing whatever happens to present itself rarely works. It's gets very tiring to constantly learn new things and not to build on your previous experiences.

"Other threads that appear in both stories are:

"You came up with an idea and did it. You had to be convincing. There was a lot of creativity and coordination. You showed initiative in both stories.

"I'm struggling to find a subject matter that appears in both. This may have no significance at all, but politics appears in both. In one story, you had to deal with the government, and in the other, you watched the state legislature for two sessions.

"Another possible thread having to do with subject matter is 'the press.' In the first story, you dealt with the press. In the second story, you were the press."

As I showed Chiron my thought patterns, he could decide whether or not what I was saying had any significance. He could think more about his own experiences. Then he could decide what was important about them and come up with conclusions of his own.

The Third Story

Kate: "Tell me your third accomplishment."
   Chiron: "Last year, I started my own book-keeping business for a grocery store."
Kate: "Tell me about this one."
Chiron: "I needed something to do. I had lost my job. Friends and I brainstormed ideas. I liked the idea of performing a service that people would appreciate. I also like food, and I have an M.B.A., so doing bookkeeping for a food business seemed logical."
Kate: "What for you was the real accomplishment?"
Chiron: "I started the business from nothing. I built it myself. And now it's successful.

When I collect the money every week, it tells me that I made this thing work."

Kate: "Even if you've already told me, what about this did you enjoy the most?" Chiron: "It was 'my thing,' and I made money from it."

When all is said and done, you have just one irreplaceable resource: this particular, unique, unrepeatable lifetime of yours.
What were you meant to do with it?

WILLIAM BRIDGES, JOBSHIFT: *HOW TO PROSPER IN A WORKPLACE WITHOUT JOBS*

Other Accomplishments

Chiron then went on to tell four additional stories. For example, the fourth was when he ran a successful political campaign for someone who was running for city council. At this time, Chiron was only about 26 years old.

After we reviewed all seven stories, I told Chiron that I noticed that three had government or politics or power in them. They all showed his ability to convince and required creativity, organization, and initiative.

In the bookkeeping business, he did not mention any interaction with the people—the people he did the bookkeeping for or even the bookkeepers he had hired to help him. In all of the other stories, he had mentioned enjoying the people: meeting new people through journalism, working with the legislature and the folk groups, or recruiting and organizing volunteers in the political campaign. This people orientation was an important element missing in the bookkeeping business. My impression was that he did not like the business. What he liked was the idea that he had started it and made it work well enough.

Other strong threads appeared to be:

- running a campaign,
- being a natural leader,
- being a major influencer,

- developing strategies, and
- doing his own thing.

What did Chiron have to say about this? He was solemn and intense: "Yes. I see myself as the General. In the army, there's a platoon leader who deals with day-to-day tactics. I'm the General who sees the overall picture. I'm making only $60,000 a year, but I really feel that I should be making double this."

I replied, "Based on what you've told me, I too see you as the General. You seem to be the type of person who has to lead, to develop strategies, to influence people. It may be that the subject matter doesn't matter much—as long as you feel you're contributing to the public good—providing a service."

That's it for his Seven Stories Exercise. The other assessment results were also important, although I won't go into them here. I did find it significant that he has an M.B.A.

As I review the results, I look to make sure all of the results are in agreement. For example, if a person says he or she does not value money, but imagines living in a palatial house, I would want to know how he or she planned to afford such a place. Most often, people's results are in sync. That is, there is usually some correlation among the various exercises.

Unresolved conflicts can hold a person back. In Chiron's case, there were a number of conflicts. The most important showed up in his Values exercise. Chiron places a very high value on his lifestyle. In fact, he and his wife go away just about every weekend to the cabin they have in the woods. They are able to do this because it doesn't cost much, and Chiron essentially works only 36 hours a week in both of his jobs combined. He leaves work early every Friday so they can go to the country. In addition, he takes French horn lessons and goes to the gym once a week. Traveling is another interest of his. At present, his lifestyle is important, and he is not willing to give it up. Yet he also wants to make $120,000 a year.

That's a lot of money. People who make that much—even far less than that—work very hard and tend to work long hours. Chiron would have to resolve this conflict of wanting to maintain his lifestyle, work a 36-hour week, and yet make a large amount of money. This rarely happens unless a person develops some highly valued expertise.

It Is Not Easy to Find Out What Is Holding a Person Back

Chiron's conflict may seem obvious to you: How could he not see the problem? *You* can see Chiron's problem because I'm spelling it out for you. However, I may be wrong. It may be that the real problem is not apparent to me. Chiron is the only one who can know for sure why he is not reaching the level to which he aspires.

Perhaps you too have something that is holding you back. It may not be obvious to you or to anyone else. Our conflicts and beliefs are subtle and often rigid. Most people do not recognize their own conflicts. Even when a conflict is pointed out to them, it is difficult to take the steps necessary to correct it. People usually continue to do what they have been doing. Changing one's beliefs takes a great deal of insight and courage.

It would take some time for Chiron to resolve this conflict in his values. So we moved on to the next part of the process. We worked on Chiron's Forty-Year Vision. He came up with a number of possibilities. It's best if you too come up with a number of scenarios for yourself. Then you can match them against your requirements. To be thorough, Chiron also filled out the Brainstorming Possible Jobs worksheet. Across the top of the worksheet, I noted his assessment results: his Seven Stories, his interests, values, education, and so on. That worksheet is shown on the next page.

Down the left-hand side of the worksheet, Chiron brainstormed possible jobs, and also asked his friends to think of job possibilities for him. Those suggestions helped him think of still others. Then he put checkmarks wherever a job possibility fit in with a characteristic. This helped him get rid of possibilities that would not fit most of his requirements.

The Three Scenarios

After all of this, Chiron came up with three possibilities that he thought he would find satisfying. He also thought that all three of these could happen within the next five years—when he would be 45 years old. The three possibilities were:

- be president of my own company
- be political director of a large national organization
- be COO of the medical not-for-profit for which he now worked.

We examined each of these so he could realistically see what would be involved—at least at the start. Then he could research each further, and think more about the direction he really wanted his life to take.

Brainstorming Possible Jobs Worksheet

Possible Jobs	Driving force: idealism	Service orientation	Artistic	Enterprising	Writer/journalist	Sales/influencing	Leader/the "General"	Strategist	Meet with leaders	"Business owner"	Advisor	Politics/government	Food/health	Nonbureaucratic	M.B.A.	Earn $100,000/yr.	Make large impact	Complex problems				Total Check-marks Across
Lobbyist	✓				✓	✓		✓	✓		✓	✓										7
Bookkeeping business		✓		✓						✓	✓											4
Political campaign mgr.	✓	✓		✓	✓	✓		✓	✓		✓	✓										9
Executive, present co.	✓	✓	✓	✓	✓	✓	✓	✓	✓	✓	✓	✓			✓	?	✓	✓				15
Development director	✓	✓		✓	✓	✓		✓	✓		✓						✓					9
Journalist	✓				✓	✓		✓	✓			✓										6
Political activist	✓	✓			✓	✓	✓	✓	✓		✓	✓										9
Union organizer	✓	✓			✓	✓	✓	✓	✓		✓	✓										9
Arts organization	✓	✓	✓		✓	✓	✓	✓	✓		✓	✓										10
Fund-raiser; music	✓	✓			✓	✓		✓	✓		✓	✓										8
Pres. of my own co.	✓	✓		✓	✓	✓	✓	✓	✓	✓			✓	✓	✓	?	✓					13
State senator	✓	✓				✓	✓	✓	✓		✓	✓										8
Pol. Director, large org.	✓	✓		✓	✓	✓	✓	✓	✓		✓	✓				?	✓					11
. . . and so on																						

> *Not everything that is faced can be changed; But*
> *nothing can be changed until it is faced.*
>
> JAMES BALDWIN

Analyzing the Possibilities

Let's take a look at each possibility. Chiron and I had a preliminary discussion so he could get a feel for how long it would take for him to move to the level he described in each of the three scenarios. In real life, a person has to do a Preliminary Target Investigation by talking to people in those fields and assessing the likelihood of being able to make such a transition.

Scenario 1: "Be president of my own company"

I asked Chiron what kind of company he could see himself heading up. He thought a new media publishing company sounded good. What size staff would he have? He thought 10 to 20 people. What kind of publishing company? He thought a magazine, such as in the health, cooking, or travel area. He imagined it as being a few monthly publications, subscription only.

It takes most people about two years from the time they decide to start their own small business until the time they actually start it. They have a lot of research and planning to do: Who else is in that market? How are they doing? What are they doing? How much will it cost? Where will I get the money? Even if a person works 15 hours a week on the new business while working full-time doing something else, it still takes two years.

Therefore, by the time Chiron is 42, he will be able to start the business—probably on the side while continuing to work at his day job. He could run it for a few years part-time until it is far enough along that he could tackle it full-time. Then he would be 44 or so. It is unlikely that he would have a staff of 10 to 20 at that time. It is more likely that it would be five or so employees— if he is lucky.

Even if Chiron opted to raise the money instead of trying to finance the enterprise himself, that still takes lots of time.

The question is whether Chiron has the discipline to investigate this idea objectively, plan it, and carry it out. If not, he should not go impulsively into this business just because it sounds like a fine idea to him. He will only repeat past mistakes where he tackled something without being properly prepared.

Scenario 2: "Be political director of a large national organization"

Chiron imagined himself in an organization that has a corporate staff of 12 or so. He would be the chief lobbyist with a staff of four to six. I asked him to pick an organization—any organization— just to make this example more real. He selected the National Association of Manufacturers, which is headquartered in Washington, D.C. Let's brainstorm this scenario.

Of course, Chiron would have to be willing to live in Washington at some point. After removing that barrier in his own mind, one scenario for moving ahead with this vision would be to get a job as a junior lobbyist *in an area that would be of interest to the organization he eventually targeted.* It would not be good enough to get lobbying experience, for example, in the utilities or tobacco field. He would need relevant experience because his future employers would want to capitalize on the contacts he had made. Then he could become a more powerful lobbyist, and he would be desirable to organizations such as the one he mentioned.

Chiron would have no trouble getting his first lobbying job. After all, it would not be that high level, and Chiron is very convincing in interviews. But since it would require a geographic move, that step could take a year. Then he would have to do extremely well in that field so he would have a few things to brag about. That would take two or three years, for sure. Then he would have to get into the right organization, and move up within it. That would be a few more years. I guessed that Chiron would be in his ideal job, making the kind of money he wanted in nine years, at age 50.

I think it's doable, and he has plenty of time, since most of us are living longer. The question, again, is one of commitment.

The third scenario will take the same length of time to achieve and require the same commitment. Life takes time. Making good money takes most people a lot of time and commitment. Chiron needed to decide what his priorities were. That also would take time.

Chiron had always prided himself on his ability to learn things quickly. However, at a certain age, those areas that were our greatest strengths can become our greatest weaknesses if we don't watch out. Chiron tends to not learn any area in depth, keeping him stuck at $60,000 or so a year.

There is no end to this story yet. We will all have to wait and see what Chiron decides to do with his life.

In a fight between you and the world,
bet on the world.

Franz Kafka

Chiron's Options

Lucky Chiron has many options. Many people would envy the life he and his wife have created for themselves. Chiron and his wife do not work long hours, earn decent money, go to the country every weekend, and have time to pursue other interests. Sometimes people are unhappy with their lives until they complete the assessment and discover they don't have it so bad after all. In Chiron's case, he and his wife can keep their lives—and their income—essentially as is. To gain the career stability Chiron wants, all he needs to do is stick with something long enough to become expert. Then he will have the kind of life many Americans want.

On the other hand, he could join the rat race with the rest of us. He may choose to do that because, for example, he thinks he needs the money to have and raise children (although people do raise children on what Chiron makes, and most wives work today).

If he wants to make a good deal more than he does now, he will have to work a good deal harder. Those who have spent years becoming expert in a marketable area can work less hard. But Chiron still has to develop marketable skills to command more money. Within that, he has many choices.

He has energy and brains and talent. He needs direction and hard work. That's not so bad.

For each of the three scenarios he targeted, he could develop a plan similar to the one Deborah did in Developing a Detailed Plan, a few chapters back. That would help him to chart a course that he could then stick to if he is committed enough. The sooner he makes a commitment to a clear direction, the more likely he is to achieve that direction. If he keeps on hedging, his energies will continue to be dispersed. In his present job, he could develop a skill that he feels sure would also help him later.

If the direction he selects later proves to be wrong, Chiron will still be better off for having chosen something and for developing a marketable skill. Then he can build on his new marketable experience.

As far as the bookkeeping business is concerned, I think Chiron should keep at it until he has made a commitment to a new path. Otherwise, he may continue his pattern of jumping from one thing to another without properly researching it. Although the bookkeeping business is not the right career path for him, the more important lesson he needs to learn is commitment. Then the future will look bright for Chiron.

You too have many options. And you too have plenty of time in which to achieve them. But you too must investigate them, and make a commitment. And give yourself a break. Remember that life takes time.

You do not sing because you are happy;
you are happy because you sing.

WILLIAM JAMES

I arise in the morning torn between the desire to
improve the world and a desire to enjoy the world.
This makes it hard to plan the day.

E. B. WHITE

Some luck lies in not getting what you thought you
wanted but in getting what you have, which once you
have got it you may be smart enough to see is what
you would have wanted had you known.

GARRISON KEILLOR

The
Five
O'Clock
Club

Having a Balanced Life

Let our advance worrying become advance thinking and planning.

WINSTON CHURCHILL

It is very easy to have a life that is out of balance. Some people intentionally have an *out-of-balance life* so they may achieve in a specific area. Or a person's life may become out of balance in one area for a certain length of time so that he or she may *catch up* in that area. However you decide to live your life, it is still good to know what you are missing.

> ***Pay attention to all areas.***
> ***For a balanced life, grow in all areas:***
>
> - **Spiritual**
> - **Financial**
> - **Career**
> - **Health and fitness**
> - **Recreation**
> - **Family**
> - **Social**

People need to pay attention to their careers to meet their basic obligations. But be sure you have a *career* and not just *work*. Career has a concept of personal development. Work has a concept of "I need money to do something else with."

The more time we spend planning a project, the less total time is required for it. Don't let today's busywork crowd planning time out of your schedule.

EDWIN C. BLISS, *GETTING THINGS DONE*

To grow in every area:

1. Have goals in every category.
2. Set priorities.
3. Develop a plan.
4. Live.
5. Review. (Go back to step 1.)

Man dreams dreams, but God directs his steps.

PROVERBS 16:9

It's a good idea to review annually what you did last year and what you plan for next year. Keep your plans in a folder and review them over the years. Look for growth in each area. Or do it twice a year. You can pick a theme for the year—something that needs extra focus. Some people do a 5-year or 10-year plan.

Set goals for yourself. The goals you set must be measurable: you must be able to tell when you've accomplished a particular goal.

Set goals that make you stretch. All successful people have failed. It's how you deal with it that's key. If you've never failed, you've never reached.

Life planning is a lot like business planning. A common approach is this one:

1. Get a dream/vision. Formulate a purpose.
2. Write it down.
3. Create long-term, measurable goals.
4. Create a series of strategies and action steps to get there.

5. Evaluate these goals and strategies: Make sure they represent a stretch, yet are reasonable.
6. Share these goals with someone.
7. Get some good counsel and advice. (Be prayerful about it.)
8. Act on it.

The Secrets of SUCCESS

Someone found this on a plane and passed it on to me:

S— Sense of purpose—written goals.

E— Excellence—commitment to be the best at whatever you do.

C—Contribution.

R—Responsibility for your actions—you don't work for a company; you work for yourself.

E— Effort.

T— Time management.

S— Stay with it.

Write down your goals for each area, and your steps for reaching your goals in each area. Some people review their lives once or twice a year. Some families develop a plan together every year. Pay attention to all areas. Feel free to add extra areas that have specific importance to you. For a balanced life, *grow* in all areas:

Area to Plan/Grow	Goals for Each Area	Steps for Getting There
• Spiritual _____		
• Financial _____		
• Career_____		
• Health and fitness _____		
• Recreation _____		
• Family _____		
• Social _____		
• Other _____		

BIFF: And suddenly I stopped, you hear me? And in the middle of that office building, do you hear this? I stopped in the middle of that building and I saw—the sky. I saw the things that I love in this world. The work and the food and time to sit and smoke. And I looked at the pen and said to myself, what the hell am I grabbing this for? Why am I trying to become what I don't want to be? What am I doing in an office, making a contemptuous, begging fool of myself, when all I want is out there, waiting for me the minute I say I know who I am!

ARTHUR MILLER, *DEATH OF A SALESMAN* (PENGUIN BOOKS)

The most difficult thing—but an essential one— is to love Life, to love it even while one suffers, because Life is all. Life is God, and to love Life means to love God.

LEO TOLSTOY, *WAR AND PEACE*

It is often said that accomplishment makes [dying] easier, that those who have achieved what they set out to do in life die more contentedly than those who have not.

JUDITH VIORST, *NECESSARY LOSSES*

What You Can Do in Your Present Situation

What has changed most fundamentally is the greater responsibility being given to workers to take charge of ensuring higher quality and to take a proactive role in organizing their own work—responsibilities that in the past management jealously kept for itself.

HEDRICK SMITH, *RETHINKING AMERICA*, (AVON BOOKS)

Now you have a vision of your future, and a plan of what you should do to achieve that vision. You will need new skills and new relationships. To advance, you may feel as though you must get out of the job you are in right now. However, you may be able to add skills, experience, and a knowledge base without leaving your current position. Look at the following list of ideas. You may want to add some of these to your Career Plan.

- Talk to colleagues about needs in your present company. Make plans to fill those needs.
- Make a Google alert about your present company so you know what's going on.
- Expand the network of people with whom you interact internally and externally.
- Develop a professional-looking LinkedIn page.
- Join LinkedIn groups having to do with your industry and profession.
- Join an association that fits in with your long-term goals; get on a committee.
- Find out what people in your function do outside of your present company (or the function you are interested in long term).
- Learn a new technical skill.
- Manage a project.
- Volunteer for a task force.
- Train staff on new software.
- Select/determine software or equipment.
- Write a proposal to fill a need.
- Make a presentation.
- Take some classroom training.
- Substitute for your manager in a meeting.
- Run a meeting.
- Assist with the budgeting process.
- Organize a community activity or do volunteer work to gain a new marketable skill.
- Train a new person.
- Research and write a report.
- Write and implement a "what if" suggestion.
- Observe the demeanor of someone in a high-level position (even if only via video).
- Continue to develop your plan.
- Think of what may stop you from reaching your goals, and overcome those barriers.

The first seven or eight items are generally considered to be the most important. These are action steps that will usually help you to do better in your career—no matter what your career goals are. Consider adding them to your list if they are not already on it.

Language reflects social reality, and the reality of the pre-nineteenth-century world was that people did not "have" jobs in the fixed and unitary sense; they "did" jobs in the form of a constantly changing string of tasks.

WILLIAM BRIDGES, *JOBSHIFT: HOW TO PROSPER IN A WORKPLACE WITHOUT JOBS*

The Five O'Clock Club®

Life Takes Time

Great ideas come into the world as gently as doves.
Perhaps then, if we listen attentively, we shall hear,
amid the uproar of empires and nations, a faint flutter
of wings, the gentle stirrings of life and hope.

ALBERT CAMUS

To sum up, here is the process:

Step 1: Understand yourself: your values, interests, skills, and so on. The better you understand yourself, and the more honest you are about it, the better you will be able to assess the opportunities that will come your way.

Step 2: Figure out what you want. What on this earth would you be best served doing? What should your future be like?

Step 3: Figure out how to get there. Later on, we will show you how to develop a Career Plan for yourself.

Step 4: Figure out what within yourself might stand in your way. Chiron had a conflict in values, and also a tendency to lack commitment to a specific path. If he can resolve these issues, nothing can stand in his way.

Internal Issues

Here are some common examples of internal issues that hold people back:

- Conflict in values. "I want to earn $300,000 a year as an exporter in Montana (where there are few export jobs), work a two-day week, and spend three years with someone like Mother Teresa."

- Lack of self-esteem. People rise to their level of self-esteem. If you have low self-esteem, stop thinking about yourself, and instead think of what you were put on this planet to do. Do what you were meant to do. God did not mean for you to bury your talents, but to use them and make them multiply.

- Inability to imagine a more fulfilling future; depression. Get some help with your Forty-Year Vision. Start writing. Think about meeting with a Five O'Clock Club career coach.

- Lack of focus. Some people see too many possibilities and cannot decide what to do. They flit from one thing to another and do not become an expert at anything.

- Lack of possibilities. Other people imagine doing the same thing for 30 years. They need to explore more and see what's out there.

- Too many skills; master of none.

- Too few skills or need to bring them up to date.

- Too tense; don't have enough fun.

- Too much fun; don't buckle under and work.

Add your own thoughts to this list. There are plenty of things that hold people back.

External Issues

In addition, most job hunters have something that they think will keep them from getting their next job. It could be that they feel they are too young or too old, have too little education or too much, are of the wrong race, creed, nationality, gender, sexual orientation, weight, or height, or are very aware that they have a physical disability.

While it is true that there is prejudice out there, job hunters who are too self-conscious about their perceived handicaps will hold themselves back. In addition, they may inadvertently draw attention to their *problem* during the interview. Your attitude must be: "What problem? There is no problem. Let me tell you about the things I've done."

Now let's move on to look at some of the things *you've* done.

A competitive world has two possibilities for you. You can lose. Or, if you want to win, you can change.

LESTER C. THUROW, DEAN, SLOAN
SCHOOL OF MANAGEMENT, M.I.T.

Monitor how you're thinking and behaving, and try to stop negative thoughts and behaviors in their tracks. Ask yourself: Why am I thinking or behaving this way? What's the positive alternative? What might make it easier for me—now and in the future—to think or act positively in this type of situation?

JACK MAGUIRE, *CARE AND FEEDING OF THE BRAIN*
(RANDOM HOUSE, INC.)

How to Decide What You Want to Offer

The fastest way to succeed is to look as if you're playing by other people's rules, while quietly playing by your own.

MICHAEL KORDA

Your enjoyable skills and your dreams help you set your long-term direction. In order to go somewhere, you must know where you are right now. In this chapter, you will look down and see where your feet are. You will become more pragmatic. What have you done so far in your life? What do you have to offer the world?

What Do You Have to Offer?

In deciding what you want to offer, first list all you have to offer—a menu to choose from. When you go after a certain kind of position, emphasize those parts that support your case. If you decide, for example, to continue your career in the same direction, you will probably focus on your most recent position and others that support that direction.

If most of your satisfaction as an adult has occurred outside your job, you may want to change something about your work life. If you decide to change careers, activities outside your regular job may help you make that change.

Thirty years ago, when I was interested in changing from computers to advertising, I offered as proof of my ability the three years I had spent at night promoting nonprofit organizations, and my portfolio of press coverage for those organizations. Later, when I wanted to work as a career coach, my proof was my many years' experience in running The Five O'Clock Club at night, the seminars I had given on job hunting and career development, and so on. When I wanted to continue working in business management, I simply offered my on-the-job experience in making companies profitable.

If you have available the entire list of what you have to offer, you can be more flexible about the direction in which you want to go.

Before I was a genius I was a drudge.

IGNACE PADEREWSKI

How to State Your Accomplishments

Present what you have to offer in terms of accomplishments. Tell your story in a way that will provoke interest in you and let the *reader* know what you are really like. Accomplishment statements are short, measurable, and results oriented. We each handle the situations in our work lives in different ways. What problems have you faced at work? How did you handle them? What was the effect on the organization?

Some of us are project-oriented and others are process-oriented. If you are project oriented, you will tend to take whatever is assigned to you, break it into *projects* in your mind, and then get those projects done. You like to solve problems, and you get bored when there are none. Your accomplishments will state the problems you faced, how you solved them, and the impact you had on the organization.

On the other hand, if you are process oriented, you like to run the day-to-day shop. You can be trusted to keep an existing situation running smoothly, and your accomplishments will reflect that. You like stable situations and systems that work. You will state that you ran a department of so many people for so many years.

Work on this exercise now. Start with any of your Seven Stories that are work related. Note the way you wrote about each accomplishment when you were telling your story. Chances are, it was a more exciting way to describe that accomplishment than the way you would normally write about it on a résumé or talk about it in an interview. Use those stories as your starting point, and be sure to include details so the reader will be able to see what you actually did. After all, they were important enough for you to include them in your Seven Stories. Don't ignore them now.

Next, write down your current or most recent position. State your title and your organization name, and list your accomplishments in that position. Do not worry right now if you do not like your job title, or don't even like your job. In our résumé book we will change your title to make it reflect what you were actually doing, and we can emphasize or de-emphasize jobs and responsibilities as you see fit. Right now, get down on paper all of your accomplishments. Then we will have something to work with.

A project-oriented accomplishment could look like this:

- Designed and directed a comprehensive and cost-effective advertising and sales promotion program that established the company as a major competitor in the market.

A process-oriented accomplishment could look like this:

- Reviewed ongoing market performance of investor-owned utility securities. Used multiple equity valuation techniques. Recommended redirection of portfolio mix to more profitable and higher-quality securities.

After you have completed your accomplishment statements for your present or most recent position, examine the job before that one. State your title and your organization name, and list your accomplishments.

Work on as many accomplishments as make sense to you. Some people cover the past 10 years in depth. If you can, cover your entire career, because you never know what may occur to you, and you never know what may help you later. In doing this exercise, you may remember jobs you had completely forgotten about—and pleasant and satisfying accomplishments. Ask yourself what it was about that job that was so satisfying. Perhaps it is another clue about what you might do in the future.

Do not wish to go back to your youth. What was challenging then will probably not satisfy you today. Look for the *elements* of those early jobs that satisfied you. These elements should be compared with your list of enjoyable skills to determine lifelong interests.

You will feel better after you have completed this exercise. You will see on paper all that you have to offer. And your accomplishments will be stated in a way that will make you proud.

Discipline yourself to do this exercise now, and you will not have to do it again.

After you have listed your work experiences, list accomplishments outside work. These, too, should be short, measurable, and results oriented. These outside experiences can help you move into a new field. In fact, that's how I—and many others—have made career transitions. By volunteering to do advertising and public relations work at night, I developed a list of accomplishments that helped me move from computers to advertising. In those days, my outside experience went like this:

Walnut Street Theatre Gallery
- Planned, organized, and promoted month-long holography exhibition. Attendance increased from fewer than 100 visitors per month to more than 3,000 visitors during the month of this exhibition.

YMCA
- Handled all publicity for fund-raising campaign. Consulted with fund-raising committee on best techniques for them to use. Received plaque in recognition.

United Way
- Received four United Way awards for editorial work in 1979; two awards the prior year. Spoke at the United Way's Editors' Conference.

Network for Women in Computer Technology
- Chair of the Program Committee.

Later, career coaching became my volunteer work, and that eventually helped me move into the field I am now in. In the early days, my outside experience was stated like this:
- Organized and ran The Five O'Clock Club. Conducted weekly groups, as well as individual coaching. Trained people in career decisions, marketing techniques, and practice interviewing. Brought in outside lecturers.

I also listed the organizations for which I had done job-hunting seminars, and stated my relevant work experience—such as when I was a training manager.

List all of your accomplishment statements. Depending on the positions you are going after, these accomplishments may be included or not. They may, for example, be unimportant for 10 years, and later on become important again, depending on your job target.

Your volunteer work may be important, just as mine was. Summer jobs can count, too.

To get better at stating your accomplishments—no matter what your level or experience—read The Five O'Clock Club's book on résumés.

This is *your* chance to brag—everyone else does. You will rework the wording of your accomplishment statements, and make them sound great, as long as they are truthful. When you have done this, you will feel terrific because you will be represented well on paper.

For now, think about what you've really done. For most people, the problem is not that they stretch the truth on their résumés; the problem is that they don't say what they've *really* done.

Figuring out what you've really done is much more difficult than simply reciting your job description. That's the importance of doing the Seven Stories exercise. It helps you step back from a résumé frame of mind so you can concentrate on the most important accomplishments of your life (in terms of what you really enjoyed doing and know you also did well). Then the exercise helps you think about each accomplishment in terms of what you *really* did: What led up to the accomplishment, what your role was, what gave you satisfaction, what your motivation was, and so on.

Where I was born and where and how I have lived is unimportant. It is what I have done with where I have been that should be of interest.

Georgia O'Keeffe

If You Think You Haven't Done a Thing with Your Life

Many people are intimidated when they see other people's accomplishments. They think they have none of their own. Chances are, you aren't thinking hard enough about what you have done. If you think you haven't done much, think again. If you are reading this book, we already know that you are competent, ambitious, and intelligent. Even people in the lowest-level jobs have accomplishments they are proud of. At all levels in an organization, people can be presented with problems and figure out how to handle them.

Don't compare yourself with others, and don't worry about what your boss or peers thought of what you have done: Maybe they did not appreciate your talents. Brag about what you have done anyway—even though your boss may have taken credit for the work, and even though you may have accomplished it with the help of others. Think of problems you have faced in your organization. What did you do to handle them? What was the result for your organization? Think of an accomplishment. Write it down. Then pare it down until you can show the reader what you handled and the impact it made.

Finally, don't say anything negative about yourself. Don't lie, but don't hurt yourself either.

In this chapter, you were to write down everything you've done so that it will serve as a menu you can draw on, depending on the kinds of jobs you are going after. In our résumé book, you will see how people struggle to develop well-written accomplishment statements. In the next chapter, we will become more focused: Your goal during your search process is to start out thinking broadly, and then focus.

The next thing most like living one's life over again seems to be a recollection of that life, and to make that recollection as durable as possible by putting it down in writing.

BENJAMIN FRANKLIN

How to Target the Job You Want

I always wanted to be somebody, but I should have been more specific.

LILY TOMLIN

You are on your way to finding your place in the world. Using the Seven Stories and other exercises, you made a list of your enjoyable skills and what you want in a job, and then you brainstormed a number of possible job targets that might fit in with your enjoyable accomplishments and/or your vision of your future. Some of these targets may be very long term. Then you thought about what you would be willing to offer. (You took it an extra step by stating these as accomplishments.)

Now we will work on firming up your job targets. You will do some preliminary research on each target through the Internet and by talking to people to see if these areas still interest you and are practical. Then you will *focus* by selecting two, three, or four areas on which to concentrate, based on what appeals to you and what you think you have that is marketable. Then you will conduct a thorough campaign aimed at each area. Because each campaign takes a lot of work, it is best if we spend some time refining your targets.

Selecting Job Targets—Your Key to Job-Hunting Success

Selecting a job target means choosing: a specific geographic area, a specific industry or organization size, and a specific position within that industry. A job target must have all three.

Select your targets. Using our book *Shortcut*

Your Job Search, conduct a campaign aimed at each. Concentrate your energies, and you increase your chances for success.

Approach each target with an open mind. Commit to a target, but only as long as it makes sense. You can change your mind after you find out more about it. It makes no sense to strive to be a ballerina after you find you have absolutely no ability as a dancer. Commitment to a target lets you discover your real possibilities and increases your chances of landing a job of your choice. The unsuccessful ballet student may have something else of great value to offer the world of dance—such as the ability to raise funds or run a ballet company.

The Results of Commitment

Commitment increases the chance that you will come across clearly and enthusiastically about the industry and the position you seek; it will help you do a thorough job of networking in the chosen area, of investigating and being knowledgeable about the area, of conducting a thorough search, and of being successful in that search.

If the result of your initial commitment is that you realize a job target is not what you thought it would be, you have resolved the issue and can move on.

Jim, a marketing manager, had targeted four industries: environmental, noise abatement, shipping, and corporate America, a backup target in case the other three did not work. He conducted an excellent search aimed at the environmental target, an area he had always wanted to explore.

It was only after a brief but committed job search that he found the environmental area was not for him: The people in it were different from what he had expected. He would not be able to do the things he had imagined he would do there. That target no longer interested him. The noise abatement and shipping industries, however, were very exciting to him, and he found a good match for himself. Later, his exploration of the environmental area paid off. He was employed by a shipping company in the containment of oil spills.

Commitment to a target means you'll give that target your best shot—and results in a better job hunt than if you had no target at all.

Target a Geographic Area

Targeting a geographic area is usually the easiest part of the targeting process. Some people decide that they want to work near their present homes, while others decide that they would be willing to move where the jobs are. Are you willing to move anywhere? Are a small town and a big city the same to you? Would you move to the coast? To Arizona? Would you rather be near your family? If you want to stay where you are now, target that area as your first selection—and you'll have a better chance of getting offers there. If you really care about where you live, *target it.*

Think about where you stand on this. You will be assigning yourself an impossible task if, for example, you want to be an export manager but want to work only in a geographic area where there are no export-management positions. If you must live in a particular area, be realistic about the kinds of jobs open to you there.

Resolve this issue. Then you will know if you'd be willing to change your target industry so you can live where you want, or change your geographic area so you can work in the industry or function that interests you.

It is therefore vital that each of us examine the values by which he lives, to decide what is truly important and what will ultimately give him feelings of fulfillment and well-being.

MICHAEL LYNBERG, *THE PATH WITH HEART*

Target an Industry and a Function in That Industry

Many people say they don't care what industry they work in. When pressed, they usually have stronger opinions than they thought.

If you think any industry would be okay for you, let's find out. Would you work in the not-for-profit sector? If so, where? In education? A hospital? How about government? A community organization? Does it matter to you?

Would you work for a magazine? A chemical company? The garment industry? How about a company that makes cardboard boxes? Or cheese? Does it matter to you?

"One day I just woke up and said to myself-- hey, thanks to the computer, I can work anywhere."

Does it matter if the organization has 40 employees? What about 40,000? 400,000? Does it matter to you?

If you're completely stumped about the kind of industries you could work in, take a look at the *brief* industry list at the back of this chapter, as well as the extensive bibliography at the back of the *Shortcut Your Search* book and in the Members Only section of our website.

You've Selected a Target If . . .

...you can clearly state the industry or organization size in which you'd be interested, your position within each industry, and some guidelines regarding geographic location.

For example, if you're a junior accountant, you may already know that you want to advance in the accounting field. You may know that you want to work for a small service organization as an assistant controller in the geographic area where you are now living.

If you have clearly selected your targets, then you can get on with finding interviews in your target area. To do that, you would conduct a campaign in your target area. (Job-hunting campaigns are covered in our book *Shortcut Your Search*.)

Here is one person's target list:

By geographic area:
- Washington, DC
- New York City

By industry:
- Book publishing
- Magazine publishing
- Advertising
- College administration (weak interest)
- Administration of professional firms (weak interest)
- Nonprofit associations
- Direct-marketing organizations

By function:
- Business manager/general manager—publishing
- International controller
- Corporate-level financial planning analysis
- General V.P. finance/general manager—nonprofit organizations

Other Issues You May Want To Consider Even If You Have a Target

Does the style of the organization matter to you? Would you rather be in a fast-paced, dynamic organization with lots of headaches or one that's more stable and slow paced, with routine work as the norm? Which would you prefer?

What kind of people do you want to work with? Friendly people? Sharp, challenging people? People interested in making a fast buck? People who want to make the world a better place? Think about it. You may have said before that you just want a job—any job—but is anything still okay with you?

If you want to be in sales, for example, would it matter if you were selling lingerie or used cars or computers or large office building space? What if you were selling cats? Rugs? Butter? Saying you want to be in *sales* is not enough.

Let's take it a step further. If what appeals to you about being a salesman is that you like to convince people, why not be a politician? Or a clergyman? Or a doctor? Or if what appeals to you is money, why not become a trader? Or a partner in a law firm? Remind yourself where your heart lies.

Case Study: William Finally—An Organized Search

William wanted a job—just about any job he saw in job postings. He spent months answering those ads. He thought he was job hunting, but he wasn't. He was simply answering ads for positions for which he was unqualified. William didn't stand a chance.

After a long time, William gave up and agreed to follow The Five O'Clock Club system. At first he resisted because, like so many job hunters, he did not want to *restrict* himself. William thought that focusing on only two or three job targets would limit his opportunities and lengthen his search. He wanted to be open to whatever job came his way.

Many job hunters, like William, simply want a job. But William needed to put himself in the position of the hiring manager: Why would he want to hire William? In his cover letters, William took the *trust me* approach. He did nothing to prove his interest in the industry, the organization, or even the position for which he was applying. His credentials matched the ad requirements only by the greatest stretch of the imagination.

A shotgun approach like William's may lead to a job offer, but it may also lead your career in a direction that is not what you would have preferred. Later, you may find yourself back in the same boat again—wondering what to do with your life, wanting to do almost anything but what you are doing, hoping your next job will miraculously be in a field that will satisfy you.

William's basic problem was not that he wanted to change careers, but that he didn't know what he wanted to do. He was willing to do anything—anything except focus on a specific area and go after it.

William eventually narrowed himself to two targets in which he was truly interested. Then he worked to find out his chances for getting jobs in those fields. William did the exercises in this book, and came up with this list to focus his search:

What I want in a job:
- A challenge in meeting new situations/ variety
- A complex situation I can structure
- Something I believe in
- A chance to express my creativity through my communication skills
- A highly visible position
- An opportunity to develop my leadership and motivational skills
- Sole responsibility for something

What I have to offer (that I also want to offer):
- Enthusiasm for the organization's basic mission/purpose
- Penetrating analysis that finds the answer
- The ability to synthesize diverse parts into a unified whole
- An ability and desire to be in new/untested situations
- Effective in dealing with many kinds of people
- Strong oral and written communication skills

Goal: A small- or medium-sized organization where I can feel my impact:

- Service
- Health care
- Human care
- Science
- Academia and learning
- Human understanding

Description of targeted areas:
- **Targeted geographic areas:**

Major East Coast cities or locales:
  - ✓ New York
  - ✓ Philadelphia

Boston
  - ✓ Baltimore
  - ✓ Washington

Targeted industries:
- First priority is health care:
  - ✓ Pharmaceuticals companies
  - ✓ Biotechnology companies
  - ✓ Hospitals
  - ✓ Maybe research labs
- Second priority is not-for-profit community organizations.

Targeted positions:
  - ✓ marketing/competitive analysis
  - ✓ organizational positioning
  - ✓ operations planning

William's first campaign was aimed at pharmaceuticals companies. He discovered what they looked for in new hires, and how he could get a position. In addition, he pursued his second objective: not-for-profit community organizations.

The result: As usual, a career transition takes time. William discovered he could make a transition into the pharmaceuticals industry, but decided not to take the backward step that would require. He learned of a job being created in a not-for-profit organization. Although he was not qualified for this position, he knew he could handle it, and it matched the list of what he wanted.

William went through the steps described in the chapter *How to Change Careers*, to convince his prospective employer he could indeed handle the job and was eager to have the chance to do it. This was difficult because the other candidates were better qualified than William—they had been in this kind of job before. For William, it was a career change.

William decided to write a number of proposals. To write them, he first needed to do research, which would not be easy. After some internet and library research, he called the heads of development at six major not-for-profits. He told them he was hoping to get a position at a certain organization, and wanted some ideas of how he could write a proposal of what he would do if he were hired.

Amazingly, his sincerity won the day. All six gave him information over the phone. Because he had done research, William was able to ask intelligent questions. He wrote a proposal, stating in his cover letter that he had spoken with the heads of development at major not-for-profits, and asked for another interview. It would be nice if that were all it took: William got another interview, but was rejected a *number* of times. Yet he continued to do research, and eventually showed enough fortitude and learned enough that he was hired.

The position was just what he wanted: a brand-new marketing research position at a major not-for-profit organization. He would head his career in a different direction and satisfy his enjoyable skills. His career was back on track, under his own control. And he's still with the organization today.

Let not my thinking become confused by listening to too many opinions, but let me consider each one individually, to see if it can be of help to me. To make good choices, I must develop a mature and prudent understanding of myself that will reveal to me my real motives and intentions.

PARAPHRASED FROM THOMAS MERTON,
NO MAN IS AN ISLAND (MARINER BOOKS)

Select Your Targets

The only difference between caprice and a lifelong passion is that the caprice lasts a little longer.

OSCAR WILDE

List your targets in the order in which you will conduct your search. First list the one you will focus on in your first campaign. If you are currently employed and have time to explore, you may want to select as your first target the most unlikely one. (Job hunters sometimes want to target areas they had only dreamed about before.) Concentrate on it and find out for sure whether you are truly interested and what your prospects are. If it doesn't work, you can become more realistic.

On the other hand, if you must find a job quickly, concentrate first on the area where you stand the best chance of getting a job—perhaps the field you are now in. After you are settled in your new job, you can develop yourself in the area that interests you in the long run. Remember, it's okay to take something less than your ideal job; just keep working toward your dreams.

Someone who made this work is Nat, who wanted to work for a Japanese company. He thought the Japanese culture suited his temperament. Yet Nat was forced to take a job at another organization because the Japanese process was slow (approval had to come from Tokyo).

Still, Nat kept pursuing the position with the Japanese firm.

Eventually, his dream job came through—at much more money than he had been making. The Japanese company realized that Nat's personal style, uncommon in America, meshed with Japanese management methods. His maturity—he was 55 years old—was also a plus. Nat, his new job, and his new employer were a good fit. Despite many obstacles, Nat pursued his dream and got it. And it was worth it in job satisfaction and in having some say over what happened in his own life.

If you are targeting a geographic area different from where you are now, be sure to conduct a serious, complete campaign aimed at that target. For example, you will want to contact search firms in that area, do library research, perhaps conduct a direct-mail campaign, and network. For in-depth information on all of these topics, please consult our book *Shortcut Your Job Search*. Use the worksheets on the following pages to plan your targets.

Our doubts are traitors,
And make us lose the good we oft might win
By fearing to attempt.

WILLIAM SHAKESPEARE, *MEASURE FOR MEASURE*

Measuring Your Targets

You've selected one to five targets on which to focus. Will they be enough to get you an appropriate job?

Let's say, for example, that your first target aims at a small industry (10 organizations) having only a few positions that would be appropriate for you. Chances are, those jobs are filled right now. In fact, chances are there may be no opening for a year or two. The numbers are working against you. But if you have targeted 20 small industries, each of which has 10 organizations with a few positions appropriate for you, the numbers are more in your favor. On the other hand, if one of your targets is large and has a lot of positions that may be right for you, the numbers are again on your side.

A Rule of Thumb

A target list of 200 positions results in seven interviews, which result in one job offer. Therefore, if there are less than 200 potential positions in your targets, develop additional targets or expand the ones you already have. Remember that when aiming at a target of less than 200, concentrated effort will be required.

However, sometimes one organization by itself may be enough. What if a very qualified administrative assistant wanted to work for a regional telephone company? What are the chances she would find a job there? A regional telephone company may have *thousands* of administrative assistants, and a qualified person would certainly be able to find a job there within a reasonable time frame.

In a tight job market, however, you will probably need to *expand your job-hunting targets*. If you are searching only in Chicago, or only in the immediate area where you live, think of other geographic areas. If you are looking only in large public corporations, consider small or private companies, or the not-for-profit area. If you are looking for a certain kind of position, what other kinds of work can you do? Think of additional targets for your search, and focus on each target in depth.

In *Shortcut Your Job Search*, you will learn how to position yourself for each of these targets. That way, when you go after a target, you will have a better chance of looking appropriate to the people in each target area.

Live all you can; it's a mistake not to. It doesn't so much matter what you do in particular, so long as you have had your life. If you haven't had that, what have you had? What one loses one loses; make no mistake about that.

HENRY JAMES, *THE AMBASSADORS* (RANDOM HOUSE, INC.)

Target Selection

After you have done some preliminary research, select the targets that you think deserve a full campaign. List first the one you will focus on in your first campaign. If you are currently employed and have time to explore, you may want to select as your first target the most unlikely one, but the one that is the job of your dreams. Then you can concentrate on it and find out for sure whether you are still interested and what your prospects are.

On the other hand, if you must find a job quickly, you will first want to concentrate on the area where you stand the best chance of getting a job—probably the area where you are now working. After you get that job, you can explore your other targets. (To expand your targets quickly, consider broadening your search geographically.)

If you are targeting a geographic area different from where you are now, be sure to conduct a serious, complete campaign aimed at that target. For example, you will want to contact search firms in that area, do Internet or library research, perhaps conduct a direct-mail campaign, and network.

Target 1: Industry or organization size: _____

     Position/function: _____

     Geographic area: _____

Target 2: Industry or organization size: _____

     Position/function: _____

     Geographic area: _____

Target 3: Industry or organization size: _____

     Position/function: _____

     Geographic area: _____

Target 4: Industry or organization size: _____

     Position/function: _____

     Geographic area: _____

Target 5: Industry or organization size: _____

     Position/function: _____

     Geographic area: _____

Measuring Your Targets

You've selected one to five (or more) targets on which to focus. Will this be enough to get you an appropriate job?

Let's say, for example, that your first target aims at a small industry (10 organizations) having only a few positions that would be appropriate for you.

Chances are, those jobs are filled right now. In fact, chances are there may be no opening for a year or two. The numbers are working against you. Now, if you have targeted 20 small industries, each of which has 10 organizations with a few positions appropriate for you, the numbers are more in your favor.

On the other hand, if one of your targets is large and has a lot of positions that may be right for you, the numbers are again on your side. Let's analyze your search and see whether the numbers are working for you or against you.

Fill out the following on your own target markets. You will probably have to make an educated guess about the number. A ballpark figure is all you need to get a feel for where you stand.

Target 1:   Industry or organization size: _____

               Position/function: _____

               Geographic area: _____

How big is the market for my service in this target?
A. Number of organizations in this target market: _____
B. Number of probable positions suitable for me in the average organization in this target: _____
A x B = Total number of probable positions appropriate for me in this target market: _____

For Target 2:   Industry or organization size: _____

               Position/function: _____

               Geographic area: _____

How big is the market for my service in this target?
A. Number of organizations in this target market: _____
B. Number of probable positions suitable for me in the average organization in this target: _____
A x B = Total number of probable positions appropriate for me in this target market: _____

For Target 3:   Industry or organization size: _____

               Position/function: _____

               Geographic area: _____

How big is the market for my service in this target?
A. Number of organizations in this target market: _____
B. Number of probable positions suitable for me in the average organization in this target: _____
A x B = Total number of probable positions appropriate for me in this target market: _____

Rule of thumb:

A target list of 200 positions in a healthy market results in seven interviews, which result in one job offer. Therefore, if there are fewer than 200 potential positions in your targets, develop additional targets or expand the ones you already have. Remember: When aiming at a target of less than 200 potential positions, a more concentrated effort is required.

Preliminary Target Investigation: Jobs/Industries Worth Exploring

Until you know that life is interesting—and find it so—you haven't found your soul.

GEOFFREY FISHER, ARCHBISHOP OF CANTERBURY

Although it takes up only a few paragraphs in this book, Preliminary Target Investigation is essential.

Your Preliminary Target Investigation could take only a few weeks if you are high in energy and can devote full time to it. You have to test your ideas for targets in the marketplace to see which ones are worth pursuing. As you research at the library, on the web, and by meeting with people in your fields of choice, you will refine those targets and perhaps develop others. Then you will know where to focus your job search, and the search will be completed much more quickly than if you had skipped this important step.

People who conduct a Preliminary Target Investigation while employed sometimes take a year to explore various fields while they continue in their old jobs. If you are not at all familiar with some of the job targets you have selected, do some Preliminary Target Investigation *now* through the web, library research (be sure to read this section), and networking. You will find that some targets are not right for you. Eliminate them and conduct a full campaign in those areas that seem right for you and that offer some reasonable hope of success.

Whether you are employed or between jobs,

Preliminary Target Investigation is well worth your time and a lot of fun. It is the difference between blindly continuing in your old career path because it is the only thing you know, and finding out what is really happening in the world so you can latch on to a field that may carry you forward for many, many years. This is a wonderful time to explore—to find out what the world offers. Most job hunters narrow their targets down too quickly, and wind up later with not much to go after. It is better for you emotionally as well as practically to develop more targets than you need *now* so you will have them when you are actively campaigning. If, on the other hand, you do not have the inclination or time to explore, you can move on. *Just remember, you can come back to this point if your search dries up and you need more targets.*

Most job hunters target only one job type or industry, take a very long time to find out that this target is not working, get depressed, try to think of other things they can do with their lives, pick themselves up, and start on one more target.

Life is God's novel. Let him write it.

ISAAC BASHEVIS SINGER

Instead, **brainstorm as many targets as possible before you begin your real job search.** *Then you can overlap your campaigns, going after a number of targets at once. If some targets do not seem to be working as well for you as others, you can drop* *the targets in which you are no longer interested. And when things don't seem to be going well, you will have other targets to fall back on.*

1. **List below all of the jobs/industries that interest you at this point.**
2. If you are not at all familiar with some of the targets you have selected, do some Preliminary Target Investigation *now* through the internet, library research or networking. Eliminate the targets that are not right for you, and conduct a full campaign in those areas that do seem right for you and seem to offer you some reasonable hope of success.

   As you find out what is happening in the world, new fields will open up for you. Things are changing so fast that if you conduct a serious search without some exploration, you are probably missing the most exciting developments in an area.

   Spend some time exploring. Don't narrow your targets down too quickly; you will wind up later with not much to go after. It is better for you emotionally, as well as practically, to develop more targets than you need now so you will have them when you are actively campaigning. If, on the other hand, you do not have the time or inclination to explore, you can move on to the next step. **Just remember: you can come back to this point if your search dries up and you need more targets.**

JOBS/INDUSTRIES THAT INTEREST ME AT THIS POINT:

(Conduct a Preliminary Target Investigation to determine what is really going on in each of them.)

_____

_____

_____

_____

_____

_____

_____

_____

_____

_____

_____

_____

_____

Counterbalance sources of stress in your life with sources of harmony. Develop closer ties to the people you love. Set up dependable routines in your schedule to which you can look forward during times of stress: a few moments each evening in a hot bath, regular nights to eat out, one day per month in bed, seasonal vacations. Create environments around you that are physically and emotionally restorative: a peaceful workspace, a blossom-filled window box you can see from where you eat, a permanent exercise nook. Regularly perform simple tasks that you can be certain will give you a sense of accomplishment.

Jack Maguire, *Care and Feeding of the Brain* (Random House, Inc.)

Targeting: The Start of an Organized Search

Dream. Dream big dreams! Others may deprive you of your material wealth and cheat you in a thousand ways, but no man can deprive you of the control and use of your imagination. Men may deal with you unfairly, as men often do; they may deprive you of your liberty; but they cannot take from you the privilege of using your imagination. In your imagination, you always win!

JESSE JACKSON, *Brother's Keeper: Words of Inspiration for African-American Men*, RODERICK TERRY, ED. 1996

To organize your targeting:

1. Brainstorm as many job targets as possible. You will not conduct a campaign aimed at all of them, but will have backup targets in case certain ones do not work out.
2. dentify a number of targets worthy of preliminary research. (If they are large targets and represent a lot of job possibilities for you, you will need fewer targets.)
3. Research each one enough—through the Internet, the library, and a few networking meetings—to determine whether it is worth a full job-search campaign. This is your Preliminary Target Investigation.
4. If your research shows that a target now seems inappropriate, cross it off your list, and concentrate on the remaining targets. **As you continue to network and research, keep open to other possibilities that may be targets for you. Add those to your list of targets to research.**

As you add new targets, reprioritize your list so you are concentrating first on the targets that should be explored first. Do not haphazardly go after everything that comes your way.

5. If you decide the target is worth pursuing, conduct a full campaign to get interviews in that area:
   • Develop your pitch.
   • Develop your résumé.
   • Develop a list of all the companies in the target area and the name of the person you want to contact in each company.
6. Then contact each organization through networking, direct contact, ads, or search firms.

Serendipitous Leads

Make a methodical approach the basis of your search, but also keep yourself open to those serendipitous *lucky leads* outside of your target areas that may come your way. In general, it is a waste of your energy to go after single serendipitous leads. It is better to ask yourself if this lead warrants a new target. If it does, then decide where it should be ranked in your list of targets, and research it as you would any serious target.

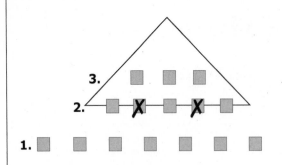

The boxes above represent different job targets. The triangle represents your job search. As you investigate targets, you will eliminate certain ones and spend more time on the remaining targets. You may research your targets by reading or by talking to people. The more you find out, the clearer your directions will become.

During Targeting Step 1 *you brainstormed lots of possible job targets, not caring whether or not they made sense.*

During Targeting Step 2 *you conducted preliminary research to determine whether or not you should mount a full campaign aimed at these targets.*

During Targeting Step 3 *you will focus on the targets that warrant a full campaign. This means you will do full research on each target, and consider using all of the techniques for getting interviews: networking, direct contact, search firms, and ads.*

The Five O'Clock Club®

Ready for the Next Step

Out of every crisis comes the chance
to be reborn...

NENA O'NEILL

By selecting and ranking your targets, you have completed a very important task. If your targets are wrong, the campaigns you aim at those targets are wrong. Maintain an exploratory mindset—assessing the targets you are pursuing, and being open to others.

Next you will start to develop your Targeting Map, essential when you are really ready to search (and you'll use our book *Shortcut Your Job Search*). Chances are, you can't fill in your Plan until you do some research, which is covered next in this book.

Make an organized search the basis for your campaign. Some lucky job hunters know lots of important people and just happen on to their next jobs. Sometimes those jobs are even satisfying. If that has happened to you in the past, count your blessings, but do not rely on that approach to work for you in the future. The world has changed, and organizations are more serious about whom they hire.

In our book *Shortcut Your Job Search*, you will begin an intensive campaign to get lots of interviews in each of the targets you have selected. The campaigns will overlap so you will be able to compare the performance of each and gain perspective. You can begin your campaign right now, by reading the next few chapters—about conducting research.

> **Do not think that you have to complete your research before you start reading *Shortcut Your Job Search*. The job-search process is largely a research process. You will continually refer to the research portions of this book throughout your campaign.**

This is the true joy in life, the being used for a purpose recognized by yourself as a mighty one, the being thoroughly worn out before you are thrown on the scrap heap; the being a force of nature instead of a feverish selfish little clod of ailments and grievances complaining that the world will not devote itself to making you happy.

GEORGE BERNARD SHAW, *MAN AND SUPERMAN*

True commitment transforms you. You really know where you stand. You have a base on which to build your life. You're not in shifting sand anymore.

CHRISTOPHER REEVE, FORMER STAR OF *SUPERMAN*, IN AN INTERVIEW WITH BARBARA WALTERS—REEVE BECAME A QUADRIPLEGIC AFTER A HORSEBACK-RIDING ACCIDENT

We will make the best possible life out of this life that we now have and there's no question that he will continue to be a leader and continue to be a strong person and a funny person and a lively person.

MRS. CHRISTOPHER REEVE (DANA),
IN THAT SAME INTERVIEW

We must not be afraid of the future. We must not be afraid of man. It is no accident that we are here. Each and every human person has been created in the "image and likeness" of the One who is the origin of all that is. We have within us the capacities for wisdom and virtue. With these gifts, and with the help of God's grace, we can build in the next century and the next millennium a civilization worthy of the human person, a true culture of freedom. We can and must see that the tears of this century have prepared the ground for a new springtime of the human spirit.

POPE JOHN PAUL II, SPEECH TO THE UNITED NATIONS
GENERAL ASSEMBLY, *LIBRERIA EDITRICE VATICANA*,
OCT. 5, 1995

The Five O'Clock Club®

Researching Your Job Targets

*Natural talent, intelligence, a wonderful
education—none of these guarantees success.
Something else is needed: the sensitivity to understand
what other people want and the willingness to give it to
them. Worldly success depends on pleasing others. No
one is going to win fame, recognition, or advancement
just because he or she thinks it's deserved.
Someone else has to think so too.*

JOHN LUTHER, PLAYWRIGHT

Why Is Research Important?

Research can help you decide which fields
and industries you want to work in. In our book
Shortcut Your Job Search we'll tell you how to
research those targets, eliminate some, add others, and develop a detailed list of organizations
to contact and how to contact them. But for right
now, you simply want a list of tentative targets.
You need to explore what kinds of positions may
be appropriate for you. Which industries? Which
geographic areas?

During the course of your research, look for
the following about each industry in your tentative target list:

1. trends and future prospects in a particular
    industry;
2. areas of growth and decline in that industry;
3. the kinds of challenges the industry faces
    that could use your skills;
4. the culture of the industry;
5. the major-league organizations in the
    industry, of course, but also the second- and
    third-tier firms as well.

In the bibliography at the back of our *Shortcut

Your Job Search* book and the Members Only section of our website, you will find many sources for
exploring these issues and concerns. Having a lot
of information will help you determine whether
or not you are in sync with a particular industry
and whether or not there is a place for you. It generally requires only a small amount of information to decide that an industry should go on your
tentative target list. You will continue to research
throughout your search because, as you will see,
the entire job-search process is a research process. You will continue to refine your targets and
your list of organizations as you go forward.

Internet and other Research at the Library

Many libraries now have developed "job
search" sections. Find a university or big-city
library that's conveniently located and has an
extensive business collection. The great thing
about libraries is that you will not be on your own:
Librarians are usually experts at helping job hunters, so plan to spend some time with the business
reference librarian. Be specific. Tell the librarian
what you want to accomplish. I have always said,
"The librarian is your friend." They also have
computer terminals and extensive databases to
help you in your search. I personally love libraries.
I was a librarian in both high school and college.
Get comfortable with the environment. Spend time
using the computer databases and the reference
books. Photocopy articles you can read at home.

If electronic information at the library is a
new frontier for you, do not be intimidated. Ask
for assistance. Computer-aided research will make
your work immeasurably faster, easier, and more

accurate. Let it work for you. If you are of a certain age or inclination and *don't like computers*, the best advice I can give you is: Get over it. In about any field I can think of, information sharing is now done by computer—you will need to adapt.

There are going to be no survivors.
Only big winners and the dead.
No one is going to just squeak by.

RONALD COMPTON, CEO, AETNA INSURANCE COMPANY

Basic Research

Set aside at least two full days strictly for library or Internet research. If you are not sure of the industry you want to pursue, you can spend two days just researching industries (or professions). One of my favorite tools is the *Encyclopedia of Business Information Sources.* It lists topics, such as oil or clubs or finance or real estate. Under each topic, it lists the most important sources of information on that topic: periodicals, books, and associations. Using this resource, you can quickly research any field in depth. This encyclopedia may also be available online at your library. You also may want to read the U.S. Department of Labor's reports on various industries or professions (www.bls.gov/emp and www.bls.gov).

Two important Internet resources on careers are www.vault.com and www.wetfeet.com.
Vault.com provides information on more than 1,200 organizations. Vault.com doesn't offer information on minor industries, but its goal is to provide you with the *inside scoop* on key industries *from a job hunter's point of view.* There are plenty of sites where you can find out about an industry from the financial investor's point of view, but Vault.com offers the employee perspective.

Vault.com covers the following industries: accounting, advertising and PR, consulting, entertainment, fashion, government, health/ biotech/ pharmaceutical, investment banking, investment management, law, media and market-

ing, nonprofit, real estate, technology, television, and venture capital.

Wetfeet.com is a good site to find information about various types of careers, the latest industry news, and the key players in each area. Wet Feet covers the following industries and professions: accounting, advertising, biotech and pharmaceuticals, brand management and marketing, consulting, entertainment, financial services, health care, human resources, law, manufacturing, information technology, nonprofit and government, oil and gas, and real estate. Some of the industry and field information used to be available for free, but it seems as though they now charge for it.

Another way to select tentative industries and fields is to go to Salary.com. There, for free, they have job descriptions and the salary amounts for your targeted geographic areas.

Once you have selected tentative industries, you will network to find out issues, trends, and buzzwords, and all this will help you refine your pitch. In addition, networking at this point may uncover other tentative targets, which you may simply add to your list of targets, or you may research them at this time.

While networking, you may find someone who will give you a list of people in a targeted field—perhaps an association membership list. Or perhaps someone will invite you to an association meeting and you can find lists and newsletters there. You may need to spend time in the library to gather the list of organizations. You may use an industry directory or local business publications that provide listings of organizations.

If you think you can work in many industries, get a sense of those that are growing and also fit your needs.

Few executives yet know how to ask: What information do I need to do my job? When do I need it? And from whom should I be getting it?

PETER F. DRUCKER, "BE DATA LITERATE—KNOW WHAT TO KNOW," *THE WALL STREET JOURNAL*, DECEMBER 1, 1992

Where Else Can You Find Information?

• **Associations.** Almost every profession imaginable has an association—sometimes several—and these are important sources of information. If you don't know anything at all about an industry or field, these groups are often the place to start. They tend to be very helpful, and will assist you in mastering the jargon so you can use the language of the trade. *The Encyclopedia of Associations* (available at your library) is a massive list of professional groups. If you are interested in the rug business, there's a related association.

Just by their very nature, associations are welcoming—so call them. If they have lots of local chapters, chances are there's one near you, and it will be a great place to network. Contact the headquarters, and ask for information and the name of the person to contact in your area. Then call that person, and say you are interested in the association and would like to attend its next meeting. If there is no local chapter in your area, associations can still send you information.

• Use the **Internet** to find associations and information on your target industries and fields. To zero in on key associations, go to Google, key in the field or industry in which you are interested, and the word association. For example, key in the words accounting association and you'll get a listing of 25 or so. Or try www.business.com, which includes links to hundreds of associations.

• **The press**. Read newspapers (online and in print) *with your target in mind*, and you will notice all kinds of things you would not otherwise have seen. Contact the author of an article in a trade magazine or blog. Tell him or her how much you enjoyed the article and what you are trying to do, and ask to get together just to chat. I've made many friends this way.

• **Chambers of commerce**. If you are doing an out-of-town job search, call the chamber of commerce in your targeted area. Ask for a list of industries and organizations in their area.

• **Universities** have libraries or research centers on fields of interest. A professor may be an expert in a field you are interested in. Contact him or her.

• **Networking** is a great research tool. At the beginning of your search, network with peers to find out about a field or industry. When you are in full job search, network with people two levels higher than you are.

Avoid the crowd. Do your own thinking independently. Be the chess player, not the chess piece.

RALPH CHARELL

Get Sophisticated about Using Reference Materials

Research will result in your Targeting Map, which you will see later in this book and which will guide you through your search. But you'll need more research to construct it.

Need more help researching your targets? Go to the Members Only section of our website: www.FiveOClockClub.com. You will see a 111-page bibliography of research sources—the best available— organized by industry and by field. You will also find all of our worksheets, which you may download.

CASE STUDY: Denise
Brainstorming Possible Industries

Developing your list of tentative targets takes creativity as well as research. The worksheet in this book, Brainstorming Possible Jobs, is an important start. Denise was a relatively recent graduate who knew she liked writing and computers, and had her undergraduate degree in agriculture. She had no geographical restrictions, and would actually enjoy relocating. Which industries should she target? The question could be put this way: *Who employs people to communicate with the agriculture and farming communities?* The world is big, and even though the agriculture market is declining in the U.S., it's a big market internationally. Who knows where this research could take her? Here are a few ideas for starters:

- The government—local, state, and federal—e.g., the U.S. Department of Agriculture (USDA).
- Chemical companies such as Monsanto.
- Financial services companies that specialize in mortgages and loans to farmers.
- Publishers that aim at the agriculture or food market, such as Rodale (Organic Gardening magazine).
- Advertising agencies and pubic relations firms that aim at that market.
- United Nations, AID, World Health Organization, and other governmental and quasi-governmental organizations that help farmers in Third World countries.
- •Associations, for example, Future Farmers of America. Some may be too small to have paid employees, but other associations are worth exploring.
- Agriculturally focused events, such as World Food Day.
- Denise can go to **www.About.com**, key in *agriculture* or *farming*, and see what comes up.

Denise will next try to come up with a list of specific employers, by industry and sub-industry. So, for example, under *government*, she would list all of the government agencies that are appropriate. Under *chemical companies*, she would list as many as possible, and not focus only on the big names that make the news every day. If the list contains only *recognized* names that everyone has heard about, Denise did not do a good research job. She must go after the small and mid-sized firms as well.

If I were Denise, I'd spend *at least* 15 hours researching the market—probably more. We're lucky to have the Internet so we can just sit at home and build the list. Later on, Denise will probably need library research and she'll also have to actually talk to people to find out what's going on. But right now she needs to find out how big her universe of potential employers is.

After Denise has a list of tentative targets, she'll conduct a Preliminary Target Exploration aimed at each of the industries to see which industries/sub-industries appeal to her the most. She also needs to know where she might stand the *best chance* of starting her agriculture communications career. For example, she may think that the USDA sounds appealing, but after conducting a preliminary exploration, she may find that her preconception was completely wrong. Or, Denise may think at this point that a large chemical company would be the best place for her. But after meeting with a few people in that industry, she may change her mind and decide that it is the worst place for her.

Salary Information

At www.Salary.com you can find job descriptions and salary ranges for hundreds of professions by geographic area. You can get a brief look at various fields. But remember, you have a unique background and bring specific experience to the situation. So what *others* are paid might not reflect what *you* are worth—salary negotiations must be based on many factors—not just standard industry ranges.

Other Sources

On **www.business.com's** home page there is a list of about 25 industries, each broken down into three or more subcategories, i.e., financial services is broken down into banking, insurance, and investment. For banking, the subcategories include: associations, banking institutions, banking law, certificates of deposits, employment, online banking, small business, and software, among others. A section called Popular Searches has links to banking for small business, the banking industry, foreign banking, and sweep accounts, plus more.

Google– again. Key in "job fields list" or "job careers." You should get list of fields and careers published by About.com and the Bureau of Labor Statistics (BLS).

> If you have no idea what you want to do with your life, print out a list of careers from About.com or the Bureau of Labor Statistics (or our list below) and put a line through any career that does **not** interest you at all. It's easier to decide what you **don't** want to do than what you **do** want to do. You should have three or four careers left that you can investigate. And be sure to see which ones fit in with your Seven Stories Exercise results and your Fifteen- or Forty-Year Visions.

Government websites. Do you want to work for the government? Even at the state level, you will find abundant information. For example, if you want a job in Tennessee, try **www.tennessee. gov** and click on *A to Z Departments and Agencies*. It's exciting to see the list of departments. Starting with "A," the listings include the Appellate Courts, the Department of Agriculture, the Alcoholic Beverage Commission, the Arts Commission, and the Attorney General. Review the various departments and see if there are a few that are of interest to you. At the top of the home page is a link to *employment*. You can search for the jobs and submit an application. But you can also target specific agencies that interest you, send your résumé directly to them, or call them and tell them that you are specifically interested in their agency. If you have a specific agency or two in mind, add them to your target list.

The choice of a career, a spouse, a place to live; we make them casually, at times, because we do not know how to articulate the choices....I believe that people often persuade themselves that their decisions do not matter, because they feel powerless to make the best decision. Some of us feel that, no matter what we do, our decisions won't matter much.... But I believe that we know at heart that decisions do matter.

PETER SCHWARTZ, THE ART OF THE LONG VIEW
(RANDOM HOUSE, INC.)

A Brief List of Industries To Consider

If you are completely stumped about the industries in which you might like to work, the following list is a starting point. Just say *yes* or *no* to each one, selecting the ones that may hold even a slight interest for you. You will investigate them further. Eliminating industries is just as important as selecting industries.

Of course, if there are no companies in your targeted geographic area for the industries you've chosen, you'll have to change the industries or your targeted geographic area.

Also be sure to look at the bibliography at the back of our *Shortcut Your Job Search* book or in the Members Only section of our website.

Academic and Education
Accounting
Advertising, including Graphic Art and Design
Aging Workers
Apparel, Textiles, Fashion, and Beauty
Art and Design
Associations
Automotive
Aviation and Aerospace
Banking, Finance, Investing, Securities, Trading, Credit, and Other
Biotechnology
Business/College/Liberal Arts/Recent Graduates
Communications Equipment and Services, including Telecommunications
Construction and Building
Consulting

Disabled

Diversity and Minorities (except Gay and Lesbian)

Electronics

Energy, Alternative Energy, and Utilities

Engineering

Entertainment, including Media (Broadcasting and Publishing)

Environmental

Ex-Inmates

Food and Beverages

Franchising

Furniture

Government

Health Care and Medicine

Human Resources

Information Technology/High-Tech (Computers, Technology, and e-Commerce)

Insurance Law

Law Enforcement and Criminal Justice

Library Science

Manufacturing

Nonprofit

Nursing

Public Relations

Publishing (Books, Magazines, Newspapers, Other)

Real Estate

Retailing

Sales and Marketing

Small Business

Transportation (Shipping, Marine, Freight, Express Delivery, Supply Chain)

Travel, Leisure, and Hospitality (including Hotels, Food Service, Travel Agents, Restaurants, and Airlines)

Veterans

Vocational (no Four-Year College Degree)

Volunteering

Wholesaling and Distributing/Importing and Exporting

Sample Targeting Map

Targeting Map: Joe Doakes

TARGET FUNCTIONS: VICE PRESIDENT/DIRECTOR/MANAGER

- Management Information Services
- Applications Development
- Information Systems
- Information Systems Technology
- Systems Development
- Business Reengineering

RESPONSIBILITIES:

- Identification of new information systems technologies and how they could affect the profitability of a company.
- Management of projects for the implementation of information systems or new technologies.
- Providing for and managing a business partner relationship between the information systems department and the internal company departments that use their services.
- Implementing and managing a business partner relationship among the company and its primary vendors and its customers using systems technologies, such as EDI (Electronic Data Interchange).

TARGET COMPANIES:

Attributes

- People oriented
- Growth minded through increased sales, acquisitions, or new products
- Committed to quality customer service
- Receptive to new ideas on how to do business use new technologies

Location

- Primary—Northern New Jersey or Westchester/Orange/Rockland Counties in New York
- Secondary—New York City, Central New Jersey, or Southern Connecticut, Eastern Pennsylvania
- Other—anywhere along the Eastern Seaboard

TARGET INDUSTRIES:

Consumer Products:	Pharmaceuticals:	Food/Beverage:	Chemicals:	Other:
Unilever Kimberly-Clark	Merck	Pepsico	Castrol	Medco
Avon	Schering-Plough	T.J. Lipton	Witco	Toys-R-Us
Carter Wallace	Warner-Lambert	Kraft/General Foods	Allied Chemical Olin	Computer Associates
Sony Products	American Home	Nabisco	Corp.	Becton Dickinson
Minolta	Bristol-Myers Squibb	Hartz Mountain	Union Carbide	Siemens
Boyle Midway	Pfizer	Continental Baking	Air Products	Dialogic
Revlon	Jannsen Pharmaceutica	Nestlé	General Chemical	Automatic Data Proc.
L&F Products	Hoffmann-LaRoche	Haagen-Dazs	Englehard Corp.	Vital Signs
Houbigant	Ciba-Geigy	Tuscan Dairies	BASF Corp.	Benjamin Moore
Mem	Sandoz	Dannon Co.	Degussa Corp.	
Chanel	A.L. Laboratories	BSN Foods	GAF Corp.	
Airwick	Smith Kline Beecham	Campbell Soup	Lonza Inc.	
Church & Dwight	American Cyanamid	Cadbury Beverages	Sun Chemical	
Johnson & Johnson	Boeringer Ingelheim	Labatt		
Reckitt & Colman	Roberts Pharmaceuticals	Arnold Foods		
Philip Morris	Glaxo	S. B. Thomas		
Clairol	Block Drug	Sunshine Biscuits		
Estee Lauder	Hoechst Celanese			
Cosmair	Ethicon			
	Winthrop Pharmaceuticals			

Sample Targeting Map

Targeting Map: Jane Doe

TARGET FUNCTIONS: VICE PRESIDENT/DIRECTOR/MANAGER

• Marketing	• Strategic Planning	• New Business Development

Target Industry:	**Target Industry:**	**Target Industry:**	**Target Industry:**	**Target Industry:**
#1 Carriers/Telecom	#2 Internet	#3 Online Finance	#4 Content/Media	#5 Information, etc.
Reasoning:	**Reasoning:**	**Reasoning:**	**Reasoning:**	**Reasoning:**
Have industry experience. Growth likely, esp. wireless. Concern: That I get a pure marketing job.	To learn fast, if equity situation. Or be high up in a larger co. Overlap with other industries.	Related to my exp. Concern: There may be a separate area for the Net at larger cos.	I'm interested. Concerns: Nature of large cos. in it; the opportunity startups will have.	List of random affinities that can't be classified elsewhere.
Sub targets:	**Sub targets:**	**Sub targets:**	**Sub targets:**	**Sub targets:**
1. Wireless/line carriers 2. Cable companies 3. Satellite cos.	1. Content providers 2. Net-related startups 3. Convergence players 4. E-business	1. Venture capital or addtl. contacts 2. Companies doing e-commerce	1. New media/ Publishing 2. Data 3. E-commerce 4. Related cos.	1. New product incubators 2. Information providers 3. Advertising

Company Names:	**Company Names:**	**Company Names:**	**Company Names:**	**Company Names:**
Omnipoint	N2K	**1.**	ABC, NBC, CBS	**1.**
ATT CellularSprint	Airmedia	Scottrade	Google	Idealab
BT/MCI	WebGenesis	Vanguard	Apple	**2.**
Cablevision	Gist	Charles Schwab	Dow Jones	Gartner Group
Comcast	Mercury 7	Fidelity Investments	Reuters	Yankee Group
Qwest	Multex	Sharebuilder	Amazon	Jupiter Comm
Tel-Save	e-Share	**2.**	Time Warner	Find/SVP
Telligent	GoAmerica	TD Ameritrade	Microsoft	Forrester Research
RAM Mobile Data	Razorfish	Bloomberg	Find/SVP	Giga
Metromedia	Juno	S&P	Advance Publ.	Meta
Periphonics	Relevant Knowledge	T.Rowe Price	Bertelsmann	D&B
Brite	I-Pro	E*Trade Financial	CPC	McGraw Hill
Lucent	PC Meter	Merrill Lynch Direct	Ziff Davis	DM-related firms
AT&T	Nielsen	Ameriprise Financial	Dow Jones	PC Meter/NPD
Road Runner	Physicians Online	**3.**	EMI	**3.**
Iridium	IDT	Other online financial	Forbes	Yoyodyne
Globalstar	ICon	companies	Harcourt General	Poppe Tyson
Consat	BroadVision		Hearst	Modem Media
Community Tele.	Firefly		McGraw-Hill	CKS
Geotek	DoubleClick		Polygram	Group Cortex
NTL	Burst!		Primedia	I-traffic
PanAmSat	Commonwealth Net		Readers Digest	SiteSpecific
Cellular Vision			Reed Elsevier	Margenotes
			Sony	
			Viacom	
			Disney	
			Washington Post	

PART FOUR

How to Manage
Your Future

New Shapes in Careers: How to Repackage the Work You Want To Do

Betsy Jaffe, Ph.D.

The man without purpose is like a ship without a rudder—a waif, a nothing, a no man. Have a purpose in life, and, having it, throw such strength of mind and muscle into your work as God has given you.

THOMAS CARLYLE, *MAN WITHOUT PURPOSE*

Who can forget that line inspired by the movie *Jaws?*..."Just when you thought it was safe to go back in the water...?" Just when you'd figured out how to survive in the workplace, the rules change... again. There's no escaping that sense of impending change, the uncertainty of what's next in these global business waters we find ourselves in. Nothing about managing a career seems the same.

That classic, up-the-ladder career with a place for everything and everything in its place is gone. Rarely, now, are there clearly defined, structured positions to move into. The organization person who built a solid career one block at a time has disappeared. Now, there's no sense of security about the route you can take or the connections you need to make, and there's no sense of being set for life.

Technological, global, and economic trends have played havoc with the best of five-year plans. Because of these and other changes, five new career shapes have emerged, each requiring a new look at how work is done, how income is earned, and what's required to succeed. There are new opportunities in each shape, new ways to package what you do. Think of these shapes in terms of your own career.

The New Classic Career

First, the New Classic Career in large organizations incorporates a much flatter ladder (if there still is one!). The steps take longer and are tougher to climb, and there are fewer rungs. New hollow, virtual, or boundaryless organizational structures are continually evolving, so that they are now more psychological than hierarchical. In this information age, the company's assets reside mostly in the minds of employees and walk out the door every night.

Horizontal networks, cross-functional teams, and strategic alliances call for new strategies. Surviving feels more like swinging on a trapeze, from opportunity to opportunity, role to role, project to project, so skills must be portable across functions. And there's no certainty of who's in charge anymore.

Instead of looking to fill a box on an organizational chart, you're looking for a situation where you can build your knowledge, skills, and experience. And you have to make it happen. If you wait to be told what to do, you'll be out on the street asking, "What happened?"

> **Surviving feels more like swinging on a trapeze, from opportunity to opportunity, role to role, project to project.**

At a financial services company in Dallas, a vice president of new product development pulls together teams from top management, former competitors, and functional specialists, as needed, to launch new pension products. He researches customer needs, talks to professionals in his field, then makes a presentation to sell his ideas... without having a staff! He has to make it happen, and he has a lot of freedom to do so. It's risky, but without the red tape of old structures, he and his company are introducing more new services faster.

Career survival in large organizations now depends on your having flexibility, adaptability, the ability to scale steep learning curves and to play on ever-changing teams. You may need to form key alliances with former rivals, break through Chinese walls at your company, and you must be able to demonstrate the value you bring to a project. It's not the way you operated five years ago. It's a different mentality—not *the way we've always done it*.

The opportunities are tremendous as regulations change, underdeveloped countries take off, and technology continually evolves, but you've got to sell yourself differently to make the cut. You've got to be a problem solver in operations as well as in finance, in marketing as well as in manufacturing. You've got to be more nimble in switching hats across those former functional lines. Those who can are more quickly reemployed. Companies are skimming off the cream, even as they cut.

> **There are 27 million self-employed, part-time, and temporary workers.**

On the other hand, what if you've had it with large organizations and crave more autonomy, multiple streams of income, and a more flexible lifestyle? Over the last decade, professionals have quietly reshaped their lives and careers. New patterns and themes have emerged as people have moved between sectors of the economy, formed their own businesses, and achieved the balance they want between their career and life priorities.

With 27 million self-employed, part-time, and temporary workers, it's no wonder that Classic

Careers are becoming the exception rather than the rule! You are less likely to find an employment situation just like the last one you had.

Besides the New Classic Career, there are four other new shapes—Concentric, Concurrent, Combination, and Contingency. They align on a change continuum between structured, organized careers characterized by moderate changes at one end, and careers that are more tumultuous and uncertain at the other.

Concentric Careers

Concentric Careers look like bull's-eyes. They build on a core, like with a business or product line. Your main product or area of expertise is in the center. As you expand in products or skills, concentric circles are added beyond the core. Organized people are particularly good at structuring Concentric Careers, and many managers and executives move to such careers when they form their own consulting firms, becoming manufacturers' reps or building a line of products or services.

A former IBMer in Michigan began with a line of home security items that she marketed through catalogs. As the business grew, she added guard services, home security audits, and consultations to businesses about security issues. She expanded on her core of products and services, weeding out losers and adding potential cash cows.

You, too, can take stock, add to your core of expertise, or delete those less promising lines of endeavor. If you're a profit center in a larger organization, you can use this strategy, too.

Concurrent Careers

People with Concurrent Careers have two or more parallel, major activities in tandem. These careers may balance each other, bring in added income, or be a rehearsal for a career change. People who like variety and the stimulation of multiple activities create such arrangements. The engineer studying for a master's degree in social work, the lighting consultant serving on his co-op board before moving on to building management, and the working new parent all come to mind. (Indeed, parenting often feels like a second career!)

Over 7 million people hold down more than one job.

You need a lot of energy, support systems, and drive to handle it all, but more than seven million people hold down more than one job. I know of one couple who worked five jobs between them to make ends meet! Another balances seasonal businesses, alternating efforts between construction and winter sports events management.

A journey of a thousand miles must begin with a single step.

LAO-TZU

Combination Careers

These include a mix of unrelated activities and may make little sense to others. They resemble a pizza—a little of this and a little of that. People who want to escape routine, who crave autonomy, and like a variety of short-term challenges have careers like these. Their résumés look like career patchwork quilts!

One part-time editor for an Atlanta-based corporate newsletter moved to New York, Houston, and back to Atlanta, all while raising two kids, studying for a degree in psychology, and volunteering with the homeless, not to mention being a corporate spouse. Pre-retirees find this a good model for the mix of travel, hobbies, part-time work, and volunteering they want in their lives. Though not synergistic, each activity adds to their overall satisfaction.

The new career shapes are: new classic, concentric, concurrent, combination, and contingency.

To pull off a Combination Career, you, of course, need financial resources in the form of multiple streams of income, pensions, and health coverage. It helps to form alliances with others in the same boat, or with those who can provide services that make it all work.

Contingency Careers

The final shape looks like broken lines on a highway. These careers are full of stopgaps and fallbacks to earn money while you hope to get a break doing what you love. Interim management companies and temp agencies provide work for all kinds of professionals: budding entrepreneurs trying to make a go of a new business, consultants between projects, and performing artists waiting for that next gig. Artists have worked as receptionists, proofreaders, and salespeople for years while they auditioned for plays, built up portfolios, and honed their skills on the side. Now, professionals are doing it.

One voice-over artist installs sound systems as a fallback. A public relations specialist turns her home into a bed-and-breakfast. Others barter services until things pick up. Skills like writing, consulting, and computer and presentation skills are transferable and can help bring in income when times are tough.

Analytical and organized people seem to lean toward classic, concentric, and concurrent careers. Creative types often have combination and contingency careers.

So no matter what your preference for security or risk, careers can be and are being fashioned in any of these new shapes. Analytical and organized people seem to lean toward Classic, Concentric, and Concurrent Careers, because they are more structured and predictable. Creative and more "emotional" types often have Combination and Contingency Careers, which entail more upheaval, risks, ambiguity, insecurity, and variation in ways to earn money.

You may have had a mix of several in your career history, or you may opt to in your next move.

Knowing that there are new options, even as the ground shifts beneath your feet, can be a lifesaver. Just be sure to make it happen.

Betsy Jaffe, Ph.D., is the author of *Altered Ambitions— What's Next in Your Life?* This article originally appeared in *The Five O'Clock News.*

A Reminder of Some Basic Career Principles

Keep your boss's boss off your boss's back.

Here are a few more basic career principles—just to keep you on your toes:

1. Don't let others define you. Set your own standards. Don't measure yourself against others.
2. Know yourself and be yourself.
3. Develop a philosophy of your life as you want it. Be selective about how you spend your time. Make your own choices. Decide what you want to commit to. We each have the same amount of time.
4. Make a plan. If you don't know where you're going, chances are you won't get very far. Make a résumé of yourself five years from now, do your Forty-Year Vision, and develop a Career Plan. Identify what you will need to get there. But keep your options open, and don't stay too long in a job. Keep on developing yourself with an eye on your own future.
5. Be willing to take a risk. Make sure your next position relies on your strengths and your basic skills, and also contains a little risk— some new growth area. The jobs or assignments you take should have all three, and they should fit in with your Forty-Year Vision. You need the new growth areas so you will progress and advance.

6. Look for jobs that can provide quantifiable measures of your accomplishments, and look for companies that fit your style.
7. Learn how to manage or change your environment, rather than being a victim of your environment.
8. Get help. Join associations. Meet others in the company. Stay in touch. Don't go through your career alone.
9. Pick a few role models—not just one. Select the characteristics you like from each one. Observe their demeanor, dress, vocabulary, and speech patterns.
10. Don't let your guard down just because you have a new job or assignment. Always have a backup plan in mind—just in case. Keep yourself marketable, and treat your employer as if you were a consultant. This position is not permanent.

**Can't do a lot of career planning?
That's okay.
Just aim for the second job out.**

When you are trying to decide on your next move, think of how that step will position you for the one after that. Even if you can't do a Forty-Year Vision—or a detailed Career Plan—you will still be better off than most people if you think at least two steps ahead.

For example, if one option is to take a position in management consulting as a sales representative, and if you think you may work for another 15 years, what would be your next step if you lost that job—say, four years from now? If you think you would be marketable in that same kind of position, then you have developed at least a four-year career plan. If you think this job would not position you well for the next job, then it may not be a good move. This kind of thinking is the start of solid career planning.

How to Keep Your Life Course in Mind

I learned three things in Zurich during the war.
I wrote them down. Firstly, you're either a
revolutionary or you're not, and if you're not
you might as well be an artist as anything else.
Secondly, if you can't be an artist,
you might as well be a revolutionary.
I forget the third.

Tom Stoppard, *Travesties* (Grove/Atlantic, Inc.)

Sometimes we forget our important thoughts, or we remember them and they sound strange, or we become afraid of them. Afraid of success. Afraid of failure. Like writing my first book. Some days I became nauseated at the thought of working on it. On other days, I simply *forgot* I was writing it, or I became afraid that it all sounded stupid, harsh, boring, trite. Often, I couldn't remember why I was doing it; then I was afraid I would never finish.

Writing a book is a lot like job hunting. Some days you forget why you're doing it—you just know that you must. Or you become sick at the thought of it. You can sometimes become afraid that you sound stupid, or are doing the wrong things, or will embarrass yourself, or you'll never finish.

But somehow—one day at a time—it gets done. A job hunter makes a phone call, writes a proposal, researches an organization. Every day you make a new decision to do your best no matter how you feel about it. You sit down and do what you must do. That is discipline: to continue to job hunt—or to continue to write—regardless of how you feel. And then you get into it and it flows.

You have to remember where you were trying to head. Job hunting—or writing a book—was supposed to take you somewhere.

When one lives without a clear value structure, it is both difficult to direct life in the long run and difficult to experience a sense of meaningfulness that comes from following a prescribed course. It is possible to sail a boat, for example, without charts or a compass. However, the absence of a chart prevents the possibility of a journey. One is limited to "day" sailing, so that new destinations and new challenges are out of reach. Eventually the same seascape and circumstances will produce a tedium not unlike the absence of meaning associated with a present-centered existence.

Herbert Rappaport, Ph.D., *Marking Time*

Everyone is running to and fro, pressed by the stomach ache of business.

Frédéric-Auguste Bartholdi,
French sculptor of Statue of Liberty
Letter to his mother, June 12, 1871

It is easy to get caught up in your day-to-day activities. Your life can get off course; you become distracted. You may even discover you have veered from your true path for a number of years. That's okay. Bring yourself back and walk toward your goal. Stay with your own direction—the one that is in your heart. Deep down, you know when things are right and when things are not. Keep walking toward your goal.

Don't be bound by your past. It is important to remember that you are not whatever your jobs have been. We don't exist on a sheet of paper, a résumé. Don't identify too strongly with it. Stay fluid behind those words on the page. They are not you, but simply a sales tool.

The power is in what you are doing now and in your pull toward the future. The power is in the act of living each day to the fullest. It is the direction in which we are each heading that is important. Look to the future. We constantly gain new insights, new visions.

Taking the long view can give you satisfaction. A stonemason working on the Cathedral of St. John the Divine was asked how he could keep on cutting those stones year after year. He said he was not cutting stones—he was building a cathedral.

Of journeying, the benefits are many; the freshness it brings to the heart, the seeing and hearing of marvelous things...the meeting of unknown friends...

Sadi

Interviewing can soften you. It can broaden your horizons and make you realize there is a big world out there with lots of interesting things to do. In talking to people, you can see that it is not all so pat—so clearly spelled out—what a person should be. There are endless variations, and when you realize how much variety there is, you also realize that, in the end, it is largely up to you to choose what you will be. We each have a place. Find your place. Live your part.

I have a dream that my four little children will one day live in a nation where they will not be judged by the color of their skin but by the content of their character.I have a dream.

Rev. Martin Luther King, Jr.
Speech to 200,000 civil rights demonstrators,
Washington, DC, August 28, 1963

Rev. Martin Luther King, Jr., was driven by his dream. *Your* main drives and inclinations also have

power. You will come back to them again and again in your life because you are driven to do these things. They will come out. Why not harness that energy and direct it consciously rather than letting it rule you? In the right situations, your drives are a benefit and can add to your success. But in the wrong situations, they will still appear over and over, and they can harm you.

Better to find out clearly what they are, and go where they are valued. Then you will have a happy marriage between you and your environment. Then you will no longer be swimming against the tide, but will let the tide take you to new heights and a new sense of satisfaction.

They say, "Go with the flow." Go with your own flow. Go in the direction you were meant to take. Find out what it is that motivates you, and go with it.

Everyone has a talent. What is rare is the courage to follow the talent to the dark place where it leads.

Erica Jong

... [T]endencies and aspirations are more important...it is more important what people want to be than what people actually are.

John Lukacs, *A History of the Cold War*

When you find out what you are inside, it will give you great energy and a happy obsession to realize it. When this happens, people say that their jobs are fun, and not work at all. There is nothing else they would rather be doing.

There is a freedom in fulfilling your function in the world—to know you are in the right place, doing what is right for you. You are fulfilled when you know what you are, know what you are supposed to be doing on this earth, and are doing it. When what you should be doing hits you, and you make it a conscious part of yourself, you won't get easily sidetracked. You will know what's right for you, and you will care.

Many of us live as though the momentum in our lives is generated by others. There is often a sense of anguish when the realization emerges that we have to generate our own momentum by the images we have of ourselves and the future.

Herbert Rappaport, Ph.D., *Marking Time*

Accept yourself as you are and be grateful. Then go for it. Be who God made you and do it all the way. Don't hold yourself back, but turn to face the world. Take your dreams and goals seriously, and your life will be simpler and have direction.

If you don't know what your dreams and goals are, then think about yourself. Do the Seven Stories exercise and observe the real you—the *you* who does certain things no matter what. Ask a friend to help you, and find the threads running through your life.

You have plenty of time. How many more years do you have left? Let's say you'll be very active until the age of 70, 80, or more. How many years is that? Perhaps I have 20 more active years—maybe 30. A lot can happen in 20 or 30 years. Is it too late for me? Is it too late for you? Probably not.

Don't rush toward your dreams, but savor every step and enjoy the present. Reaching your goal is not the point. In fact, it does not matter whether you ever reach your goal. Just live each day.

Live your life, enjoy, and make the most of each day. Your goal is simply a guide—not a do-or-die phenomenon. If you can have a goal and enjoy the process of getting there, you have truly lived. It's the *process* that's important.

Why, sometimes I believed as many as six impossible things before breakfast.

Lewis Carroll, *Alice in Wonderland*

It's your life. Play a little. Take chances. You will succeed if you aren't too rigid about succeeding. Test things out. See what works. Don't try to hold on too tightly.

Our dreams recur. Perhaps yours are so deep and so quashed that you don't know what they are. Let them come out, then test them later to see how true they are for you. Dreams are serious things, and you might as well live them. Because, when you are old, you will find great satisfaction in having lived your dreams—in having lived your life. If you don't try to live your dreams, you may later be filled with regret.

One of the common themes among depressed adults who I see in my practice is the deep sense of regret for not "stretching oneself" at different stages of life.

Herbert Rappaport, Ph.D., *Marking Time*

There is only one success—to be able to spend your life in your own way.

Christopher Morley

Advance steadily in the direction of your goal, and don't worry about how long it will take you to get there. You will get there as soon as you can anyway. I've seen people advance steadily for many, many years. They somehow wound up doing amazing things that would have seemed impossible and frightening if they had concentrated on them earlier. By taking life one step at a time, and not getting anxious about the future, they moved ahead, taking small steps, but lots of them. The steps that followed seemed smaller still, and not frightening, and they became the persons they were meant to be. They followed their own, not completely defined dreams. As they lived each step, the next step became more clear.

Goals evolve as we test and see what feels right for us. We try a step, and sometimes step back rather than take our lives in a direction that we thought would be right but was not. And then, after a number of years, we look back, amazed at our own progress and surprised that this could

165

happen to us—sure of our direction, still taking the steps one at a time, and testing our direction as we go.

And so our lives unfold. The excitement is in the present—the hope is in the future, and we know we are truly part of the universe as much as each star and each tree. We belong here—doing our part, full of life and living what was once a dream, and unafraid of failure.

Ah, but a man's reach should exceed his grasp,
Or what's a heaven for?

ROBERT BROWNING, "ANDREA DEL SARTO"

There are some elemental truths about yourself that define the real you. You may have buried them over time, but now stay tuned in and see if you can uncover them. Sometimes these deep dreams of yours may shock your family and friends, and may even shock you. Better that you should know what they are.

I once had a client who had very low self-esteem, and had been doing safe work at a major corporation. He would sit hunched, with his head turned up toward where I was sitting, and he would meekly talk about the interviews he was going on. He didn't have a clue about what he should do with his life. There was so much confusion between what he thought he should do and what he had done in the past, it was very difficult for him to find some direction to head toward.

Then one day, as we were discussing all the usual things, this timid, hunched-over person said in a bland tone, "You can't imagine how thrilled I'd be if I could be the leader, running the entire thing and being completely in control."

It seemed impossible that these strong words were coming out of this person's mouth. Looking at him made it seem even more unlikely, yet there was some deep, elemental truth about what he wanted for himself. I wrote down what he said because it was one of those truths that can be so easily lost—so easily dismissed with a "Let's be realistic, honey."

I believe that if this person keeps his dream in mind, he will someday be an incredibly dynamic person, *in charge of the whole thing*— whatever that may be. He will learn to hold himself better, to sound more dynamic, and to look the part. And when this dynamic winner emerges, it will be the real him. I believe that the timid, play-it-safe person is not the real him, but some twisted person that emerged when the real him was submerged.

And, if this person remembers his dream, he will surely advance toward it. Ten years from now, he will look back and find it hard to believe that he is the same person. The living comes not in finally reaching his dream—the living comes in becoming the kind of person he truly is deep inside. The living comes in his day-to-day life as he simply lives it.

Those words were the most important he ever said during the many hours I spent with him. It will take him years to be the real him—that's been buried for so long. But what a happy way to spend 10 years. I can't think of a better way to live them—concentrating each day on the task before him, but remembering the person he was meant to be—finding his own place in the universe and being proud of it.

I spent a large part of my life being a loser, which I think adds an interesting dimension to my personality.

MICHAEL CAINE, *Acting in Film*

As you're the only one you can really change, the only one who can really use all your good advice is yourself.

JOHN-ROGERS AND PETER MCWILLIAMS

Congratulations!

Dear Reader:

Congratulations on completing this program. You have just taken an important step toward achieving greater professional satisfaction and success. Because of your efforts, you have increased your understanding of yourself and your goals. This will lead to more effective career decisions.

I know this has been a very intensive process. You are to be congratulated for taking some time out of your busy schedule simply to think about yourself—what's important to you, what you want to achieve, and how you might do that.

Next Steps

What happens next depends on the goals you have set for yourself. You may choose to make improvements in your present position—to make it better suit your long-term goals.

You may want to work with an individual Five O'Clock Club career coach—to review your results and get a professional's point of view.

You may also wish to read the other books in the career-development series provided by The Five O'Clock Club, starting with *Packaging Yourself: The Targeted Résumé*.

Finally, you may want to join The Five O'Clock Club's weekly small-group strategy sessions. Join other ambitious, intelligent people like yourself. You will receive guidance and have fun while you are learning how to manage your career.

Membership in The Five O'Clock Club is for life—it's your Club for improving your career. We are dedicated to giving you the specific information you need to survive and thrive in this changing economy.

Here's to continued success in your career. We wish you growth—in personal satisfaction, inner peace, and financial comfort. We'd like to continue to travel along with you. I hope you feel the same.

Love and cheers!
Kate

The
Five
O'Clock
Club®

PART FIVE

THE FIVE O'CLOCK CLUB

APPROACH TO
JOB SEARCH

An Overview of
The Five O'Clock Club Process

Facts are friendly. Facts that tend to reinforce what you are doing and give you a warm glow are nice, because they help in terms of psychic reward. Facts that raise alarms are equally friendly, because they give you clues about how to respond, how to change, where to spend the resources.

IRWIN MILLER, FORMER CEO, CUMMINS ENGINE CO.,
THE RENEWAL FACTOR (RANDOM HOUSE, INC.)

Start Here:

1. Targeting a Great Career

- Figure out who you are, what you enjoy doing, and what you want to do with your life—and your career.
- Develop your job targets by industry, field or profession, and geographic area.

2. Packaging Yourself: The Targeted Résumé

- Develop a résumé that separates you from your competition and makes you look appropriate to your targets.

- Then you'll be desirable when you go in for an interview.
- Remember, the average résumé is looked at for only ten seconds.

3. Shortcut Your Job Search: Get Meetings That Get You the Job

- Use the Internet and other techniques properly.
- Get lots of interviews.
- Refer to the extensive bibliography to uncover lists of organizations in your target market.

4. Mastering the Job Interview and Winning the Money Game

- Turn those job interviews into job offers.
- Answer those difficult interview questions The Five O'Clock Club way.
- Use our Four-Step Salary Negotiation Method to get what you deserve.
- Start out on the right foot in your new job.

5. Navigating Your Career: Develop Your Plan, Manage Your Boss, Get Another Job Inside

- Learn how to get ahead in your present organization.
- Enhance your interpersonal skills.
- Have a career-development discussion with your boss.
- Get the assignments you really want.

6. WorkSmarts: Be a Winner on the Job

- Build Relationships; Achieve Results
- Navigate Politics and Personalities
- Manage Conflict with Style

And be sure to listen to our terrific audio CDs (or downloads) on each of 16 topics. Most people play them over and over.

He that will not apply new remedies must expect new evils.

FRANCIS BACON, ENGLISH PHILOSOPHER

Here's an *overview* of the entire job-search process—the Five O'Clock Club way. The Five O'Clock Club uses a methodical, organized approach to job search. Each topic in this section is covered in much greater detail in our job-search book series and CDs. The techniques we teach work for those who are looking for consulting work, as well as those who want an on-payroll job. In fact, 15% of the people who attend The Five O'Clock Club are looking for consulting work.

These techniques work when you're looking for consulting work, too. However, our book, *Your Great Business Idea: The Truth About Making It Happen*, covers everything you need to know about starting a business of any kind.

We have come out of the time when obedience, the acceptance of discipline, intelligent courage and resolution were most important, into that more difficult time when it is a person's duty to understand the world rather than simply fight for it.

ERNEST HEMINGWAY

Most people *think* they're job searching when they get an interview and go on an interview. That's not a job search. That's just getting interviews and going on interviews. They're just hoping they'll get lucky and that somebody will hire them.

Most people follow the latest fads, expecting something magical to save them from having to do a full search. Over the years, job hunters have debated such things as using a certain color of résumé paper to give them an edge. One of the most recent fads was answering ads on the Internet, but studies have shown that only 4 percent of active job hunters get jobs that way. *The Wall Street Journal* once featured a middle-aged professional man who stood on a street corner wearing a sandwich board with the message that he wanted to work. Did he get a job that way? No, but he could then claim that he had tried *everything* and nothing had worked.

So, forget fads and gimmicks and do it our way. There is no harm in trying something faddish (say, 1 percent of your time!), but make The Five O'Clock Club approach the basis for your search.

And remember, to get momentum going, someone who is unemployed should spend 35 hours a week on his or her search. There's much more to do than you can imagine. Those who are working full time need to spend 15 hours a week on a part-time search, but most of those hours will be in the evenings and on weekends, doing research, writing emails and letters, and following up after meetings.

The members of your small group are all using our methodical, organized approach to job search. You can land that dream job at any point in your search, but don't skip a step in the process. Your search will actually go more quickly if you touch every step. What's more, with the Five O'Clock Club approach, you'll be able to tell if things are working for you or not.

Self-respect is the fruit of discipline; the sense of dignity grows with the ability to say no to oneself.

ABRAHAM J. HESCHEL, QUOTED IN RUTH M. GOODHILL, ED., *THE WISDOM OF HESCHEL*

Here's one way to look at the process:
1. **Figure out the kind of job you want.**
2. **Develop a résumé that makes you look appropriate.**
3. **Get lots of interviews.**
4. **Measure how well you are doing.**
5. **Interview like a consultant.**
6. **Follow up intelligently.**
7. **Have fun!!!**

You've got to get obsessed and stay obsessed.

JOHN IRVING, *The Hotel*

First, figure out the kind of job you want by going through the exercises in this book—especially the Seven Stories Exercise and the Forty-Year Vision. You'll come up with job targets—the kinds of places where you want to work in the long run—and be better able to focus on the kind of work you'd like to do in your next job.

Then, you'll develop a *résumé* that makes you look appropriate to these targets—so that you'll be desirable when you go in for an interview.

Next, we'll help you get plenty of *interviews* in your target markets. And, we'll show you how to measure how well you're doing in your search, so you can determine whether or not you're meeting the right people and how well you're doing in those meetings.

We'll teach you how to interview like a consultant, which will keep you calm—and help you ask the right questions during the interview.

Then we'll show you how to follow up intelligently—so you can turn those job interviews into offers and get the salary you deserve.

And, finally, we want you to have FUN in the process. If you're not keeping some fun in your life, you won't interview well, and you'll take longer to get a job.

The world fears a new experience more than it fears anything. Because a new experience displaces so many old experiences....The world doesn't fear a new idea. It can pigeon-hole any idea. But it can't pigeon-hole a real new experience.

D. H. LAWRENCE

What Is a Target?

Everything starts with your job targets. We say, "If your targets are wrong, everything is wrong." Nothing in your search is going to work out well if your targets are vague or ill-defined for long. Targets are the starting point, the basis for everything else you do in your search.

If your targets are wrong, everything is wrong.

Every man is born into the world to do something unique and something distinctive and if he or she does not do it, it will never be done.

BENJAMIN E. MAYS, "I KNEW CARTER G. WOODSON," *NEGRO HISTORY BULLETIN*, JANUARY-MARCH 1981

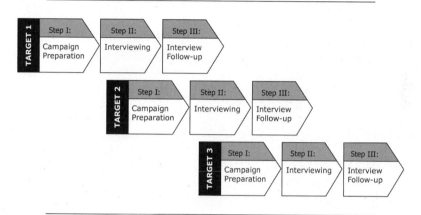

ASSESSMENT

Consists of:

- The Seven Stories Exercise
- Interests
- Values
- Satisfiers and Dissatisfiers
- Your Fifteen- or Forty-Year Vision

Results in:

- As many targets as you can think of
- A ranking of your targets
- A résumé that makes you look appropriate to your first target
- A plan for conducting your search

TARGET 1

Step I:	Step II:	Step III:
Campaign Preparation	Interviewing	Interview Follow-up

TARGET 2

Step I:	Step II:	Step III:
Campaign Preparation	Interviewing	Interview Follow-up

TARGET 3

Step I:	Step II:	Step III:
Campaign Preparation	Interviewing	Interview Follow-up

RESULTS

Step I:
Campaign Preparation.
Results in:
- ❏ Research (list of companies)
- ❏ Résumé
- ❏ Cover letter
- ❏ Plan for getting interviews
  - networking
  - direct contact
  - search firms
  - ads

Step II:
Interviewing.
Results in:
- ❏ Giving them information to keep them interested in you
- ❏ Getting information so you can "move it along"
- ❏ Plan for follow-up (You may do several in-depth follow-ups with each person)

Step III:
Follow-Up.
Results in:
- ❏ Aiming to have 6 to 10 things in the works, and

Job Offers!

A job target consists of:

- an industry or company size where you think you'd like to work, let's say for example, banking or health care;
- a specific position within those industries, something that you think you'd enjoy doing, such as marketing; and
- a certain geographic area, let's say St. Louis.

Those *three* elements make up a target, and, as you will see, each target may have 5, 10, 20, or more positions. In the beginning of your search, come up with as many targets as you possibly can in case you need more targets later on in your search. You'll conduct a Preliminary Target Investigation (through the Internet and networking) on your first list of targets. This will help you refine your Targeting Map, which will guide your search. Of course, we'll show you how to do all of this.

If you will be working with a private coach in addition to your small group coach: Prior to the first private coaching session, send your coach your current résumé, no matter how good or bad it may be, and the results of the Seven Stories Exercise. You and your coach can discuss your Fifteen- and Forty-Year Vision and brainstorm potential targets. Your coach may assign you other exercises or instruments that are right for you, and will help you with your résumé.

Prepare Your Résumé

There's a lot of talk about self-esteem these days. It seems pretty basic to me. If you want to feel proud of yourself, you've got to do things you can be proud of. Feelings follow actions.

OSEOLA MCCARTY, A WASHERWOMAN WHO GAVE HER LIFE SAVINGS OF $150,000 TO HELP COMPLETE STRANGERS GET A COLLEGE EDUCATION.

When you have completed the exercises in this book, you will be in a better position to develop a résumé that makes you look appropriate to your targets. Then you will be desirable when you go in for a meeting. Remember, the average résumé is looked at for only 10 seconds. So, it's vital that key ideas or words pop out. Can the reader *easily* figure out your level? If you say, I "install computer systems," you could be making anywhere from $15,000 to $200,000. Is your résumé accomplishment oriented or just a job description? Work with your private coach and your small group to make your résumé stand out. It will not stand out if it reads like a job description.

Résumés are a complicated matter, and that's why we have an entire book on the subject.

Duty largely consists of pretending that the trivial is critical.

JOHN FOWLES, *THE MAGUS*

Starting Your Targeting Map

Once you've thought of a few tentative job targets, you are ready to work on your Targeting Map. This Map will guide you throughout your entire job search.

In my small group, I often ask someone to name something that he or she is targeting and the group helps that person brainstorm how to go after that target. Let's say Joe is targeting *investment advisor*—a job that involves giving investment advice. Jim and his group might start brainstorming where a person could do investment advisory work: perhaps commercial banks, investment banks, hedge funds, insurance companies, or mutual funds.

So far, Joe is targeting a position (investment advisor) and the industries that we just named. Finally, the formula is complete when he names the geographic area. Joe said he was interested in both New York and Chicago.

Develop *Your* Targeting Map Based on Targets

The position:

"Investment advisor"—a job where I would give investment advice

The industries:

commercial banks
investment banks
hedge funds
insurance companies
mutual funds

The geographic areas:

New York and Chicago

Segmenting Your Targets

A person may say that she wants to work in the not-for-profit area. This is not a target because it's too broad.

Not-for-profit could include associations, hospitals, universities, the government—and each of those sub-targets is huge!

Breaking your targets into manageable sub-targets is called *segmenting your targets*.

"Not-for-profit" is too broad to be useful.

It could include:
- associations
- hospitals
- universities
- the government
—and all of those sub-targets are huge!

What if Susan wants to target health care? Health care is unwieldy as a target! It could include, for example, hospitals, home health care, HMOs, pharmaceutical companies, nursing homes, hospice care, health insurance companies, crisis intervention programs, congregate care facilities, medical billing, health-care consulting firms, medical device manufacturers, and distributors. (Who makes the catheters? And who makes the beds?)

You could go on and on. Health care could also be anything having to do with the aging of America, for example. You could brainstorm lots of other job targets having to do with health care itself.

We'll talk more about Susan's search later, but let's go back to our investment advisor example. I would say to Joe, "How many commercial banks would you say are appropriate for you to consider? Name a number, any number." (Of course, job hunters don't really know, but I want them to name something.) And Joe would give me a rough guess. "Let's say there are approximately 24 commercial banks," he would say. "Twenty-four investment banks, twenty hedge funds—all within my targeted geographic areas. Let's also say there are six insurance companies, eight mutual funds, and so on."

Break Your Targets Down into Sub-targets

Health care, for example, could include:
- home health care
- HMOs
- pharmaceutical companies
- nursing homes
- hospice care
- health insurance companies
- crisis intervention programs
- congregate care facilities
- medical billing
- health-care consulting firms
- medical device manufacturers
- distributors
- government agencies
- quasi-governmental agencies

Rank Your Targets—To Organize Your Work

The only joy in the world is to begin.

CESARE PAVESE, ITALIAN WRITER

So Joe, our investment advisor, has a lot of targets: commercial banks, investment banks, hedge funds. It's just too much. In addition to segmenting his targets, he also has to rank his targets. If he doesn't rank them, he will be scattered and ineffective. His list is too big and too unwieldy.

Health care could also include:
- Anything having to do with the aging of America
- Vitamin companies
- Health-care publishing
- Lots of other subcategories, depending on your interests

Joe must organize his work. My next question is: "What is your target #1?" Joe says his target #1—the place where he would most like to work—is commercial banking. So I respond, "Let's analyze commercial banks. How many positions would a typical commercial bank have that would be appropriate for you?" Joe doesn't really know the answer. Would there be one position or ten? We're talking about *positions*, not job openings. Positions.

Sub-targets For Our Investment Advisor Example

"How many commercial banks are appropriate for you to consider? Name a number, any number." Approximately:

- 24 commercial banks
- 24 investment banks
- 20 hedge funds—all within your targeted geographic areas
- 6 insurance companies
- 8 mutual funds—and so on

Joe doesn't really know the answer, but I push him to guess. Joe says, "Well, out of 24 commercial banks that I'm targeting, I think each one might have an average of 10 positions that are appropriate for me" (*positions*, not openings). So Joe is targeting 240 positions at just those 24 banks. That is a lot of positions!

In fact, we know from our research that, to be successful in your search in a reasonable time frame, you must target 200 positions. So you can see that Joe is going after 240 positions in just this one target area, increasing the likelihood of a successful search. So you can see that if you are targeting a *smaller* number of positions, you will have a longer search. Chances are, *you* can come up with targets with a total of at least 200 positions. Of course, this takes a lot of research and hard work. You will find a 111-page bibliography of job-search resources in the Members Only section of our website (www.FiveOClockClub.com) and also in our book *Shortcut Your Job Search*.

Target #1: Commercial Banks

"How many *positions* would a typical commercial bank have that would be appropriate for you?"

So rank your targets. Decide which targets you want to go after first, second, third, fourth. It may be, if you are desperate, you'll focus first on the target where you are most likely to get a job. If you are not desperate and have time to explore—maybe you're employed right now— then maybe your first target is your dream job, the thing you've always wanted to explore. So your first step is to rank your targets.

Then measure your targets. If the total number of positions you're going after is fewer than 200, that's not good.

Remember that we are not totaling job openings, but *positions*. And it does not matter if the positions are filled right now. You are trying to avoid targets that are just too small. Those searches are doomed from the start.

Target #1: 24 Commercial Banks

An average of 10 positions at each bank Joe is targeting 240 positions at just these 24 banks. That is a lot of positions!

As a separate but very relevant issue, think about the state of the market within each of those targets. Some markets are growing and some markets are retrenching. If your target market is retrenching, you'll need to go after even more positions.

On the other hand, if it's growing and people are getting hired, you may be able to get away with targeting fewer positions.

> **Calculate the number of *positions*, not job openings. It doesn't matter if the positions are filled right now.**

> **To get a job within a reasonable time, target 200 positions—not openings— positions.**

Now, take a look at Joe's targets in more detail. Let's say he's targeting commercial banks as Target #1. And investment banks as Target #2. He's targeting two dozen companies in each of these targets.

> **Most people start out with targets that are just too small. Their searches are *doomed*.**

If you cannot catch a bird of paradise, better take a wet hen.

NIKITA S. KHRUSHCHEV, QUOTED IN *TIME*, JANUARY 6, 1958

Developing Your A-List, B-List, C-List

But Joe needs to divide up his list of commercial banks: The A-list includes companies he would die to work for; the companies that he would consider *okay* to go into are the B-list; and the C-list companies are actually of no interest to him.

Joe should contact his C-list companies first to get his feet wet and use them for practice. Because he does not care that much about them, he will probably be more relaxed and confident and will interview well. He is *practicing*. He will also be testing his market to see if he gets a good response from these C-list companies.

Many are stubborn in pursuit of the path they have chosen, few in pursuit of the goal.

FRIEDRICH NIETZSCHE

If the companies on Joe's C-list are not interested in him, that's important for him to know. He needs to talk to the people in his small group to find out what he is doing wrong. However, if he is well received by the companies on his C-list, then Joe can contact the companies on his B-list. He could say something like, "I am already talking to a number of companies in your industry (which is true), but I didn't want to accept a job with any of them (which is also true) until I had a chance to talk with you." This script is just one approach. Be sure to talk to your small group about the right things for you to say to those on your B-list.

> • **Your A-list: You'd love to work there.**
> • **Your B-list: They're okay.**
> • **Your C-list: They don't interest you.**

Your search will have more impact if it is focused by targets and segments of targets. For example, if Susan is going after the health-care market, talking to all of the hospitals on her list within a certain period gives her credibility. She can say, "Oh, I talked to..." and name the hospital that she talked to yesterday, "and what is happening there is this. I am really interested in working for a hospital." It makes her sound believable.

> **Contact C-list companies first.**

Remember what we said above about segmenting your targets. The pitch that you use with one of these targets, say, hospitals, will be very different from the pitch you would use-with a different target, say, health-care manufacturers.

> **"I am already talking to a number of companies in your industry, but I didn't want to accept a job with any of them until I had a chance to talk with you."**

Your approach cannot be casual—even in the initial stages of your search. You might be tempted to say in an interview, "I don't care whether I work for a hospital or a manufacturer, so long as I have some connection to health care. I can do what I want to do just about anywhere." You may not care, but your prospective employers care. They want to know that you understand—and care about—*their* industry.

> **If you are well received by organizations on your C-list, move on to your B-list.**

The Five O'Clock Club

Getting Lots of Meetings

If I try to use human influence strategies and tactics of how to get other people to do what I want, to work better, to be more motivated, to like me and each other—while my character is fundamentally flawed, marked by duplicity and insincerity—then, in the long run, I cannot be successful. My duplicity will breed distrust, and everything I do—even using so-called good human relations techniques—will be perceived as manipulative....
Only basic goodness gives life to technique.

STEPHEN R. COVEY, *THE SEVEN HABITS OF HIGHLY EFFECTIVE PEOPLE* (CBS CORPORATION)

Developing a Detailed Targeting Map

It's best to focus on one target for a condensed period. For example, Susan can make a list of all of the hospitals within the geographic area she's interested in. This list will become her Targeting Map. Let's say there are 80 hospitals that are appropriate for her; she would put those on her list. Then she would mount a campaign to get plenty of meetings in that target area, hospitals. A second target could be health-care manufacturers. She would make a second list, this one containing manufacturers she considered appropriate for her in her geographic area

> **Make a list of organizations within each target. Eighty hospitals in Susan's geographic area are appropriate for her.**

Then, *stagger* your targets so you can focus on each target in turn. Susan will focus on the hospitals first, and when that's under way, she'll start on the health-care manufacturers. To get plenty of meetings, she'll consider all four basic techniques for getting meetings in her target markets. The techniques are:

- Networking—that is, using someone's name to get a meeting,
- Contacting people directly when you don't have a networking contact,
- Answering ads, and
- Talking to search firms.

The opposite of love is not hate, it's indifference.
The opposite of art is not ugliness, it's indifference.
The opposite of faith is not heresy, it's indifference.
And the opposite of life is not death, it's indifference.

ELIE WIESEL

If you try all four techniques, you can see which techniques result in meetings for you. Use more of *those* techniques. Use Internet ads, for example, *if* they result in meetings for you. If they don't result in meetings, concentrate on other approaches.

> **Make sure every *manager* in your target market knows that you exist.**

Susan has 80 hospitals in her first target. Remember that the managers in those hospitals don't even know that she exists. You want potential employers to hear about you within a reasonable time. Certainly you can contact search firms and answer ads, but only 20 percent of all jobs are filled through search firms and ads. So consider two other techniques— networking and contacting organizations directly. Your goal is to make sure that as many managers as possible know about you within a reasonable time.

Methods for Getting Meetings in Your Target Areas:

- Networking (40 percent of meetings)
- Direct contact (40 percent)
- Search firms (10 percent)
- Ads (print and Internet) (10 percent)

Let's reemphasize an important distinction here. Networking means using someone else's name to get a meeting ("Sue suggested I contact you."). Direct contact means pursuing people whom you may have known in the past, but especially people you have never met: association members, or key people identified on the Internet, through newspaper or magazine articles, or from library research.

Heroes come in all sizes, and you don't have to be a giant hero. You can be a very small hero. It's just as important to understand that accepting self-responsibility for the things you do, having good manners, caring about other people—these are heroic acts. Everybody has the choice of being a hero or not being a hero every day of their lives.

George Lucas, *Time*, April 26, 1999

By the way, when we say that you should "make sure everyone on your target list knows that you exist within a reasonable time," we mean *managers*. We don't mean human resources, unless you want a job in human resources.

But you cannot *network* into 80 organizations within a reasonable time. The last thing you want is to find out you're too late! If you rely primarily on networking, you may get around to contacting an organization three months into your search and hear one of them say,

---

"We just filled a position. I wish we had met you before."

So, if you have a list of 80 companies you want to contact, divide up your list. Perhaps you can network into 5 or 6. If you know someone who can refer you in, use his or her name, contact the hiring manager, and say, "Jim Smith suggested I contact you."

That would leave 75 more organizations out of your list of 80. Select 20 of those that you really want to get in to see, even though you don't have a connection. It doesn't matter if they don't have any openings—you don't know that anyway. To these 20, you would send a *targeted* mailing and follow up with a phone call.

That would leave 55 organizations on your list. For the remaining 55, you could do a direct-mail campaign. That is, you would send your cover letter and résumé, but you would not follow up with a phone call. You're just letting them know that you exist, so if they have a need for someone like you, they'll give you a call. By combining these various job-search techniques, you will be able to contact all of the organizations on your list within a reasonable time.

Get Lots of Meetings

ABC company
Avrey
Acme
Allister Metal
Goopers
Haskell
Jesking
Alcoa
Fortunoff
Patricin
Costco
Hormell
DiscCity
Oliphant
Divide up your list. If you have a list of 80 companies:

- **Network** into **5 or 6** if you can
- Send a **targeted mailing** to 20 (with a phone call follow-up)
- For the remaining **55**, use a **direct-mail campaign** (with NO follow-up)

My Own Case Study

When I was working for a tiny advertising agency in Lancaster, Pennsylvania, a very long time ago, I needed to move to New York because of a family situation. I didn't know anyone in New York, so I could not have networked into any companies there.

I did my research and identified about 60 advertising agencies in New York, as well as the correct people to contact. For the *large* advertising agencies, I identified the names of three managers who seemed appropriate—the president would have been too high up for me to contact. For the small and mid-sized agencies, I wrote directly to the president.

Part of the challenge in your search is picking the right person to contact, say a department head or division head.

For my own search, I identified 60 advertising agencies. and the correct person to contact at each.

- **For the large advertising agencies, three names of managers who seemed appropriate to me.**
- **For the small and mid-sized agencies, I wrote to the president.**

Direct-mail campaigns formed the basis of my search. That is, I wrote to the appropriate people in those companies, but did not make follow-up phone calls. Out of 60 companies, I got about five phone calls saying,

"Why don't you come in for a meeting?"

When I went in for the meetings, I treated them exactly like networking meetings—not job interviews. When I was there, I tried to network into *other* firms in New York. That was my total campaign. Because I was searching from out-of-town, I took off from work every other Friday. Then I could say to a company, "I'll be back in town again in two weeks. Is there anybody else I could meet with in your firm?" *This* technique is networking: getting in to see someone by using someone else's name.

You can see that I got momentum going by combining direct contact with networking. My search started when I contacted companies directly, met with people, and asked them to help me network into other companies. Or you can start your search by networking into organizations and asking them for a list of other organizations you can contact directly without using that person's name.

> **These meetings are not job interviews, treat them like networking meetings.**
>
> - **Try to network into other firms.**
> - **"I'll be back in town in two weeks. Is there anybody else I could meet in your firm?"**
> - **"Here's a list of companies I'm interested in. What do you think of them?" (Show your Targeting Map.)**
> - **Combine direct contact with networking.**

So consider all four techniques for getting interviews in your target areas: Get momentum going by contacting search firms, answering ads, networking, and, most importantly, by contacting companies directly.

I have seen the future, and it's a lot like the present, but much longer.

DAN QUISENBERRY, PROFESSIONAL BASEBALL PLAYER

This Information Is Based on Over 25 Years of Research

I know this is a lot for you to digest, but there's even *more* to tell you. And, in the long run, our approach is much more efficient than simply hitting the *send* button on your computer and waiting for a reply. Historically, the average person attending The Five O'Clock Club has found a new job or is in the negotiating stage within 10 weekly sessions.

Most members read the books, listen to the lectures on audio CDs, and attend the weekly small-group strategy sessions at the same time. Our various resources complement each other. Furthermore, your small-group members as well as your career coach will keep you on track and help you with your specific situation. You will master the material over time, and *your future job searches* will be easier because you will use the same methodology the next time you search.

Our methodology is based on more than 25 years of research, and we continually conduct research to develop the best techniques. Let's put this in perspective. During the depths of the 1987 to 1992 recession, when the average American was taking 8.1 months to find a job, the average Five O'Clock Clubber found a new job in just 10 weeks! Even those who had been unemployed 9 to 18 months when we met them found jobs in just 10 weeks. And this was at a time when there were few jobs available.

Not only did these long-term unemployed people find jobs, they found jobs that paid what they were worth in the market. They did *not* take pay cuts just because they had been unemployed a long time.

So you see, there's hope even for those who are targeted to give up hope. Your situation might not be dire. Or perhaps your situation is dire for your market and for the kind of job you're looking for. But the Five O'Clock Club can give you hope. Now you know that there's a methodology you can follow—one that's proven to work. We have specialized in tough searches!

> **During depths of a bad recession (1987-1992):**
> - **Average American took 8.1 months to find a job.**
> - **Five O'Clock Clubbers found a new job in an average of just 10 weekly sessions—even those who had already been unemployed 9 months to 1.5 years when we met them.**
> - **They got paid what they were worth in the market—despite their long-term unemployment.**

When You've Lost the Spirit to Job Hunt

Everyone else seems to be doing terrific! You're barely hanging on. You used to be a winner. Now what can you do?

1. **Put things in perspective.**
   You've worked 10 or 20 years, and you're not done yet. You do have a future, you know. Being unemployed and depressed can make it hard to see this truth.
2. **Get support.**
   Join the Club! Relying solely on yourself is not the answer. Job hunters can feel vulnerable and uncared for. They walk into walls and have accidents.
3. **Remember that this is part of a bigger picture.**
   Learn from this experience and make some sense of it. Decide what is important to you now.
4. **Continue to do your job—which is job *hunting*!**
   Sometimes you didn't feel like doing your *old* job, but you did it anyway. Now your focus is finding something new, so get it done! Organize. Make that call. Have fun.

It's true that when God closes a door, He opens a window. But the hallways are hell.

SOL WACHTLER, CHIEF JUDGE, STATE OF NEW YORK COURT OF APPEALS, AFTER SERVING TIME IN JAIL

I do not believe they are right who say that the defects of famous men should be ignored. I think it is better we should know them. Then, though we are conscious of having faults as glaring as theirs, we can believe that that is no hindrance to our achieving also something of their virtues.

W. SOMERSET MAUGHAM, *THE MAUGHAM READER* (DOUBLEDAY)

So, let's see where you are. So far:
1. You've brainstormed your targets. That is, you've thought about the industries and the fields you want to go after. And you've brainstormed as many targets as possible—with the help of your coach or you small group.
2. You've ranked your targets: *Hospitals* is your first target. *Health-care manufacturers* is your second.
3. You're aiming to have a focused, compact search. You've decided to go after all the hospitals at the same time so you can say, "I'm talking to so-and-so at Presbyterian Hospital right now." This gives you credibility.

That's where you are in your search. Now we'll talk about how you can plan and organize your entire job-search campaign. In our books and CDs, we cover each of these areas in great detail: how to do your résumé; how to interview; how to negotiate salary.
But here we are presenting an overview of the entire job search.

It is work, work that one delights in, that is the surest guarantor of happiness.

ASHLEY MONTAGU, *THE AMERICAN WAY OF LIFE*

Job-Search Campaign Management

Every man is born into the world to do something unique and something distinctive and if he or she does not do it, it will never be done.

Benjamin E. Mays, "I Knew Carter G. Woodson," *Negro History Bulletin*, January-March 1981

Campaign Overview

Conduct a Campaign Aimed at Each Target (industry, position, field)

Now we'll give you an overview of how to plan and organize your entire campaign and bring it all together. The goal of your campaign is to get lots of meetings. You may get excited when you line up one job interview, but when that interview falls apart, you have to start all over again to get another one. Because of the lack of momentum, this kind of one-at-a-time search can last for many, many months.

We're trying to increase your chance for success, so you'll have three concurrent offers and then you can *pick the job that will position you best*

for the long term. So just hang in there. Trust us on this, and follow the rest of the process.

Here's what a campaign aimed at one target might look like. Let's say that target #1 for you is hospitals. There's a planning step, an interviewing step, and a follow-up step.

In the Planning Step:

- **Make a list of all the hospitals** that are appropriate for you in your targeted geographic area. We talked about this earlier.
- **Develop what we call your Two-Minute Pitch**. That is, in the hospital market, how do you respond when people say, "Tell me about yourself." For example, your pitch to hospitals might be, "I have 10 years of marketing experience in the health-care indus-

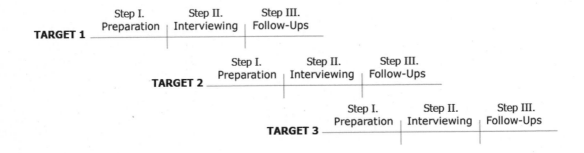

try. In fact, at one company, I increased sales by 50 percent in one product line." Your pitch to hospitals might be very different from your pitch to manufacturing companies in the health-care field. For that target, you may want to emphasize different accomplishments.

- **Be sure your *résumé* makes you look appropriate** to the hospital market. If you've never worked in a hospital before, get rid of jargon that applied to your old industry, and use the jargon of the hospital industry.

- Next, you'll **develop your plan for getting meetings** in this target market. That is, make a short list of search firms you can contact, scrutinize the ads for information and find those that would require a direct-contact approach, identify the organizations you'll be able to network into, and directly contact the others.

The Two-Minute Pitch

The way you position yourself is used throughout your search:

- at the top of your résumé,
- in your interviews,
- in your networking meetings, and
- in your cover letters (second paragraph).

It is the response to "So, tell me about yourself." A great pitch helps people see you as appropriate for the kind of job you are going after. At The Five O'Clock Club we say, "If your pitch is wrong, everything is wrong." That is, if the way you are positioning yourself is wrong, you're derailed from the start and everything else about your search will be wrong. It can't work.

The top of your résumé is your written positioning. The Two-Minute Pitch is your oral positioning. And they must correspond. So, in spite of having spent the past four years in the mortgage industry, the top of Elliott's résumé could read:

**Domestic and International Marketing Manager
with 15 years' experience in the
leisure and sporting goods industry**

This will help him get back into the field he loved. In an interview, when an employer asks, "So tell me about yourself," Elliott could start with the verbal version of that same pitch: "I'm a domestic and international marketing manager with more than 15 years' experience in leisure and sporting goods. I've always emphasized quality and productivity. For example,..." And then he could talk about examples of his accomplishments, which would correspond to some of the bulleted accomplishments at the top of his résumé. When your pitch is correct, you will use it throughout your entire search.

I found that values, for each person, were numerous. Therefore, I proposed to write my value names and to annex to each a short precept—which fully expressed the extent I gave to each meaning. I then arranged them in such a way as to facilitate acquisition of these virtues.

BENJAMIN FRANKLIN

The Interviewing Step

After the Planning Step, you'll be in the Interviewing Step. With the help of your group, you've figured out how to get meetings in your target market.

In the **Interviewing Step**:

- Get information and give information.
- *Don't* try to "close" too soon to get the offer.
- Get another meeting.

Most people think interviews result in job offers. But there are usually a few intervening steps before a final offer is made. Interviews should result in getting and giving information.

- Did you learn the issues important to each person with whom you met?
- What did they think were your strongest positives?
- How can you overcome the decision makers' objections?

Most people try to get offers too early. Instead, try to get the next meeting. After all, most organizations need to see you more than once. Keep in the running.

Don't think like a job hunter who is trying to coax people to hire him. Think like a consultant trying to land a $40,000, $90,000, or $150,000 consulting assignment—whatever your salary is. Job hunters are commonly too passive, fielding questions as best they can. They leave interviews thinking, "I did *so* great answering those questions."

Instead, be more proactive in the interview. Have a pad and pen in hand for taking notes. Find out what's *going on* in the company. Ask

about their *needs*. How can you satisfy those needs? Who's doing what in this organization? How might you fit in? What are the most important problems the organization faces right now?

A consultant takes notes because a consultant knows he has to *analyze* what happened during the meeting and later make a proposal about how to handle the job. Here is the drill for consultants:

- Research the organization thoroughly.
- Dress and look the part.
- Prepare a 3x5 card including the Two-Minute Pitch, as well as several key points.

Find out:

- What is going on? What are their needs?
- How can I satisfy those needs?

Work to outclass your competition.

- Ask how you stack up against others.
- Make sure you have all the information you need.
- Find out when they hope to decide.
- Find out if they have any objections to you.

Plan your follow-up.

- Get and give information.
- Don't try to get an offer right now.
- Get the next meeting.
- Consultants write proposals. So will you!

Think about your competition.

You do have competition, you know. And if you *think* you're the only one being interviewed, you could come away dumb and happy—confident that you did a great job. But you won't know how you stack up *against others* unless you ask! Say to the hiring manager:

- Where are you in the hiring process? Am I first? Second? Last?

- How many other people are you talking to?
- And how do you see me compared with the other people you're talking to?

Ask yourself: Have I gathered all the information I need to write a good proposal about what I would do for this organization? Find out if they're ready to decide now, or if it will take a few months.

Do all you can to keep in the running.

> **Everything you need to know about interviewing, following up after the interview, and salary negotiation is covered extensively in our book *Mastering the Job Interview* and *Winning the Money Game*.**

Just a few other points before we go on to the Follow-Up Step:

Handling Difficult Interview Questions

> **Do not allow the interview to get off track. When the interviewer brings up something that takes you in a direction in which you don't want to go, briefly give a response that satisfies the interviewer, and then get back on track.**

> **Give your answer, and then say, for example, "But I really wanted to tell you about a special project I worked on." It is your responsibility to get the conversation back on track.**

Conduct a campaign aimed at a company.

If Miss Gold is the hiring manager, don't try to see her just yet. Surround the hiring manager. Meet with others, so when you finally get in to see her, you will have several advocates and know a lot about the organization.

Dig for the information you need.

Say to the person who set up the meeting: "I'd like to go in prepared. With whom will I meet?" Ask:

- names and job titles
- issues important to each of them
- what they are like
- tenure with organization

Uncover their objections, just as a consultant would:

- Where are you in the hiring process?
- How many others are you considering?
- How do I stack up against them?
- Is there any reason why you might be reluctant to bring someone like me on board?

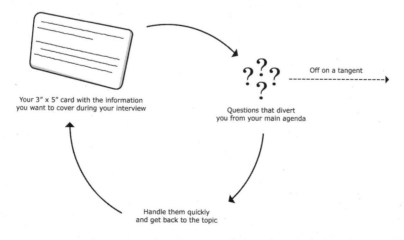

Your 3" x 5" card with the information you want to cover during your interview

? ? ? Off on a tangent

Questions that divert you from your main agenda

Handle them quickly and get back to the topic

Get each interviewer to see you as the ideal.

If you speak to several people, you want each one to advocate having you on board. If anyone objects to you, handle it now.

Cartoon Courtesy © Jerry King

"Relax, Mr. Gray, this is just a simple job interview for a sales position. So, please stop pleading the 5th everytime I ask you a question."

Always have 6 to 10 possibilities going:

- Always try to get the offer—even at companies you don't want to work for. Otherwise, you'll never get 6 to 10 possibilities. That's what momentum is all about.
- Even when an offer seems certain, do not drop other search activities.

Chaos often breeds life, while order breeds habit.

HENRY ADAMS, AMERICAN HISTORIAN

In the interviewing step, you're also *planning* your follow-up. You're not sitting there thinking,

"I hope they make me an offer." Instead you're thinking, "I wonder what I should do to follow up after this interview."

Great is the art of beginning, but greater the art of ending.

HENRY WADSWORTH LONGFELLOW

The Follow-Up Step

After the Planning and Interviewing steps, now you're in the Follow-Up Step. This is the brainiest part of the process. In our book *Mastering the Job Interview and Winning the Salary Game*, you'll read lots of case studies to help you understand this part. But here's a brief story right now.

By the time Jeffrey came to The Five O'Clock Club, he had been interviewing with a telemarketing company for *four* months for the job of marketing head. Yet he wasn't getting an offer. So his small group said to him, "Jeffrey, what do you think might be their *objection* to bringing someone like you on board?" He said, "They're afraid that I don't understand their industry."

Jeffrey's situation was easy for his small group: He needed to let his prospective employer know that he understood their industry. The group suggested he do some research, and find out about the company's competitors. So after doing that, Jeffrey wrote the hiring team a letter that essentially said, "If I came in as head of marketing, here's what I would do." He identified their competitors, how he saw them stacking up against their competitors, and what he would do as head of marketing. They offered Jeffrey a job immediately—*once* he had overcome their objections.

Actually, you'll be doing this intensive follow-up with 6 to 10 different prospective employers at the same time. It's a lot of hard work and brainpower. In fact, you should put as much time and energy into the follow-up step as you did into the planning and interviewing steps.

Five O'Clock Clubbers know that they must put more effort into this part of the process—more than any of their competitors do. They want to make sure their follow-up is better than anyone else's. Then they have a better chance of turning their job interviews into job offers.

Change does not roll in on the wheels of inevitability, but comes through continuous struggle. And so we must straighten our backs and work for our freedom. A man can't ride you unless your back is bent.

REV. MARTIN LUTHER KING, JR., "THE DEATH OF EVIL UPON THE SEASHORE," SERMON GIVEN AT THE CATHEDRAL OF ST. JOHN THE DIVINE, NEW YORK CITY, MAY 17, 1956

Follow Up:

1. The brainiest part of the process:

- **Takes as much time as getting interviews and interviewing.**
- **Keep things alive with 6 to 10 organizations.**
- **Requires brainpower—be sure to get help from your group.**

2. Do not write silly *thank-you* notes after job interviews. Instead, write thoughtful letters and proposals to influence the decision makers.

Using all of these techniques will help you to turn job interviews into OFFERS!

The more I want to get something done, the less I call it work.

RICHARD BACH, *ILLUSIONS*

It's takes brainpower because the kind of follow-up you do depends on:

- the kind of organization you're interviewing with,
- your personality,
- the number of times you've met with the prospective employer (Have you met with five people for one hour each, or have you met with just one person for half an hour?),
- the information you've gathered in those meetings, and
- who your competitors are.

Tell your small group what's going on and get their help to decide what you should do next.

Give every step of your job search the attention it requires, and do as well as you can in each area of your campaign: Planning, Interviewing, Follow-Up. Don't skip any step in the process.

Passion costs me too much to bestow it on every trifle.

THOMAS ADAMS

Step III: Interview Follow-Up
(including salary negotiation)

Follow-Up after a Job Interview

- This is the brainiest part of the process.
- It takes as much time as getting interviews and interviewing.
- Work to keep things alive with 6 to 10 organizations.
- Don't write a silly **thank-you** note after a job interview. Instead, write an **influence** letter or proposal.
- Tailor the follow-up to each situation.
- Build a relationship. If the company says there won't be any hiring until February, that's okay— just keep in touch.
- Whether to call, write, or email is not the issue. Uncovering possible objections to you and *proving* you can do the job are the issues.
- Try to find out: Would *you* be the person chosen when the hiring decision is made?
- Your coach will want to know:
  — Who did you meet with?
  — What are each person's key issues?
  — Why would each want you there?
  — What are each person's objections to you?
  — What can you offer vs. competition?
- Decide the next steps, such as:
  — another meeting; meeting w/others,
  — an in-depth review of documents,
  — developing a few ideas and then meeting, and/or drafting a proposal.
- State the *next steps* in your follow-up note. For example, "I'd like to get together with you to discuss my ideas on..."
- Influence the influencers.
- Be in sync with their timing, not yours.
- If unemployed, be open to consulting work.

Salary Negotiations

- Starts with your first meeting: position yourself so they see you at an appropriate level.
- Mantra: "Salary will not be a problem."
- Manage the process to get the right offer
  — If original offer is too low, that is okay for now.
  — Don't try to close too soon and ruin the deal.
- The Four-Step Salary Negotiation Process:
  1. Negotiate the job.
  2. Outshine and outlast your competition.
  3. Get the offer.
  4. Negotiate the salary.

- Must be done in this order. For example, don't negotiate salary if you have competitors.
- *Grow the job* to make it worth more.
- Find out your worth in the market.
  — Network: "What would you expect to pay some one with my background?"
  — Do research at Salary.com and through associations.
- Make yourself in demand: Having 6 to 10 possibilities is a must
- Don't reject the offer—talk about the job.
- Keep the process open; hear their best offer.
- Postpone salary discussion until the offer.
  — Person who names a number first loses.
  — Talk more about the job.
- Discuss salary using a collaborative tone. This may take more than one meeting.

The amount of money you receive will always be in direct proportion to the demand for what you do, your ability to do it, and the difficulty of replacing you.

DENNIS KIMBRO, *THINK AND GROW RICH: A BLACK CHOICE*

Have 6 to 10 job possibilities in the works at all times. Five will fall away through no fault of your own.

With 6 to 10 things going, you increase your chances of having three good offers to choose from.

When you are in the Interview Step of Target 1, it's time to start the Planning Step of Target 2. This will give you more momentum and insure that you do not let things dry up. Keep both targets going, and then start Target 3.

Our research shows: **Those who regularly attend a small group headed by a Five O'Clock Club coach get better jobs faster and at higher rates of pay than those who search alone or only work privately with a coach.**

Remember...

- Get 3 hours of fun a week—like it or not!!
- Job search in the summer and during holidays.
- "They" never call when they say they will, so follow up by being creatively persistent. The ball is *always* in your court.

Overlap Your Campaigns

*All changes, even the most longed for, have their
melancholy; for what we leave behind is part of
ourselves; we must die to one life before we
can enter into another.*

ANATOLE FRANCE, FRENCH WRITER

When you're in the *interviewing* step of Target
1, say, hospitals, then your main focus will be
hospitals, which means you will customize your
Two-Minute Pitch, your résumé, and your cover
letter. But once those letters are in the mail and
you have had a few meetings with hospitals, you
can start working on Target #2, say, healthcare
equipment manufacturers. When you're in the
interviewing step of Target #2, you can start
working on Target #3, say, HMOs. This staggered,
focused search will result in more meetings and
also keep your momentum going.

For each target:

- **Conduct research to develop a list of all
  the organizations. Find the names of
  people you should contact in the appropriate departments in each of those
  companies.**
- **Develop your cover letter. (Paragraph
  1 is the opening; Paragraph 2 is a summary about yourself appropriate for
  this target; Paragraph 3 contains your
  bulleted accomplishments ("You may
  be interested in some of the things I've
  done"); Paragraph 4 is the close. (Lots of
  sample letters are in our book *Shortcut
  Your Search*.)**
- **Develop your plan for getting lots of
  meetings in this target.**

Target #1: Hospitals

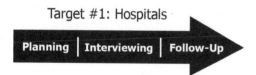

Target #2: Health-Care Equipment

Target #3: HMOs

These organized, overlapping campaigns give you a structured search, as opposed to a scattered search. If you talk to hospitals, health-care manufacturers, HMOs, and anybody else *whenever you feel like it*:

- your pitches will become blurred,
- you will sound less committed to the target,
- you'll have less powerful cover letters,
- you'll get confused,
- your search will take longer, and
- you'll get fewer offers.

Instead, have structured campaigns. So, the most effective approach is to contact every organization in your first target. Give your first target a good try, and within a week or two, you can start on your second target.

Even if you're going after very small targets, where there are only two or three very small companies in each industry, you should still focus on one target at a time.

For example, Marilyn wanted a job in high-end marketing. One of her targets was watch companies, and there were only two watch companies that were of interest to her. Marilyn was also interested in tabletop companies, that is, companies that made fine china. There were only three tabletop companies that were of interest to her in her geographic area.

These are very small targets. Still, Marilyn contacted the two watch companies at the same time, then the three tabletop companies at the same time. Altogether, she had 18 very small targets, and she focused on one at a time. Even if

your targets are very small, focus on one target at a time—even a few hours apart—and you'll do better. Your research will be better, as will your cover letters and your pitch.

> - **Conduct a structured search: Contact every organization in your first target.**
> - **Even if your targets are small, focus on one target at a time.**

...[W]e have to create a new organizational architecture flexible enough to adapt to change. We want an organization that can evolve, that can modify itself as technology, skills, competitors, and the entire business change.

PAUL ALLAIRE, CEO, XEROX CORPORATION

At the Five O'Clock Club, we:

- advocate a structured search,
- conduct targeted campaigns,
- prepare for each campaign,
- interview *well* in each campaign, and
- follow up with every person in every organization in each campaign.

As a splendid palace deserted by its inmates looks like a ruin, so does a man without character, all his material belongings notwithstanding.

MOHANDAS GANDHI

The Stages of Your Search

The last thing one discovers in composing a work is what to put first.

BLAISE PASCAL

Measure How Well You Are Doing in Your Search

So, how can you tell whether you're doing well in your search? It's *not* good enough to say, "I'll know my search was effective when I get a job." That's too late.

The first guidepost in evaluating your search is the Preliminary Target Investigation, which will help you check out your various targets and prevent you from wasting months going after targets that are inappropriate for you.

Then, we'll tell you how to measure the effectiveness of your search in terms of Stages 1, 2, and 3. It took us *four years of research* to develop this method for measuring the effectiveness of your search.

You'll find that the search process is a *research* process. As you go along in your search, try to be objective about yourself: Which targets are working for you? Which techniques are resulting in interviews for you? It's ongoing research.

Dying is no big deal. The least of us will manage that. Living is the trick.

WALTER ("RED") SMITH, FUNERAL EULOGY FOR GOLF IMPRESARIO, FRED CORCORAN

Measuring the Effectiveness of Your Search

During a five-month search, you sent 100 résumés and talked to 75 people. But was this *effective*? Measure where you are.

Stage 1 means *keeping in touch with 6 to 10 people* in your target area. Get information on the targets and feedback.

Stage 2 is the core of your search. *Keep in touch* with 6 to 10 of the right *people* at the right *level* in the right *organizations*. When they say, "I wish I had an opening right now—I'd love to have someone like you on board," you have a GREAT search. Now, aim for 10 to 20 ongoing Stage 2 contacts.

But if you're *not* getting this kind of positive feedback, your target is wrong or your positioning is wrong.

Stage 3 will happen naturally: 6 to 10 job possibilities. Aim for three concurrent offers.

Don't select the job that simply pays $2,000 or $20,000 more. Select the job that positions you best for the long term, because it probably will not be your last job. You *will* have to search again.

Stage 1: Your Preliminary Target Investigation

During Stage 1, network and make *contacts* in your target markets. As you gather information, analyze it: which markets seem worth pursuing and which do not? Don't waste months on targets that are unlikely to work out.

The Stages of Your Job Search

Most job hunters say, "I'll know my job search was good if I get a job." That's not a very good way to measure your search. You need to be able to tell **as you go along** if you have a good search. This is the test: Do you have six to ten things in the works? That is, are you talking on an ongoing basis to six to ten people who are in a position to hire you or recommend that you be hired? Which stage are *you* in? Start at the bottom of this page.

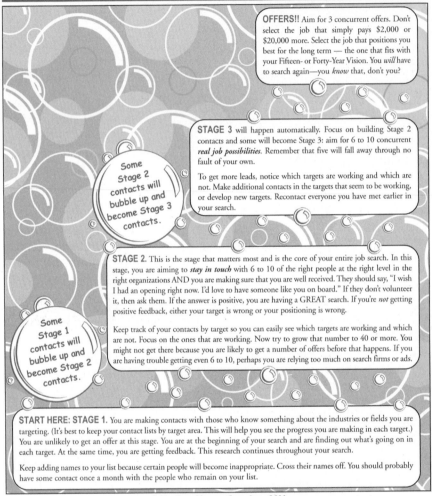

OFFERS!! Aim for 3 concurrent offers. Don't select the job that simply pays $2,000 or $20,000 more. Select the job that positions you best for the long term — the one that fits with your Fifteen- or Forty-Year Vision. You *will* have to search again—you *know* that, don't you?

STAGE 3 will happen automatically. Focus on building Stage 2 contacts and some will become Stage 3: aim for 6 to 10 concurrent *real job possibilities*. Remember that five will fall away through no fault of your own.

To get more leads, notice which targets are working and which are not. Make additional contacts in the targets that seem to be working, or develop new targets. Recontact everyone you have met earlier in your search.

Some Stage 2 contacts will bubble up and become Stage 3 contacts.

STAGE 2. This is the stage that matters most and is the core of your entire job search. In this stage, you are aiming to *stay in touch* with 6 to 10 of the right people at the right level in the right organizations AND you are making sure that you are well received. They should say, "I wish I had an opening right now. I'd love to have someone like you on board." If they don't volunteer it, then ask them. If the answer is positive, you are having a GREAT search. If you're *not* getting positive feedback, either your target is wrong or your positioning is wrong.

Keep track of your contacts by target so you can easily see which targets are working and which are not. Focus on the ones that are working. Now try to grow that number to 40 or more. You might not get there because you are likely to get a number of offers before that happens. If you are having trouble getting even 6 to 10, perhaps you are relying too much on search firms or ads.

Some Stage 1 contacts will bubble up and become Stage 2 contacts.

START HERE: STAGE 1. You are making contacts with those who know something about the industries or fields you are targeting. (It's best to keep your contact lists by target area. This will help you see the progress you are making in each target.) You are unlikely to get an offer at this stage. You are at the beginning of your search and are finding out what's going on in each target. At the same time, you are getting feedback. This research continues throughout your search.

Keep adding names to your list because certain people will become inappropriate. Cross their names off. You should probably have some contact once a month with the people who remain on your list.

So it may be that at the beginning of your search, you've brainstormed plenty of targets—maybe you've come up with 3 to 10 targets. Maybe you thought, "Gee, I think I'd like to work for a hospital." But in your Preliminary Target Investigation, you talked to managers at 4 hospitals—briefly—just to see what hospitals are like. And then you said to yourself, "Now that I have a feel for hospitals, I don't think hospitals are a good match for me." Because you've gathered some information, you can eliminate that target.

Preliminary Target Investigation

- **Networking or contacting people directly to gather information.**
- **Building contacts in your target market.**
- **Analyze your target markets: Which targets are working for you and which are not?**

All of the above will continue throughout your search.

time— going on interviews—and not even realizing that this target is not working for you.

So, eliminate inappropriate targets and decide which targets are worth a full campaign. Rank them: Target 1, Target 2, Target 3, and so on, depending on which ones you want to go after first, second, and third.

All of this happens during your Preliminary Target Investigation: brainstorm as many targets as you can, select the ones worth checking out, investigate them, eliminate some, rank the remaining ones, and mount your campaigns with overlapping targets.

Target #1: Hospitals

Planning | Interviewing | Follow-Up

Target #2: Health-Care Equipment

Planning | Interviewing | Follow-Up

Target #3: HMOs

Planning | Interviewing | Follow-Up

If you did not talk to hospitals in a concentrated way, it would be more difficult to assess whether or not you'd want to work for a hospital. You would be like all the other job hunters out there who are just going on interviews in a random manner and hoping they get an offer. Instead, assess the hospital market:

- Is this a good industry for me or not?
- Are my skills easily transferable or not?
- How can I make myself more appealing to hospitals?

With a *structured* search, you can say, "This hospital target does not work for me. I need to get rid of it!" Otherwise, you're just wasting your

You *must* stay in touch with a certain number of the people you've met during this investigative period. Those are your Stage 1 Contacts. For a good Stage 1, you need to have 6 to 10 people with whom you want to *stay in touch*. If you have no intention of staying in touch with some people you've contacted, they don't go on your Stage 1 List.

A Solid Stage 1

- **Maintaining 6 to 10 good contacts *on an ongoing basis*.**
- **You must stay in touch with them.**

Stage 2 is the meat of your search, and this is where you should put most of your effort. You're in a good, solid Stage 2 when you're talking to 6 to 10 of the right people at the right level at the right organizations. The *quality* of your contacts has changed and you're being well received. That is, they're saying to you, "I'm so sorry we don't have an opening right now. We'd love to have someone like you on board."

Stage 2—The Stage That Matters Most

Get in to see the right people
- **at the right level,**
- **at the right organizations, and**
- **make sure you are being well received.**

"I wish we had an opening right now. I'd love to have someone like you on board."

That's a solid Stage 2 search, and it means that you've got a great search going.

You're talking to the *right* people, and they *like* you; they really like you. They'd love to have someone like you on board. It just so happens they don't have an opening right now. But that's okay because the positive feedback means you're working the right targets with the right pitch.

What should you do next? Work hard to get more quality meetings: Talk to more of the right people at the right level in the right organizations.

What *else* should you do? Stay in touch with all of them—because someday they're going to need someone like you—they already said they want you!

This is the description of a terrific search! You shouldn't expect that a company would have an opening just because you happened to talk to them at this moment. Stay in touch with them—with at least 6 to 10 people *on an ongoing basis*. But if you *don't* intend to talk to them again, *they don't count* as Stage 2 contacts.

This Is a Terrific Search!
- **Although they don't have an opening for you right now...**
- **Talk with people and stay in touch with...**
- **At least 6 to 10 on an ongoing basis.**
- **Someday, they'll need you.**

Develop *more* quality contacts. That's right: 6 to 10 are not enough, 6 to 10 was a minimum range to help you test your presentation to this marketplace. It worked. Now, increase that number, and *aim for 12 to 20 or even 40*, and keep in touch with all of them. We're not suggesting the impossible! These recommended numbers are the result of solid research, which we are now passing on to you. Stage 2 is crucial: We know that Five O'Clock Clubbers who follow this methodology and generate these numbers end up with multiple offers to choose from.

Instead of 6 to 10, aim for 12 to 20, or even 40.

Refining Your Search

Look at your Stage 2 contacts by target, and notice which targets are best for you. Become a researcher on your own behalf. You might notice, "Hospitals are being responsive to me. I think I need to contact more people in the hospital market." If you notice which targets are working and which are not, you'll have a better, faster search, and you'll feel calmer in your search because you'll have more control.

Notice which targets are being most responsive to you.

If you can't get a healthy Stage 2 going—if you are not being well received—ask your small group and your coach to help you figure out what's wrong. But you have to bring them good information. For example, if you're in a meeting—not a job interview, but a meeting where there is no job opening—ask the manager, "If you had an opening right now, would you consider having someone like me on board?" If the manager is candid and gives you reasons *why not*, tell this information to your group.

This is what I love about The Five O'Clock Club process: It's a research-based approach. There can be only two possible problems here: either your *target* is wrong (you're going after the wrong industries, positions, or geographic areas), or your *positioning* is wrong (your pitch is wrong, you don't look the part, your résumé positions you incorrectly). Ask your coach and your small group for feedback.

> - **If Stage 2 is working, do more of the same.**
> - **If Stage 2 is *not* happening:**
>   - ✓ **Your targets are wrong, or**
>   - ✓ **Your positioning is wrong.**
>   - ✓ **Ask your small group and your coach what is wrong.**

If you've done Stage 2 well, Stage 3 will take care of itself. Being in Stage 3 means you're talking to 6 to 10 organizations *on an ongoing basis* about a *real* job, or the *possibility* of creating a job for you. Don't worry about Stage 3. Worry about Stage 2.

In Stage 3, we want you to aim to have 6 to 10 *job* possibilities. Don't stop at 2 or 3! That's not enough. Out of 6 to 10, *5 will fall away through no fault of your own.* So you see that two or three possibilities are not enough. Chances are they will disappear for reasons beyond your control, or as we say at the Club, "fall away through no fault of your own."

> **Out of 6 to 10 job possibilities, 5 will fall away through no fault of your own.**

To get more job possibilities, don't worry about Stage 3. Instead, develop more Stage 1 and Stage 2 contacts. Some Stage 1 contacts will bubble up and become Stage 2 contacts. Build up the number of Stage 2 contacts. Instead of 6 to 10, aim to have 20, 30, or even 40. A certain number of those will bubble up to become Stage 3 contacts—that is, where people are considering you for a real job or the possibility of creating a job for you.

Keep that momentum going. Your small group is so helpful here. Just when you think, "There's no *way* I can get more interviews," your small group will tell you how to keep the momentum going in your campaign.

We're a society that's not about perfection, but about rectifying mistakes. We're about second chances.

HARRY EDWARDS, IN "HARDLINE," *DETROIT FREE PRESS*

> **To get more job possibilities going:**
>
> - **Develop more Stage 1 and Stage 2 contacts.**
> - **Some Stage 1 contacts will bubble up to Stage 2.**
> - **Instead of 6 to 10, develop more.**
> - **A certain number of Stage 2 contacts will bubble up to Stage 3.**
> - **Keep your momentum going.**

Remember, talk about your search in terms of stages. If your small group asks how your search is going, don't say, "I don't have a job yet" or "I think I might get a job." Instead, analyze your search. Say, "My search is going great. I have 6 things in Stage 2; 12 in Stage 1; and one Stage 2 contact may become a Stage 3." If you use this mind-set and this shorthand, you will become better at analyzing how well you really are doing, and your small-group members will also be able to tell—and we can help you more.

> **How is your search going?
> Talk in terms of stages.**

Also tell your small group how you're *keeping in touch* with your contacts. It's okay if prospective employers don't have an opening right now. In another month or two, some of the organizations you're keeping in touch with *may* have an opening. So you must keep in touch with them *so they will think of you when something comes up.* Your coach and your small group can help you with this part as well.

Three Concurrent Job Offers

Yes, we want you to have three concurrent job offers. It sounds like a lot, but often the first offer you get is not the best. If you have three offers, you are in a better position to compare the jobs as well as the salaries, and you increase your chance of getting *more* offers.

Then you should pick the job that *positions you best for the long term.* Memorize that phrase! When you have choices—and we want you to have choices—don't pick the job that pays you $500 more or $5,000 more or $50,000 more! Think long term. The average American has been in his or her job only four years. Chances are, you will have to search again. So pick the job that positions you best for the long term.

> **Aim for three concurrent job offers,
> and then pick the job that positions
> you best for the long term.
> Don't pick the one that pays the most.
> Remember your Forty-Year Vision!**

Have Fun!

Finally, we want you to have three hours of fun a week—whether you like it or not. It's a little joke of ours, but the fact is, if you don't get three hours of fun a week, you won't interview well. You'll be too stressed and come across like a drone, rather than seeming like a person who everyone wants to work with.

> **Attend The Five O'Clock Club
> consistently. It's fun, and our research
> shows that those who attend on a
> regular basis get better jobs faster and
> at higher rates of pay than those
> who attend sporadically.**

We advocate a structured, disciplined search. If you think you can stop attending the club for a few weeks, and go out and search on your own for a while, you may be buying trouble. If you come back only when you *think* you have a problem, chances are your group could have helped you avoid the problem.

Attend consistently and the group will become familiar with your search and notice when you are going off track. You may even be targeting the wrong kind of job, and the group will notice that in your expression, or in your report of what happens when you go to meetings. We don't want you to just get a job—any job. We want you to get the job that's right for you. If you skip meetings and search on your own—without the benefit of weekly peer review—it's easy to get off track. Then when you finally come back to the group, everything's a *mess.*

Instead, attend The Five O'Clock Club week after week after week.

That also means you should job search in the summer and during the holidays. In fact, those are very opportune times to search. Your competition drops out of the job market because they think nothing is going on. Yet there's plenty of hiring going on during the summer and holidays.

Keep going with your job search. Don't use any excuse to drop out. In fact, Five O'Clock Clubbers put their foot to the pedal and move ahead whatever time of year it is!

- **Get three hours of fun a week— whether you like it or not!!**
- **Consistently attend The Five O'Clock Club's weekly small-group strategy sessions.**
- **Job search in the summer and during the holidays, too.**
- *They* **never call when they say they will.**

And always remember how vital it is to take the initiative and follow up. When they say, "I'll call you on Tuesday," they really mean it. But they will never call you when they say they will. **The ball is always in your court**. It is always up to you to figure out what to do next—and your small group can help you do that.

Let the past drift away with the water.

JAPANESE SAYING

Study our books as if you were in graduate school. Work with your coach and your small group. You'll *love* your small group. Everyone does. You'll be in a small group of your peers. So if you're making $60,000 a year, for example, you'll be in a group of people earning, say, $50,000 to $80,000. If you're earning more than $100,000 a year, you'll be in a group in which everyone earns more than $100,000 a year. And those earning more than $200,000 a year are in a group of *their* peers.

It's important to be in a group of your peers because everyone's brainstorming with you about what you need to do next in your search.

Cartoon Courtesy © Jerry King

"Going up?"

Now you have an <u>overview</u> of The Five O'Clock Club approach. You have a lot more ahead of you—in our other books and CDs and in the weekly meetings.

Take good care of yourself and your career. Good luck to you. And the next time you need us, we'll be here.

The price one pays for pursuing any profession or calling is an intimate knowledge of its ugly side.

JAMES BALDWIN, *NOBODY KNOWS MY NAME*

PART SIX

What is
The Five O'Clock Club

WHERE PROFESSIONAL SUCCESS
GETS PERSONAL ATTENTION

How to Join the Club

The Five O'Clock Club: Where Professional Success Gets Personal Attention

"One organization with a long record of success in helping people find jobs is The Five O'Clock Club."

FORTUNE

- Weekly Job-Search Strategy Groups
- Private Coaching
- Books, Audio CDs and audio downloads
- Membership Information
- When Your Employer Pays

THERE *IS* A FIVE O'CLOCK CLUB NEAR YOU!

For more information on becoming a member, please fill out the Membership Application Form in this book, sign up on the web at:
www.fiveoclockclub.com,
or call: 1-800-538-6645
(or 212-286-4500 in New York)

The Five O'Clock Club Search Process

The Five O'Clock Club process, as outlined in *The Five O'Clock Club* books, is a targeted, strategic approach to career development and job search. Five O'Clock Club members become proficient at skills that prove invaluable during their entire working lives.

Career Management

We train our members to manage their careers and always look ahead to their next job search. Research shows that an average worker spends only four years in a job—and will have 12 jobs in as many as 5 career fields—during his or her working life.

Getting Jobs . . . Faster

Five O'Clock Club members find more satisfying jobs, faster. The average professional, manager, or executive Five O'Clock Club member who regularly attends weekly sessions finds a job by his or her 10th session. Even the discouraged, long-term job searcher can find immediate help.

The keystone to The Five O'Clock Club process is teaching our members an understanding of the entire *hiring* process. A first interview is primarily a time for exchanging critical information. The real work starts *after the interview*. We teach our members how to *turn job interviews into offers* and to negotiate the best possible employment package.

Setting Targets

The Five O'Clock Club is action oriented. *We'll help you decide what you should do this very next week to move your search along.* By their third session, our members have set definite job targets by industry or company size, position, and geographic area, and are out in the field gathering information and making contacts that will lead to interviews with hiring managers.

Our approach evolves with the changing job market. We're able to synthesize information from hundreds of Five O'Clock Club members and come up with new approaches for our members. For example, we discuss temporary placement for executives, how to use voice mail and the Internet, the use of LinkedIn and other social media, and how to network when doors are slamming shut all over town.

The Five O'Clock Club's Weekly Small Group Strategy Sessions

The Five O'Clock Club weekly meeting includes you, 6 to 8 peers (people at your same salary level) and a senior Five O'Clock Club career coach who has been certified by us. The meeting is a carefully planned *job-search strategy program where participants go away with an assignment to help them get more interviews in their target markets or turn those interviews into offers.* We provide members with the tools and tricks necessary to get a good job fast—even in a tight market. Networking and emotional support are also included in the meeting.

Participate in 10 *consecutive* small-group strategy sessions to enable your group and career coach to get to know you and to develop momentum in your search.

Weekly Presentations via Audio CDs or audio Downloads

Prior to each week's teleconference, listen to the assigned audio presentation covering part of The Five O'Clock Club methodology. These are scheduled on a rotating basis so you may join the Club at any time.

Small-Group Strategy Sessions

During the first few minutes of the teleconference, your small group discusses the topic of the week and hears from people who have landed jobs. Then you have the chance to get feedback and advice on your own search strategy, listen to and learn from others, and build your network. All groups are led by trained career coaches with years of experience. The small group is generally no more than six to eight people, so everyone gets the chance to speak up.

Let us consider how we may spur one another on toward love and good deeds. Let us not give up meeting together, as some are in the habit of doing, but let us encourage one another.

Hebrews 10:24-25

Private Coaching

You may meet with your small-group coach—or another coach—for private coaching by phone or in person. A coach helps you develop a career path, solve current job problems, prepare your résumé, or guide your search.

Many members develop long-term relationships with their coaches to get advice throughout their careers. If you are paying for the coaching yourself (as opposed to having your employer pay), please pay the coach directly (charges vary from $100 to $175 per hour). **Private coaching is not included in The Five O'Clock Club seminar or membership** fee and the Club gets no portion of whatever you pay the coach. For coach matching, see our website or call 1-800-538-6645 (or 212-286-4500 in New York).

Fortune, *The New York Times, Black Enterprise, Business Week,* The TODAY Show, NPR, CNBC and ABC-TV are some of the places you've seen, heard, or read about us.

From the Club History, Written in the 1890s

At The Five O'Clock Club, [people] of all shades of political belief—as might be said of all trades and creeds—have met together.... The variety continues almost to a monotony.... [The Club's] good fellowship and geniality—not to say hospitality—has reached them all.

It has been remarked of clubs that they serve to level rank. If that were possible in this country, it would probably be true, if leveling rank means the appreciation of people of equal abilities as equals; but in The Five O'Clock Club it has been a most gratifying and noteworthy fact that no lines have ever been drawn save those which are essential to the honor and good name of any association. Strangers are invited by the club or by any members, [as gentlepeople], irrespective of aristocracy, plutocracy or occupation, and are so treated always. Nor does the thought of a [person's] social position ever enter into the meetings. People of wealth and people of moderate means sit side by side, finding in each other much to praise and admire and little to justify snarlishness or adverse criticism. People meet as people—not as the representatives of a set—and having so met, dwell not in worlds of envy or distrust, but in union and collegiality, forming kindly thoughts of each other in their heart of hearts.

In its methods, The Five O'Clock Club is plain, easy-going and unconventional. It has its "isms" and some peculiarities of procedure, but simplicity characterizes them all. The sense of propriety, rather than rules of order, governs its meetings, and that informality which carries with it sincerity of motive and spontaneity of effort, prevails within it. Its very name indicates informality, and, indeed, one of the reasons said to have induced its adoption was the fact that members or guests need not don their dress suits to attend the meetings, if they so desired. This informality, however, must be distinguished from the informality of Bohemianism. For The Five O'Clock Club, informality, above convenience, means sobriety, refinement of thought and speech, good breeding and good order. To this sort of informality much of its success is due.

The Schedule

See our website for the specific dates for each topic. All groups use a similar schedule in each time zone.

Fee: $49 for LIFETIME membership (includes Beginners Kit, a LIFETIME subscription to *The Five O'Clock News*, and LIFETIME access to the Members Only section of our website), **plus** session fees based on member's income (the price for the Insider Program includes audio-CD lectures, which retail for as much as $150).

Reservations are required for your first session. Unused sessions that you paid for (as opposed to employer-paid programs) are transferable to anyone you choose or will be donated to members attending more than 16 sessions who are having financial difficulty.

The Five O'Clock Club's programs are geared to professionals, managers, and executives from a wide variety of industries and professions, and also recent graduates. Most earn from $30,000 to $500,000 per year. Half of the members are employed; half are unemployed. **You will be in a group of your peers.**

> **To register, please fill out form on the web (at www.fiveoclockclub.com) or call 1-800-538-6645 (or 212-286-4500 in New York).**

Lecture Presentation Schedule

- History of the Five O'Clock Club
- The Five O'Clock Club Approach to Job Search
- Developing New Targets for Your Search
- Two-Minute Pitch: Keystone of Your Search
- Using Research and Internet for Your Search
- The Keys to Effective Networking
- Getting the Most Out of Your Contacts
- Getting Interviews: Direct/Targeted Mail

- Beat the Odds when Using Search Firms and Ads
- Developing New Momentum in Your Search
- The Five O'Clock Club Approach to Interviewing
- Advanced Interviewing Techniques
- How to Handle Difficult Interview Questions
- How to Turn Job Interviews into Offers
- Successful Job Hunter's Report
- Four-Step Salary-Negotiation Method

Audio excerpts from many of these presentations can be found on our website in the "How to Get a Job" section.

All groups run continuously. Dates are posted on our website. The textbooks used by all members of The Five O'Clock Club may be ordered on our website or purchased at major bookstores.

The original Five O'Clock Club was formed in Philadelphia in 1883. It was made up of the leaders of the day who shared their experiences "in a spirit of fellowship and good humor."

Questions You May Have about the Weekly Job-Search Strategy Group

Job hunters are not always the best judges of what they need during a search. For example, most are interested in lectures on answering ads on the Internet or working with search firms. We cover those topics, but strategically they are relatively unimportant in an effective job search.

At The Five O'Clock Club, you get the information you really need in your search—*such as how to target more effectively, how to get more interviews, and how to turn job interviews into offers.*

What's more, you will work in a small group with the best coaches in the business. In these strategy sessions, your group will help you decide what to do, this week and every week, to move your search along. You will learn by being coached and by coaching others in your group.

We find ourselves not independently of other people and institutions but through them. We never get to the bottom of our selves on our own. We discover who we are face to face and side by side with others in work, love, and learning.

Robert N. Bellah, et al., *Habits of the Heart*

Here are a few other points:

- For best results, attend on a regular basis. Your group gets to know you and will coach you to eliminate whatever you may be doing wrong—or refine what you are doing right. Our research shows that if

you attend only once a month, the group will have little or no impact on your search results.

- The Five O'Clock Club is a members-only organization. To get started in the small-group teleconference sessions, you must purchase a minimum of 10 sessions.
- The teleconference sessions include the set of 16 audio-CD presentations on Five O'Clock Club methodology. In-person groups do not include CDs.
- After that, you may purchase blocks of 5 or 10 sessions.
- We sell multiple sessions to make administration easier.
- If you miss a session, you may make it up any time. You may even transfer unused time to a friend.
- Although many people find jobs quickly (even people who have been unemployed a long time), others have more difficult searches. Plan to be in it for the long haul and you'll do better.

Carefully read all of the material in this section. It will help you decide whether or not to attend.

- The first week, pay attention to the strategies used by the others in your group. Soak up all the information you can.
- Read the books before you come in the

second week. They will help you move your search along.

To register:

1. Read this section and fill out the application.
2. After you become a member and get your Beginners Kit, call to reserve a space for the first time you attend.

To assign you to a career coach, we need to know:

- your current (or last) field or industry
- the kind of job you would like next (if you know)
- your desired salary range in general terms

For private coaching, we suggest you attend the small group and ask to see your group leader, to give you continuity.

The Five O'Clock Club is plain, easy-going and unconventional.... Members or guests need not don their dress suits to attend the meetings.

(From the Club History, written in the 1890s)

What Happens at the Meetings?

Each week, job searchers from various industries and professions meet in small groups. The groups specialize in professionals, managers, executives, or recent college graduates. Usually, half are employed and half are unemployed.

The weekly program is in two parts. First, listen to a lecture on some aspect of The Five O'Clock Club methodology. Then, job hunters meet in small groups headed by senior full-time professional career coaches.

The first week, get the textbooks, listen to the lecture, and meet with your small group and the senior coach who is leading the group. During your first session, listen to the others in your group. You learn a lot by listening to how your peers are strategizing their searches.

By the second week, you will have read the materials. Now we can start to work on your search strategy and help *you* decide what to do next to move your search along. For example, we'll help you figure out how to get more interviews in your target area or how to turn interviews into job offers.

In the third week, you will see major progress made by other members of your group and you may notice major progress in your own search as well.

By the third or fourth week, most members are conducting full and effective searches. Over the remaining weeks, you will tend to keep up a full search rather than go after only one or two leads. You will regularly aim to have 6 to 10 things *in the works at all times*. These will generally be in specific target areas you have identified, will keep your search on target, and will increase your chances of getting multiple job offers from which to choose.

Those who stick with the process find it works.

Some people prefer to just listen for a few weeks before they start their job search and that's okay, too.

How Much Does It Cost?

It is against the policy of The Five O'Clock Club to charge individuals heavy up-front fees. Our competitors charge $4,000 to $6,000 or more, up front. Our average fee is $360 for 10 sessions (which includes audio CDs (or downloads) of 16 presentations for those in the teleconference program). Those in the $100,000+ range pay an average of $540 for 10 sessions. For administrative reasons, we charge for 5 or 10 additional sessions at a time.

You must have the books so you can begin studying them before the second session. (You can purchase them on our website, at Amazon. com, or ask for them at your local library.) If you don't do the homework, you will tend to waste the time of others in the group by asking questions covered in the texts.

Is the Small Group Right for Me?

The Five O'Clock Club process is for you if:

- You are truly interested in job hunting.
- You have some idea of the kind of job you want.
- You are a professional, manager, or executive— or want to be.
- You want to participate in a group process on a regular basis.
- You realize that finding or changing jobs and careers is hard work, but you are absolutely willing and able to do it.

If you have no idea about the kind of job you want next, you may attend one or two group sessions to start. *Then see a coach privately for one or two sessions*, develop tentative job targets, and return to the group. You may work with your small-group coach or contact us through our website or by calling 1-800-538-6645 (or 212-286-4500 in New York) for referral to a private coach.

How Long Will It Take Me to Get a Job?

Although our members tend to be from fields or industries where they expect to have difficult searches, the average person who attends regularly finds a new position within 10 sessions. Some take less time and others take more. During the worst recessions, our average professional, manager and executive still found employment in an average of 16.4 weeks (as opposed to the 35 weeks that the population as a whole was taking—assuming they didn't give up on searching).

One thing we know for sure: **Research shows that those who regularly attend the small-group strategy sessions get more satisfying jobs faster and at higher rates of pay than those who search on their own, only work privately with a career coach, or simply take a course**. This makes sense. If a person comes only when they think they have a problem, they are usually wrong. They probably had a problem a few weeks ago but didn't realize it. Or the problem may be different from the one they thought they

had. Those who come regularly benefit from the observations others make about their searches. Problems are solved before they become severe or are prevented altogether.

Those who attend regularly also learn a lot by paying attention and helping others in the group. This *secondhand* learning can shorten your search by weeks. When you hear the problems of others who are ahead of you in the search, you can avoid them completely. People in your group will come to know you and will point out subtleties you may not have noticed that interviewers will never tell you.

Will I Be with Others from My Field/Industry?

Probably not, but it's not that important. If you are a salesperson, for example, would you want to be with seven other salespeople? Probably not. You will learn a lot and have a much more creative search if you are in a group of people who are in your general salary range but not exactly like you. Our clients are from virtually every field and industry. The *process* is what will help you.

We've been doing this since 1978 and understand your needs. That's why the mix we provide is the best you can get.

Career Coaching Firms Charge $4,000-$6,000 Up Front. How Can You Charge Such a Small Fee?

1. We have no advertising costs, because 90 percent of those who attend have been referred by other members or an association you belong to. (Be sure to ask your alumni or trade association to contact us for a special rate for its members.).

   A hefty up-front fee would bind you to us, but we have been more successful by treating people ethically and having them pretty much *pay as they go*.

   We need a certain number of people to

cover expenses. When lots of people get jobs quickly and leave us, we could go into the red. But as long as members refer others, we will continue to provide this service at a fair price.

2. We focus strictly on *job-search strategy,* and encourage our clients to attend free support groups if they need emotional support. We focus on getting *jobs that fit in with your career goals,* and that reduces the time clients spend with us and the amount they pay.

3. We attract the best coaches, and our clients make more progress per session than they would elsewhere, which also reduces their costs.

4. We have expert administrators and a sophisticated computer system that reduces our overhead and increases our ability to track your progress.

May I Change Coaches?

Yes. Great care is taken in assigning you to your initial coach. However, if you want to change once for any reason, you may do it. We don't encourage group hopping: It is better for you to stick with a group so that everyone gets to know you. On the other hand, we want you to feel comfortable. So if you tell us you prefer a different group, you will be transferred immediately.

What If I Have a Quick Question Outside of the Group Session?

Some people prefer to see their group coach privately. Others prefer to meet with a different coach to get another point of view. Whatever you decide, remember that the group fee does not cover coaching time outside the group session. Therefore, if you wanted to speak with a coach between sessions—even for *quick questions*—you would normally meet with the coach first for a private session so he or she can get to know you better. *Easy, quick questions* are usually more complicated than they appear. After your first private session, some coaches will allow you to pay in advance for one hour of coaching time, which you can then use for quick questions by phone (usually a 15-minute minimum is charged). Since each coach has an individual way of operating, find out how the coach arranges these things.

What If I Want to Start My Own Business?

The process of becoming a consultant is essentially the same as job hunting and lots of consultants attend Five O'Clock Club meetings. However, if you want to buy a franchise or existing business or start a growth business, you should see a private coach. Regardless of the kind of business you want to have, be sure to read our book: *Your Great Business Idea: The Truth About Making It Happen.*

How Can I Be Sure That The Five O'Clock Club Small-Group Sessions Will Be Right for Me?

Before you actually participate in any of the small-group sessions, you can get an idea of the quality of our service by listening to all 16 audio CDs that you purchased. If you are dissatisfied with the CDs for any reason, return the package within 30 days for a full refund.

Whatever you decide, just remember: **Research shows that those who *regularly* attend the small-group strategy sessions get more satisfying jobs faster and at higher rates of pay than those who search on their own, *only* work privately with a career coach, or simply take a course.** If you get a job just one or two weeks faster because of this program, it will have more than paid for itself. And you may transfer unused sessions to anyone you choose. However, the person you choose must be or become a member.

The Five O'Clock Club's Job-Search Buddy System

Do you wish you had someone to talk to —fairly often and informally—about the little things? "Here's what I'm planning to do today in my search? What are *you* planning to do? Let's talk tomorrow to make sure we've done it." You and your job-search buddy could keep each other positive and on track, and encourage each other to do what you told your small group you were going to do: Make that call, send out those letters, write that follow-up proposal, focus on the most important things that should be done—rather than (for example) spending endless hours responding to job postings on the Web.

With your buddy, practice your Two-Minute Pitch, get ready for interviews, bounce ideas off each other. Some job-search buddies talk every day. Some talk a few times a week. Most of the conversation is by phone and e-mail.

Sometimes, people match themselves up as buddies. Just pick someone you get along with in your small group. Sometimes, your coach can match you up. However you do it, stay away from negative people who talk about how bad it is out there. They will drag you down.

The small group changes over time: people get jobs; new people come in. If you lose one buddy who got a job, get another buddy.

Your buddy does not have to be in your field or industry. In fact, being in the same field or industry could keep you focused on the industry rather than on the *process*. But you *do* have to get along! The relationship may last only a month or two, or go on for years. Some buddies become friends.

Of course, you should see your Five O'Clock Club career coach *privately* for résumé review, target development, salary negotiation, and job interview follow-up. It's usually best to get professional coaching advice for these areas. And nothing beats the weekly small-group strategy sessions for making progress in the job search itself. Those who regularly attended the small group got jobs in half the time.

Using The Five O'Clock Club
From the Comfort of Your Home

A man who found the Five O'Clock Club books at his library near Denver calls to ask if there is a local branch. A woman in Seattle who bought the books on Amazon wants to know if she can attend our weekly seminars. A man in Phoenix who received *Targeting a Great Career* from his daughter also wants to attend. And an HR executive wants to know whether we can help her employees in an office closing in Miami.

In our early years, the reach of The Five O'Clock Club—because of the popular Club books—exceeded its presence, but systems have been in place for the past ten years to allow people anywhere to access the Club seminars and coaching by phone and computer.

The Launch of the Insider Groups

Teleconferencing has long come into its own, and for ten years we have offered weekly Club meetings on a nationwide basis. Our Insider Groups (via teleconference) were launched in February 2000, and the first teleconference group included executives from California, North Dakota and Maryland. Prior to the conference call, each person listens to the topic of the week on his or her audio CD or reads the topic in the books. They can listen to the "topic of the week" at their leisure and are then ready for the weekly teleconference.

Following the conference, participants can stay on the line and chat with each other—and most do. In addition, they can browse our LinkedIn Group and network with the almost 1,000 Five O'Clock Clubbers who participate. They can "reply all" to the emails sent to members of their small group and stay in touch with each other that way. And they can talk daily to their Job-Search Buddies, offering advice and encouragement that follow The Five O'Clock Club's methodology. What's more, they can talk to their private coach about a specific interview coming up, get advice on turning a job interview into an offer, or get help negotiating their compensation.

Website as a Public Service

Anyone can wander through the various areas of www.FiveOClockClub.com and tap into vast amounts of useful information—without being a member! For example, click on How To Get a Job to find a menu of 13 substantive articles that represent the heart of the Five O'Clock Club methodology. These articles cover job targeting, interviewing and salary negotiations—and how to start out on the right foot on your new job. There is also a free mini-course to help you assess the **quality** of your job search. Sure, you're working hard, but are you doing the right things?

Remember, The Five O'Clock Club is the ONLY organization devoted to conducting research on behalf of job hunters. We are the only organization with a research-based methodology for you to use rather than the vanilla job-search techniques that everyone else uses. We are the ONLY organization that has books and audios that document the methodology you should use in your job search.

In the Free Articles section you can access hundreds of articles that have appeared in our monthly magazine, *The Five O'Clock News*.

The Weekly Small-Group Strategy Sessions

You are assigned to a small group of your peers (same salary level). Each session is moderated by a certified Five O'Clock Club coach, lasts for an hour, and is guided by the same principles and techniques presented in our books and audios. These are not general discussions on job-search topics; each session moves you forward in your search by helping you to identify steps to take during the coming week. You leave the session with an assignment and proactive coaching on how to do it.

"Our group coach expects us to recap what we've done and we get an assignment. The momentum you get with The Five O'Clock Club makes the big difference," reports one Clubber.

One California Insider member said, "It's really been neat. I've been involved with other job-hunting groups, but they don't have the full breadth of job-search regimen that you have with The Five O'Clock Club. Reading the books and listening to the audios ahead of time helps keep us focused. Our coach expects us to recap what we've done and we get an assignment. The momentum you get with The Five O'Clock Club makes the big difference. I've stagnated with other groups." And he finds that there is a benefit in working with a group whose members are in California, Florida, Massachusetts and New Jersey. "It gives us a different perspective on issues. We have great rapport on the phone and we email and call each other after the session is over."

Reach Out and Touch Someone

You can get assigned to a Five O'Clock Club coach for private one-on-one coaching. Most of these match-ups result in telephone sessions—the coach may be in Maryland or Chicago, the client in California or Maine. Many clients want an hour or two of private coaching to help them determine goals and targets. You can find a sampling of coach bios and photos on our website.

Our coaches are trained in The Five O'Clock Club method and are committed to our ethical standards. At other such firms, a newly hired coach with experience is up and running that day. At The Five O'Clock Club, a coach with experience must go through our four-month certification program, un-learn what they thought they knew about job search, and master the methodology.

Seasoned career coaches are attracted to our certification program. Candidates for the Guild must study our 250-page training manual and pass exams to be admitted; they must do two "before" and "after" résumés so they don't give you a cookie-cutter résumé; they must observe 10 small-group coaching sessions and write an essay on what they have learned; and they must do an audition on some aspect of The Five O'Clock Club methodology so they can again prove that they have mastered it. With some 50 coaches in training, in addition to our certified coaches, we are in a position to meet the volume of coaching requests that may come our way in the future.

Be sure to tell your friends about us, and tell your employer that you want The Five O'Clock Club as your outplacement provider!

When Your Employer Pays

Does your employer care about you and others whom they ask to leave the organization? If so, ask them to consider The Five O'Clock Club for your outplacement help. The Five O'Clock Club puts you and your job search first, offering a career-coaching program of the highest quality at the lowest possible price to your employer.

Over 25 Years of Research

The Five O'Clock Club was started in 1978 as a research-based organization. Job hunters tried various techniques and reported their results back to the group. We developed a variety of guidelines so job hunters could choose the techniques best for them.

The methodology was tested and refined on professionals, managers, and executives (and those aspiring to be) from all occupations. Annual salaries ranged from $30,000 to $400,000; 50 percent were employed and 50 percent were unemployed.

Since its beginning, The Five O'Clock Club has tracked trends. Over time, our advice has changed as the job market has changed. What worked in the past is insufficient for today's job market. Today's Five O'Clock Club promotes all our relevant original strategies—and so much more.

As an employee-advocacy organization, The Five O'Clock Club focuses on providing the services and information that the job hunter needs most.

Get the Help You Need Most: 100 Percent Coaching

There's a myth in outplacement circles that a terminated employee just needs a desk, a phone, and minimal career coaching. The new trend is to provide job hunters with databases of fake job openings and other online help and call it "outplacement." The price is ridiculously low, but then an employer can claim that it is providing outplacement to all employees.

<u>**Our experience clearly shows that down-sized workers need qualified, reliable coaching more than anything else.**</u> Most traditional outplacement packages last only 3 months. The average executive gets office space and only 5 hours of career coaching during this time. Yet the service job hunters need most is the career coaching itself—not a desk and a phone.

Most professionals, managers, and executives are right in the thick of negotiations with prospective employers at the 3-month mark. Yet that is precisely when traditional outplacement ends, leaving job hunters stranded and sometimes ruining deals.

It is astonishing how often job hunters and employers alike are impressed by the databases of job postings claimed by outplacement firms. Yet only 10 percent of all jobs are filled through ads and another 10 percent are filled through search firms. Instead, direct contact and networking—done The Five O'Clock Club way—are more effective for most searches.

For the latest information on our outplacement services, go to our website, www.fiveoclockclub.com, and look in both the "For Employers" and "For Employees" sections.

You Get a Safety Net

<u>**Imagine getting a package that protects you for a full year**</u>. Imagine knowing you can come back if your new job doesn't work out—even months later. Imagine trying consulting work if you like. If you later decide it's not for you, you can come back to The Five O'Clock Club.

We can offer you a safety net of one full year's career coaching because our method is so effective that few people actually need more than 10 weeks in our proven program. But you're protected for a year.

You'll Job Search with Those Who Are Employed—How Novel!

Let's face it. It can be depressing to spend your days at an outplacement firm where everyone is unemployed. At The Five O'Clock Club, half the attendees are working, and this makes the atmosphere cheerier and helps to move your search along.

What's more, you'll be in a small group of your peers, all of whom are using The Five O'Clock Club method. Our research proves that those who attend the small group regularly and use The Five O'Clock Club methods get jobs faster and at higher rates of pay than those who only work privately with a career coach throughout their searches.

So Many Poor Attempts

Nothing is sadder than meeting someone who has already been getting job-search help, but the wrong kind. They've learned the traditional techniques that are no longer effective. Most have poor résumés and inappropriate targets and don't know how to turn job interviews into offers.

You'll Get Quite a Package

You'll get up to 14 hours (or more, depending on the package) of private coaching—well in excess of what you would get at a traditional outplacement firm. You may even want to use a few hours after you start your new job.

And you get one full year of weekly small-group career coaching. In addition, you get books, audio CDs, and other helpful materials.

To Get Started

The day your human resources manager calls us authorizing Five O'Clock Club outplacement, we will immediately ship you the books, CDs, and other materials and assign you to a private coach and a small group.

Then we'll monitor your search. Frankly, we care about you more than we care about your employer. And since your employer cares about you, they're glad we feel this way—because they know we'll take care of you.

What They Say about Us

The Five O'Clock Club product is much better, far more useful than my outplacement package.
SENIOR EXECUTIVE AND FIVE O'CLOCK CLUB MEMBER

The Club kept the juices flowing. You're told what to do, what not to do. There were fresh ideas. I went through an outplacement service that, frankly, did not help. If they had done as much as the Five O'Clock Club did, I would have landed sooner.

ANOTHER MEMBER

When Your *Employer* Pays for The Five O'Clock Club, *You* Get:

- **Up to 14 hours (or more, depending on the package) of guaranteed private career coaching** to determine a career direction, develop a résumé, plan salary negotiations, etc. In fact, if you need a second opinion during your search, we can arrange that too.
- **ONE YEAR of weekly small-group strategy sessions via teleconference** (average about 5 or 6 participants in a group) headed by a senior Five O'Clock Club career consultant. That way, if you lose your next job, you can come back. Or if you want to try consulting work and then decide you don't like it, **you can come back**.
- **LIFETIME membership** in The Five O'Clock Club: Beginners Kit and two-year subscription to The Five O'Clock News.
- **The complete set of our four books** for professionals, managers, and executives who are in job search.
- **A boxed set of 16 audio CDs** of Five O'Clock Club presentations.

COMPARISON OF EMPLOYER-PAID PACKAGES

Typical Package	Traditional Outplacement	The Five O'Clock Club
Who is the client?	The organization	Job hunters. We are employee advocates. We always do what is in the best interest of job hunters.
The clintele	All are unemployed	Half of our attendees are unemployed; half are employed. There is an upbeat atmosphere; networkng is enhanced.
Length/type of service	3 months, primarily office space	1 year, exclusively career coaching
Service ends	After 3 months—or before if the client lands a job or consulting assignment.	After 1 full year, no matter what. You can return if you lose your next job, if your assignment ends, or if you need advice after starting your new job.
Small group coaching	Sporatic for 3 months Coach varies	Every week for up to 1 year; same coach
Private coaching	5 hours on average	Up to 14 hours guaranteed (depending on level of service purchased)
Support materials	Generic manual; web-based info	• 4 textbooks based on over 25 yrs. of job-search research • 16 40-minute lectures on audio CDs • Beginners Kit of search information • LIFETIME subscription to the Five)'Clock Club magazine, devoted to career-management articles
Facilities	Cubicle, phone, computer access	None; use home phone and computer

The Way We Are

The Five O'Clock Club means sobriety, refinement
of thought and speech, good breeding
and good order. To this, much of its success is due.
The Five O'Clock Club is easy-going and
unconventional. A sense of propriety, rather
than rules of order, governs its meetings.

J. HAMPTON MOORE, *HISTORY OF THE FIVE O'CLOCK CLUB*
(WRITTEN IN THE 1890S)

Just like the members of the original Five O'Clock Club, today's members want an ongoing relationship. George Vaillant, in his seminal work on successful people, found that "what makes or breaks our luck seems to be… our sustained relationships with other people." (George E.Vaillant, *Adaptation to Life,* Harvard University Press, 1995)

Five O'Clock Club members know that much of the program's benefit comes from simply showing up. Showing up will encourage you to do what you need to do when you are not here. And over the course of several weeks, certain things will become evident that are not evident now.

Five O'Clock Club members learn from each other: The group leader is not the only one with answers. The leader brings factual information to the meetings and keeps the discussion in line. But the answers to some problems may lie within you or with others in the group.

Five O'Clock Club members encourage each other. They listen, see similarities with their own situations, and learn from that. And they listen to see how they may help others. You may come across information or a contact that could help someone else in the group. Passing on that information is what we're all about.

If you are a new member here, listen to others to learn the process. And read the books and listen to the presentations so you will know the basics that others already know. When everyone understands the basics, this keeps the meetings on a high level, interesting, and helpful to everyone.

Five O'Clock Club members are in this together, but they know that ultimately they are each responsible for solving their own problems with God's help. Take the time to learn the process, and you will become better at analyzing your own situation, as well as the situations of others. You will be learning a method that will serve you the rest of your life, and in areas of your life apart from your career.

Five O'Clock Club members are kind to each other. They control their frustrations—because venting helps no one. Because many may be stressed, be kind and go the extra length to keep this place calm and happy. It is your respite from the world outside and a place for you to find comfort and FUN. Relax and enjoy yourself, learn what you can, and help where you can. And have a ball doing it.

There arises from the hearts of busy [people] a love of
variety, a yearning for relaxation of thought
as well as of body, and a craving for a
generous and spontaneous fraternity.

J. HAMPTON MOORE, *HISTORY OF THE FIVE O'CLOCK CLUB*

Lexicon Used at The Five O'Clock Club

The LEXICON — to help you talk about your search

The Five O'Clock Club lexicon is a short-hand — a way to quickly analyze your search and to clearly speak about your search to other Five O'Clock Clubbers. We all speak the same language so we can help each other. Our counselors across the country also speak the same language.

Whether you are in a group or working privately with a Five O'Clock Club career counselor, you can learn our language and analyze your search. After you read the summary below, study our books "as if your were in graduate school." You will learn to better express where you are in your job search, and be better able to figure out what to do next.

The average person who attends The Five O'Clock Club regularly has a new job within just ten weekly sessions–even those who have been unemployed up to two years. Follow our method and you will increase your chances of getting a better job faster.

The following questions will help you to pinpoint what is wrong with your search.

I. Overview and Assessment

How many hours a week are you spending on your search?

Only two or three hours a week, you say? The good news is that you have not yet begun to search. That's why you're making so little progress. To develop momentum in your search, spend 35 hours a week on a full-time search; if you are employed, spend 15 hours a week for a solid, part-time search.

What are your job targets?

If your job targets are wrong, everything is wrong. A target includes:

- industry or organization size,
- the position you want in that industry, and
- your targeted geographic area.

For example, let's say you want to target the health care industry. That's not a good target. It needs to be better defined. For example, perhaps you would consider hospitals. In the metropolitan New York area, for example, there are 80 hospitals. Let's say you're a marketing person, and you would consider doing marketing in a hospital in the NY area. That's one target: Hospitals is the industry, marketing is the position, and NY area is the geographic area. You could also target HMO's. Let's say there are 15 HMO's that you consider appropriate in the NY area. You could do marketing for them. That's a second target. You could also work for a consulting firm in the NY area that does health-care consulting. That's your third target.

But let's say you and your spouse have always loved Phoenix. You think you may like to investigate all three of those industries in the Phoenix area. That's three more targets. The reason you divide your search into targets is so you can have control over it, and tell what's working and what isn't. You make a list of all of the organizations in each of your targets–we call that your "Targeting Map." Then you find out the names of the people you need to contact in each of those targets–the hiring managers of the departments or divisions you are interested in.

That's the start of an organized search. At the very beginning of your search, you can assess how good your targets are and whether you stand a chance getting a job within a reasonable timeframe. Take a look at "Measuring Your Job Targets" in our books.

How does your résumé position you?

The average résumé is looked at for only ten seconds–regardless of length. When someone looks at your résumé, will they pick up the most important information that you want them to know about you? The summary and body should make you look appropriate to your target. We recommend that the first line of your summary tell the reader exactly how they should see you, e.g., as an "Accounting Manager" or whatever. They will want to stereotype you anyway, so why not help them see you the way you want to be seen?

The second line should differentiate you from your competition: How are you different from all of those other Accounting Managers out there? Your second line could say, for example, "Expert in Cost Accounting."

That is followed by three or four bulleted accomplishments–the most important things you want them to know about you. That way, if they spend only 10 seconds on your résumé, they will see what you want them to see. For the complete Five O'Clock Club approach, see our Résumé book. It contains summaries related to over 100 industries and professions.

What are your back-up targets?

Decide at the beginning of the search before you start your first campaign. Then you won't get stuck later when things seem hopeless.

Have you done the Assessment?

If you have no specific targets, you cannot have a targeted search. Do the Assessment exercises in our books. You could see a counselor privately for two or three sessions to determine possible job targets. When a person joins the Club, we want them to do the exercises even if they are perfectly clear about what they want to do next. Doing the assessment helps a person to do better in interviews and helps them to have a better resume. Do not skip the assessment, especially the Seven Stories Exercise and the Forty-Year Vision.

II. Getting Interviews

How large is your target area (e.g., 30 companies)?
How many of them have you contacted?

When you know your targets, you can research them and come up with a list of all of the companies in your target areas. Figure out how large your target market is. If you have contacted only a few companies in your target area, contact the rest. If you haven't contacted any, contact them all. That's a thorough–and fast–search.

How can you get (more) leads?

You will not get a job through search firms, ads, networking or direct contact. Those are techniques for getting interviews–job leads. Use the right terminology, especially when speaking to someone who has already landed a job. Do not say: how did you get the job, if you really want to know where did you get the lead for that job. In our books, you will find cover letters and approaches for each of these techniques. A good search does not rely on just one technique. We want our members to consider all four techniques for getting interviews in your target markets.

Do you have 6 to 10 things in the works?

When a job hunter is going after only one position—and hoping they will get an offer—that is a weak search. Our research shows that a good job hunter has 6 to 10 things in the works at all times. This is because five will fall away through no fault of your own: Maybe the company decides to hire a finance person instead of a marketing person, or maybe they decide to hire their cousin!

Do not put all of your eggs in one basket. When one offer falls through, you will have lost months in your search because you have to gear up all over again. To avoid losing momentum, make sure you have 6 to 10 things in the works at all times—through search firms, ads, networking or direct contact. It's not as hard as it sounds. Just follow our approach.

If you have 6 to 10 things going at once, you are more likely to turn the job you want into an offer because you will seem more valuable. Don't go after only one job.

How's your Two-Minute Pitch? (Who shall we pretend we are?)

A Two-Minute Pitch is the answer to the question, "So, tell me about yourself." Practice a tailored Two-Minute Pitch. Tell the group—or a friend—the job title and industry of the pretend hiring manager. You will be surprised how good the group is at critiquing pitches. Do it a few weeks in a row until you have a smooth presentation.

Practice it again after you have been in search a while, or after you change targets. Make sure your pitch separates you from your competition.

You seem to be in Stage One (or Stage Two or Stage Three) of your search.

Know where you are in the process. If you are in Stage One—making initial contacts you will recontact later—make lots of contacts so at least 6 to 10 will move to Stage Two: the right people at the right levels in the right companies. You will

get the best job offers in Stage Three—talking to 6 to 10 people on an ongoing basis about real jobs or the possibility of creating a job.

Are you seen as insider or outsider?

Are people saying: "I wish I had an opening for someone like you." You are doing well in meetings. If your target is good, it's only a matter of time.

III. Turning Interviews into Offers

Want to go through the Brick Wall?

The brainiest part of the process is turning your job interview into an offer. First, make sure you want the job. If you do not want the job, perhaps you want an offer, if only for practice. If you are not willing to go for it, the group's suggestions will not work.

Who are your likely competitors and how can you kill them off?

"Outshine and outlast your competition" does not mean dirty tricks, but reminds you that you have competitors. You will not get a job simply because "they liked you". The issues are deeper. Ask: Where are you in the hiring process? What kind of person would be your ideal candidate?

What are your next steps?

The "next step" means: what are you planning to do if the hiring manager doesn't call by a certain date, or what are you planning to do to assure the hiring manager does call you.

Can you prove you can do the job?

Most job hunters take the "Trust Me" approach. Instead, prove to them that you can do the job, often by doing additional research or by writing a "proposal" of how you would handle the job.

Which job positions you best for the long run? Which job is the best fit?

Don't decide only on salary. Since the average person has been in his or her job only four years, you will have another job after this. See which job looks best on your resume, and makes you a stronger candidate next time. Take the job that positions you best for the long run.

In addition, find a fit for your personality. If you don't "fit," it is unlikely you will do well there. The group can give feedback on which job is best for you.

> **"Believe me, with self-examination and a lot of hard work with our coaches, you can find the job... you can have the career... you can live the life you've always wanted!"**
>
> **Sincerely,**
> **Kate Wendleton**

Membership

As a member of The Five O'Clock Club, you get:

- A LIFETIME subscription to The Five O'Clock News—10 issues a year filled with information on career development and job-search techniques, focusing on the experiences of real people.
- LIFETIME access to the Members Only section of our website containing, for example, all of our basic worksheets, our 111-page bibliography of research resources, and many other items.
- Access to reasonably priced weekly seminars featuring individualized attention to your specific needs in small groups supervised by our senior coaches.

- Access to one-on-one coaching to help you answer specific questions, solve current job problems, prepare your résumé, or take an in-depth look at your career path. You choose the coach and pay the coach directly.
- An attractive Beginners Kit containing information based on over 25 years of research on who gets jobs... and why... that will enable you to improve your job-search techniques—immediately!
- The opportunity to exchange ideas and experiences with other job searchers and career changers.

All that access, all that information, all that expertise for the one-time membership fee of only $49, plus seminar fees.

How to become a member— by mail or Email:

Send your name, address, phone number, how you heard about us, and your check for $49 (made payable to "The Five O'Clock Club") to our headquarters address: The Five O'Clock Club, 300 East 40th Street, New York, NY 10016, or sign up at www.fiveoclockclub.com. Or call us at 1-800-538-6645.

We will immediately mail you a Five O'Clock Club Membership Card, the Beginners Kit, and information on our seminars followed by our magazine. Then, call 1-800-538-6645 (or 212-286-4500 in New York) or email us (at info@ fiveoclockclub.com) to:

- reserve a space for the first time you plan to attend, or
- be matched with a Five O'Clock Club coach.

Membership Application

The Five O'Clock Club

☐ **Yes! I want to become a member!**

I want access to the most effective methods for finding jobs, as well as for developing and managing my career.

I enclose my check for $49 for a LIFETIME membership, payable to The Five O'Clock Club. I will receive a Beginners Kit, a LIFETIME subscription to *The Five O'Clock News*, LIFETIME access to the Members Only area on our website, and a network of career coaches. Reasonably priced weekly small-group strategy sessions via teleconference are held every evening across the country.

Name:_____

Street Address:_____

City:_____State:_____Zip Code:_____

Work phone: (_____)_____

Home phone: (_____)_____

Email:_____

Date:_____

How I heard about the Club:_____

TARGETING A GREAT CAREER
The following *optional* information is for statistical purposes. Thanks for your help.

Salary range:

☐ under $30,000   ☐ $30,000-$49,999   ☐ $50,000-$74,999

☐ $75,000-$99,999   ☐ $100,000-$125,000   ☐ over $125,000

Age: ☐ 20-29   ☐ 30-39   ☐ 40-49   ☐ 50+

Gender: ☐ Male ☐ Female

Current or most recent position/title: _____

Please send to:
Membership Director,
The Five O'Clock Club Headquarters
300 East 40th St.,
New York, NY 10016

The original Five O'Clock Club® was formed in Philadelphia in 1893. It was made up of the leaders of the day who shared their experiences "in a setting of fellowship and good humor."

Index

About the Author

Kate Wendleton is a nationally recognized authority on career development. She founded The Five O'Clock Club in 1978 and developed its methodology to help job hunters, career changers and employees of all levels, making The Five O'Clock Club the only organization to conduct ongoing research on behalf of employees and job hunters.

Kate was a nationally syndicated columnist for eight years and a speaker on career development, having appeared on the Today Show, CNN, CNBC, Larry King, National Public Radio and CBS, and in *The Economist, The New York Times, The Chicago Tribune, The Wall Street Journal, Fortune* magazine, *Business Week* and other national media.

For the past two years, Kate has spent every Saturday with young adults who have aged out of foster care, trying to give them the opportunity to make the most of their lives. This organization, Remington Achievers, is a not-for-profit arm of The Five O'Clock Club.

Kate also founded Workforce America, a not-for-profit Affiliate of The Five O'Clock Club, that served adults in Harlem who were not yet in the professional or managerial ranks. For ten years, Workforce America helped each person move into better-paying, higher-level positions as each im-proved in educational level and work experience.

Kate founded, and directed for seven years, The Career Center at The New School for Social Research in New York. She also advises major corporations about employee career-development programs.

A former CFO of two small companies, she has twenty years of business-management experience in both manufacturing and service businesses.

Kate attended Chestnut Hill College in Philadelphia and received her MBA from Drexel University. She is a popular speaker with groups that include associations, corporations, and colleges.

While living in Philadelphia, Kate did long-term volunteer work for the Philadelphia Museum of Art, the Walnut Street Theatre Art Gallery, United Way, and the YMCA. Kate currently lives in Manhattan with her husband, has a number of children, including young men who have aged out of foster care.

Kate is the author of The Five O'Clock Club's five-part career-development and job-hunting series for professionals, managers and executives as well as *Your Great Business Idea: The Truth About Making It Happen, WorkSmarts* (co-editor) and The Five O'Clock Club's boxed set of sixteen lectures on audio CD's as well as via downloads.

About The Five O'Clock Club and the "Fruytagie" Canvas

Five O'Clock Club members are special. We attract upbeat, ambitious, dynamic, intelligent people—and that makes it fun for all of us. Most of our members are professionals, managers, executives, consultants, and freelancers. We also include recent college graduates and those aiming to get into the professional ranks, as well as people in their 40s, 50s, and even 60s. Most members' salaries range from $30,000 to $400,000 (one-half of our members earn in excess of $100,000 a year). In addition to attending the weekly small-group strategy sessions at the Club, The Five O'Clock Club Book Series contains all of our methodologies—and our spirit.

The Philosophy of The Five O'Clock Club

The "Fruytagie" Canvas by Patricia Kelly, depicted here, symbolizes our philosophy. The original is actually 52.5" by 69" inches. It is reminiscent of popular 16th century Dutch "fruytagie," or fruit tapestries, which depicted abundance and prosperity.

I was attracted to this piece because it seemed to fit the spirit of our people at The Five O'Clock Club. This was confirmed when the artist, who was not aware of what I did for a living, added these words to the canvas: "The garden is abundant, prosperous and magical." Later, it took me only 10 minutes to write the blank verse "The Garden of Life," because it came from my heart. The verse reflects our philosophy and describes the kind of people who are members of the Club.

I'm always inspired by Five O'Clock Clubbers. They show others the way through their quiet behavior... their kindness... their generosity... their hard work... under God's care.

We share what we have with others. We are in this lush, exciting place together—with our brothers and sisters—and reach out for harmony. The garden is abundant. The job market is exciting. And Five O'Clock Clubbers believe that there is enough for everyone.

About the Artist's Method

To create her tapestry-like art, Kelly developed a unique style of stenciling. She hand-draws and hand-cuts each stencil, both in the negative and positive for each image. Her elaborate technique also includes a lengthy multi-layering process incorporating Dutch metal leaves and gilding, numerous transparent glazes, paints, and wax pencils.

Kelly also paints the back side of the canvas using multiple washes of reds, violets, and golds. She uses this technique to create a heavy vibration of color, which in turn reflects the color onto the surface of the wall against which the canvas hangs.

The canvas is suspended by a heavy braided silk cord threaded into large brass grommets inserted along the top. Like a tapestry, the hemmed canvas is attached to a gold-gilded dowel with finials. The entire work is hung from a sculpted wall ornament.

Our staff is inspired every day by the members of The Five O'Clock Club, and our mantra, which is to "always do what is in the best interests of the job hunter." We all work hard—and have FUN! The garden is abundant—with enough for everyone.

We wish you lots of success in your career. We—and your fellow members of The Five O'Clock Club—will work with you on it.

—Kate Wendleton, President

The original Five O'Clock Club was formed in Philadelphia in 1883. It was made up of the leaders of the day, who shared their experiences "in a spirit of fellowship and good humor."

THE GARDEN OF LIFE IS abundant, prosperous and magical. ❦ In this garden, there is enough for everyone. ❦ Share the fruit and the knowledge ❦ Our brothers and we are in this lush, exciting place together. ❦ Let's show others the way. ❦ Kindness. Generosity. ❦ Hard work. ❦ God's care.